BILL HALL'S

Land

and

Lakes

COOKBOOK

Dedication

To Mama, the world's best cook (except turnip greens)
the late Jerry Duncan, Jr.
Amanda Solomon
Middle Tennessee UT Extension Service
The People of the Great State of Tennessee

Cover Photo by Mark Queen
Additional Photos by Tony Gipson and Mark Peek

Special Thanks to
Tom T. and Dixie Hall
Middle Tennessee Chapter of the American Diabetes Association
Tennessee Wildlife Resources Agency

This cookbook is a collection of our favorite recipes,
which are not necessarily original recipes.

Published by: Bill Hall

Copyright© Bill Hall
WSMV Channel 4, Nashville
P.O. Box 400
Nashville, Tennessee 37202
(615) 353-2231

Library of Congress Number: 93-073580
ISBN: 0-87197-391-X

Edited, Designed and Manufactured in the United States of America by:
Favorite Recipes® Press
P.O. Box 305142
Nashville, Tennessee 37230
1-800-358-0560

First Printing: 1993 5,000 copies
Second Printing: 1995 2,000 copies

Bill Hall is among the most popular television personalities in Middle Tennessee. His show covers a wide range of outdoor topics including hunting, fishing and cooking. So it's only natural that he publish a cookbook. Bill is a natural cook and by that I mean he can cook without a cookbook. Some people, Bill at the top of the list, have a way of knowing just how "food things" go together. His fans (both TV and Cable) have been asking for this tome of wisdom for a long time.

You will not hear Bill bragging on his ribs, chops, ham, chili or any of the other recipes in this book. He is much too humble, so trust me when I say that no kitchen no matter how well it is technically or decoratively appointed, should be without this book.

You won't always find Bill in the kitchen. Likely as not, you will find him cooking on the riverbank, campsite, tailgate of a pickup or in his backyard. And any restaurant or cafe where you spot Bill Hall you can bet is a great place to pull up a chair.

My husband, Tom T., another Hall, (they all love to eat) once said "Food is like the weather, it's either good or it's not." I reminded him of what Bill says, "If you don't do the weather, I won't do the cooking." Tell the truth, I'll take Bill's cooking over his weather...any day!!

For fellow cookbook collectors this book stands alone on the shelf. I predict it will be a classic in your kitchen. Bill's mother used to tell him "don't waste stuff," so don't you waste this opportunity to add this gem to your cookbook collection.

Mrs. Tom T. (Dixie) Hall

I chose the Middle Tennessee Chapter of the American Diabetes Association as a favorite charity to share in the proceeds of our new cookbook, *Bill Hall's Land and Lakes Cookbook* because I am diabetic and because I want to help in the fight against diabetes. Like all my co-workers and fellow Tennesseans, we are continuing in the Tennessee tradition of volunteering. To me that means supporting not just one, but as many charities as possible. Diabetes professionals, my doctor, Dr. John McRae, Anne Brown, MSN and registered dietitian, Patricia Davidson are members of my "A Team." Through their help and the help of other diabetes educators I have been given another chance. I think it only fair that I help give others a chance by sharing in the proceeds of what I hope is a cookbook people will let grace their kitchen.

Bill Hall

Contents

Outdoor Tips   *Cooking Tips*

Gardening Tips   *Weather Tips*

Bill's Four Seasons Eating

January
February
March

To me the best foods of these months are those prepared the previous summer, late fall and early winter, canned or preserved from the garden and orchard, small game harvested and frozen from fall and winter hunting and hogs killed near Thanksgiving.

April
May
June

Beginning in late March or earlier, some garden produce such as spring onions, lettuce and early garden goodies are in abundance and ready to be served with just about any dish. Good blackberry pickin' is near. By the way, fishing is now pretty good most places.

July
August
September

Most produce (my favorites anyway) are available. This time of year barbecue grills and rod and reels give me the greatest thrills. My thoughts drift to fall fishing and the opening of deer season. My favorite hot peppers (a wide variety) are in abundance. My nights are very long because after leaving work around eleven o'clock I'm sure to stay up very late (sometimes 'til 2 or 3 a.m.) making pepper sauce. Fifty to seventy-five bottles will be given to special people and friends for Christmas presents.

October
November
December

One of my favorite times of the year. Already I'm excited about the new hunting seasons and late fall fishing. A time when my closest friends are preparing for every dish from small game to our deer harvests to duck breast smoked over the grill on a cold January day.

A word about fishing, I practice catch and release when it comes to bass fishing. I'll keep a few crappie, catfish or sauger to eat. Hunting? I and every friend I have and probably 98% of the people I know that hunt have not and will not harvest any game except for eating.

Tennessee Lakes and Fishing Areas

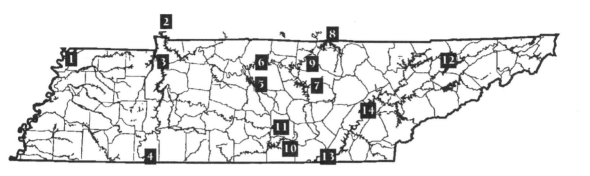

West Tennessee

1   Reelfoot Lake

2   Lake Barkley

3   Kentucky Lake

4   Pickwick Lake

Secret West Tennessee Spots

See Brenda Hicks or

John Williams at

Buchanan Resort.

East Tennessee

12   Norris Reservoir

13   Nickajack Lake

14   Watts Bar Lake

Secret East Tennessee Spots

Middle Tennessee

5   Percy Priest Lake

6   Old Hickory Lake

7   Center Hill Lake

8   Dale Hollow Lake

9   Cordell Hull Lake

10   Tim's Ford Lake

11   Woods Reservoir

Secret Middle Tennessee Spots

See Jack Christian

Alabama

Eufaula Lake

Guntersville Lake

Secret Alabama Spots

See Guide Harold Bennett

on Eufaula.

Friends of Bill

Carolyn and Bill's 25th Anniversary Party.
Since we grew up together, I guess I'd better say something nice. After being with her most of the last 32 years, I'm used to her.

Amanda Solomon. *Besides being one of Decherd's best cooks, she is the brains behind the cookbook.*

Bill and Demetria. *We served up our specialties in the Nashville Gas Kitchen at the Southern Womens Show—Greek and Soul.*

The
Vegetable Patch

The only good thing missing from this cookbook is a
recipe from my good friend Jerry Thompson.

Taffy Apple Salad

1 8-ounce can pineapple tidbits
2 cups miniature marshmallows
1 cup sugar
1 egg, beaten
1 tablespoon flour

2 tablespoons vinegar
4 or 5 large red apples, unpeeled,
   chopped
8 ounces whipped topping
1 cup chopped peanuts

Drain pineapple, reserving juice. Mix pineapple with marshmallows in medium bowl. Blend reserved juice with sugar, egg, flour and vinegar in saucepan. Cook over medium heat until thickened, stirring constantly. Chill pineapple mixture and dressing overnight. Add dressing and apples to pineapple mixture; mix well. Stir in whipped topping and peanuts. Yield: 12 servings.

Approx Per Serving: Cal 282; Prot 4 g; Carbo 47 g; Fiber 3 g;
    T Fat 11 g; 32% Calories from Fat; Chol 18 mg; Sod 15 mg.

Dietary Exchanges: Lean Meat 1/2; Fruit 3; Fat 2

Evelyn Childers, Winchester, Tennessee

Avocado and Melon Salad

1/4 cup chili sauce
1/4 cup honey
3 tablespoons white vinegar
2 teaspoons Worcestershire sauce
2 teaspoons minced onion
1/4 cup oil
Salt and pepper to taste

1/2 head butter lettuce, rinsed, drained
1/2 head red leaf lettuce, rinsed,
   drained
5 stalks celery, finely chopped
1/2 cantaloupe, cut into 1-inch cubes
1/4 cup thinly sliced red onion
1 avocado, cut into 1/2-inch cubes

Combine chili sauce, honey, vinegar, Worcestershire sauce, onion, oil, salt and pepper in small bowl; mix well. Chill in refrigerator. Tear butter lettuce and red leaf lettuce into bite-sized pieces. Toss in large salad bowl. Layer celery, cantaloupe, red onion and avocado over lettuce. Stir dressing. Pour over salad just before serving. Yield: 8 servings.

Approx Per Serving: Cal 168; Prot 2 g; Carbo 19 g; Fiber 2 g;
    T Fat 11 g; 54% Calories from Fat; Chol 0 mg; Sod 158 mg.

Dietary Exchanges: Fruit 1; Vegetable 1/2; Fat 2

Bill says that the best advice he can give anyone on growing, gardening, harvesting and canning is to call his local University of Tennessee Extension leader for answers and assistance.

Dilled Green Beans in Sour Cream

1 pound green beans
1 tablespoon dried minced onion
2 tablespoons chopped parsley
2 tablespoons butter
1 tablespoon flour

1 teaspoon dillweed
1 teaspoon vinegar
1 teaspoon each sugar and salt
1/2 teaspoon pepper
1 cup nonfat sour cream

Cook green beans in water to cover in saucepan until tender. Drain, reserving 1/2 cup liquid. Sauté onion and parsley in butter in medium saucepan until onion is tender. Stir in flour. Add reserved green bean liquid gradually, stirring constantly. Cook until sauce is thickened, stirring constantly; remove from heat. Add green beans, dillweed, vinegar, sugar, salt, pepper and sour cream; mix well. Yield: 10 servings.

Approx Per Serving: Cal 55; Prot 3 g; Carbo 7 g; Fiber 1 g;
    T Fat 2 g; 36% Calories from Fat; Chol 6 mg; Sod 256 mg.

Dietary Exchanges: Vegetable 1/2; Fat 1/2

Zesty Beets

1 16-ounce can pickled beets, drained
1 cup cooked prunes

1 7-ounce jar cream-style horseradish

Combine all ingredients in bowl; mix well. Chill, covered, in refrigerator for 24 hours. Serve with ham. Yield: 12 servings.

Approx Per Serving: Cal 107; Prot 1 g; Carbo 14 g; Fiber 2 g;
    T Fat 6 g; 48% Calories from Fat; Chol 8 mg; Sod 227 mg.

Dietary Exchanges: Bread 1/2; Fruit 1/2; Vegetable 1/2; Fat 1

Broccoli Delight Salad

1 cup mayonnaise
1/2 cup sugar
3 tablespoons apple cider vinegar
Flowerets of 2 bunches fresh broccoli

1/2 cup raisins
1/2 cup chopped purple onion
1/2 cup chopped pecans
12 slices bacon, crisp-fried, crumbled

Combine mayonnaise, sugar and vinegar in small bowl; mix well. Chill overnight. Combine broccoli, raisins, onion and pecans in serving bowl. Add dressing; mix gently. Sprinkle with bacon. Yield: 12 servings.

Approx Per Serving: Cal 273; Prot 5 g; Carbo 19 g; Fiber 2 g;
    T Fat 21 g; 67% Calories from Fat; Chol 16 mg; Sod 223 mg.

Dietary Exchanges: Lean Meat 1/2; Fruit 1; Vegetable 1/2; Fat 4

Annie Laura Hunt, Duck River, Tennessee

Broccoli and Tomato Salad

2 pounds fresh broccoli
1 large tomato, peeled, chopped
1 small onion, chopped

1 cup light mayonnaise
Salt and pepper to taste
Curry powder or garlic salt to taste

Cut flowerets from broccoli; chop stems. Cook in a small amount of water in saucepan until tender-crisp; drain and rinse with cold water. Combine broccoli, tomato and onion in salad bowl. Blend mayonnaise with salt, pepper and curry powder in small bowl. Add to vegetables; toss lightly. Chill until serving time. Yield: 12 servings.

Approx Per Serving: Cal 73; Prot 2 g; Carbo 8 g; Fiber 2 g;
   T Fat 4 g; 48% Calories from Fat; Chol 5 mg; Sod 125 mg.

Dietary Exchanges: Vegetable 1; Fat 1/2

Broccoli and Yogurt Salad

4 cups broccoli flowerets
1 cup seedless grapes
1/2 cup chopped almonds
1/2 cup sliced red onion
5 slices bacon, crisp-fried, crumbled

1/2 cup plain low-fat yogurt
1/3 cup (cholesterol-free
   reduced-calorie) light mayonnaise
2 tablespoons wine vinegar
1 tablespoon sugar

Combine broccoli, grapes, almonds, onion and bacon in bowl; mix well. Combine yogurt, mayonnaise, vinegar and sugar in small bowl; mix well. Add to salad; mix well. Chill for several hours to overnight. Yield: 12 servings.

Approx Per Serving: Cal 97; Prot 4 g; Carbo 8 g; Fiber 2 g;
   T Fat 6 g; 55% Calories from Fat; Chol 3 mg; Sod 103 mg.

Dietary Exchanges: Lean Meat 1/2; Fruit 1/2; Vegetable 1/2; Fat 1

Zesty Coleslaw

3 cups shredded cabbage
1/2 cup finely shredded carrot
1/4 cup milk
1 tablespoon sugar
Salt to taste

1/2 cup light mayonnaise
1/4 cup buttermilk
1/4 teaspoon celery seed
2 or 3 drops of Tabasco sauce
1 tablespoon minced onion

Combine cabbage, carrot, milk, sugar and salt in salad bowl; mix well. Chill, covered, for 1 hour or longer. Combine mayonnaise, buttermilk, celery seed, Tabasco sauce and onion in small bowl; mix well. Pour over chilled cabbage mixture; toss to mix. Chill until serving time. Yield: 8 servings.

Approx Per Serving: Cal 60; Prot 1 g; Carbo 7 g; Fiber 1 g;
   T Fat 3 g; 49% Calories from Fat; Chol 5 mg; Sod 96 mg.

Dietary Exchanges: Vegetable 1/2; Fat 1/2

"Fair-Weather" Cabbage and Pineapple Slaw

1 8-ounce can crushed pineapple
1/2 cup mayonnaise
3 cups finely chopped cabbage
1 red Delicious apple, unpeeled,
   chopped

12 seedless green grapes, cut into halves
1/2 cup chopped celery
1/4 cup golden raisins
1 onion, thinly sliced
1 clove of garlic, minced

Drain pineapple, reserving juice. Blend reserved juice with mayonnaise in small bowl. Combine cabbage, pineapple, apple, grapes, celery, raisins, onion and garlic in large bowl; mix well. Add mayonnaise mixture; mix gently. Chill, covered, until serving time. Yield: 8 servings.

Approx Per Serving: Cal 165; Prot 1 g; Carbo 17 g; Fiber 2 g;
   T Fat 11 g; 58% Calories from Fat; Chol 8 mg; Sod 91 mg.

Dietary Exchanges: Fruit 1; Vegetable 1/2; Fat 2

Carrie Byrne Bartlett, Gallatin, Tennessee

Sauerkraut Slaw

1 32-ounce can chopped sauerkraut
1 red bell pepper, chopped
1 green bell pepper, chopped
1 cup chopped celery

1 small onion, chopped
3/4 cup sugar
1/2 cup oil
1 tablespoon vinegar

Combine sauerkraut, bell peppers, celery and onion in serving bowl. Combine sugar, oil and vinegar in small bowl; mix well. Add to salad; mix well. Chill, covered, for 12 hours, stirring several times. Yield: 12 servings.

Approx Per Serving: Cal 151; Prot 1 g; Carbo 18 g; Fiber 2 g;
   T Fat 9 g; 53% Calories from Fat; Chol 0 mg; Sod 509 mg.

Dietary Exchanges: Fruit 1; Vegetable 1; Fat 2

Myrtle Aslee Warren, Clifton, Tennessee

Carrot and Raisin Salad

3 cups shredded carrots
1/2 cup flaked coconut
1/2 cup raisins

1/3 cup mayonnaise-type salad dressing
1/4 cup pineapple juice

Combine carrots, coconut, raisins, salad dressing and pineapple juice in bowl; mix well. Chill for 2 to 3 hours. Serve in lettuce-lined bowl. Yield: 6 servings.

Approx Per Serving: Cal 150; Prot 1 g; Carbo 24 g; Fiber 3 g;
   T Fat 7 g; 37% Calories from Fat; Chol 3 mg; Sod 115 mg.

Dietary Exchanges: Fruit 1; Vegetable 1; Fat 1 1/2

Cauliflower Salad

Flowerets of 1 head cauliflower
3 tablespoons chopped onion
1/4 green bell pepper, chopped
1 large tomato, chopped

1/2 cup nonfat sour cream
4 teaspoons white vinegar
Salt to taste

Combine cauliflower, onion, green pepper, tomato, sour cream, vinegar and salt in salad bowl; mix well. Chill for several hours to overnight before serving. Garnish with olives. Yield: 4 servings.

Approx Per Serving: Cal 54; Prot 4 g; Carbo 11 g; Fiber 3 g;
       T Fat <1 g; 5% Calories from Fat; Chol 0 mg; Sod 53 mg.

Dietary Exchanges: Vegetable 1 1/2; Milk 1/2

Cauliflower and Cottage Cheese Salad

1 head cauliflower, finely chopped
1 cup finely chopped celery
1/2 cup chopped black olives
1/2 cup chopped stuffed green olives

1/2 cup chopped green onions
16 ounces nonfat cottage cheese
1/2 cup mayonnaise
Salt and pepper to taste

Combine cauliflower, celery, black olives, green olives, green onions and cottage cheese in salad bowl; mix lightly. Add mayonnaise, salt and pepper; toss to mix. Chill, covered, overnight. Yield: 10 servings.

Approx Per Serving: Cal 139; Prot 7 g; Carbo 5 g; Fiber 2 g;
       T Fat 11 g; 66% Calories from Fat; Chol 9 mg; Sod 486 mg.

Dietary Exchanges: Lean Meat 1/2; Vegetable 1/2; Fat 2

Congealed Cranberry Waldorf Salad

1 cup cranberry juice
1   3-ounce package lemon gelatin
1 cup cranberry juice, chilled

1 cup chopped apple
1/2 cup chopped celery
1/4 cup chopped walnuts

Bring 1 cup cranberry juice to a boil in saucepan. Stir in gelatin until dissolved. Add 1 cup chilled cranberry juice. Chill until partially set. Fold in apple, celery and walnuts. Spoon into salad bowl. Chill until set. Unmold onto serving plate. Yield: 8 servings.

Approx Per Serving: Cal 111; Prot 1 g; Carbo 22 g; Fiber 1 g;
       T Fat 2 g; 19% Calories from Fat; Chol 0 mg; Sod 35 mg.

Dietary Exchanges: Bread 1/2; Fruit 1

Ann Withrow, Waverly, Tennessee

Cucumber Salad

2 cucumbers, sliced
1 red onion, sliced into rings
Salt and pepper to taste

1 tablespoon vinegar
2 tablespoons (about) sour cream

Combine cucumbers, onion rings and salt in bowl. Chill, covered, for 45 to 60 minutes; drain. Add pepper, vinegar and sour cream, stirring to coat. Chill for several hours or longer to enhance flavor. Yield: 6 servings.

Approx Per Serving: Cal 30; Prot 1 g; Carbo 4 g; Fiber 1 g;
    T Fat 1 g; 32% Calories from Fat; Chol 2 mg; Sod 5 mg.

Dietary Exchanges: Vegetable ½

Rinse those freshly harvested vegetables outdoors. The soil will stay in the garden instead of going down the drain and a thirsty garden gets a drink.

Turkish Cucumber Salad

3 large cucumbers
3 large tomatoes
2 teaspoons salt
4 bunches fresh dillweed
4 cloves of garlic, crushed

1 cup plain nonfat yogurt
¼ cup olive oil
Several drops of water
Chili powder to taste
8 Turkish black olives

Peel cucumbers and slice into quarters lengthwise, discarding seed. Slice quarters into bite-sized pieces. Peel and seed tomatoes; chop into bite-sized pieces. Combine with cucumbers in bowl. Add salt; mix well. Chill for 1 hour. Reserve several sprigs of dillweed for garnish. Chop remaining dillweed. Combine chopped dillweed with garlic, yogurt, olive oil and enough water to make of desired consistency in bowl. Add to cucumber mixture; mix gently. Chill for 2 hours. Drain well. Serve on lettuce-lined serving plate. Sprinkle with chili powder; top with black olives. Garnish with mint and reserved dillweed. Yield: 8 servings.

Approx Per Serving: Cal 109; Prot 3 g; Carbo 8 g; Fiber 2 g;
    T Fat 8 g; 60% Calories from Fat; Chol 1 mg; Sod 593 mg.
    Nutritional information includes entire amount of marinade.

Dietary Exchanges: Vegetable 1; Fat 1½

Layered Salad

1 head lettuce, shredded
1 cauliflower, chopped
1 large purple onion, thinly sliced
1 pound bacon, crisp-fried, crumbled

1/2 cup grated Parmesan cheese
1/4 cup sugar
2 cups mayonnaise

Layer first 6 ingredients in large salad bowl. Spread mayonnaise over layers, sealing to edge of bowl. Chill until serving time. Toss at serving time. Yield: 12 servings.

Approx Per Serving: Cal 381; Prot 7 g; Carbo 9 g; Fiber 1 g;
T Fat 36 g; 84% Calories from Fat; Chol 35 mg; Sod 482 mg.

Dietary Exchanges: Lean Meat 1/2; Fruit 1/2; Vegetable 1/2; Fat 61/2

Carleen Rogers, Nunnelly, Tennessee

Lettuce and Apple Salad

3/4 cup oil
1 tablespoon sugar
2 cloves of garlic, minced
Salt to taste

4 heads Bibb lettuce, torn
1 cup sliced red onion
1 cup chopped walnuts
1 red Delicious apple, sliced

Combine oil, sugar, garlic and salt in covered jar; shake well. Let stand for 1 hour; shake again. Pour over lettuce, onion, walnuts and apple in salad bowl; toss to mix well. Yield: 12 servings.

Approx Per Serving: Cal 206; Prot 2 g; Carbo 7 g; Fiber 1 g;
T Fat 20 g; 84% Calories from Fat; Chol 0 mg; Sod 4 mg.

Dietary Exchanges: Vegetable 1/2; Fat 21/2

Okra Vinaigrette

1 pound fresh whole okra
1/4 cup water
1/2 teaspoon salt
3 tablespoons oil

3 tablespoons cider vinegar
1 tablespoon Dijon mustard
1/8 teaspoon freshly ground pepper

Combine okra with water and salt in 11/2-quart glass dish. Microwave, covered, on High for 5 to 6 minutes or just until tender, stirring once. Let stand for 1 minute; drain. Whisk oil, vinegar, mustard and pepper in bowl until smooth. Combine with okra in serving bowl; mix gently. Chill, covered, for 1 hour or longer. Yield: 4 servings.

Approx Per Serving: Cal 131; Prot 2 g; Carbo 9 g; Fiber 3 g;
T Fat 11 g; 68% Calories from Fat; Chol 0 mg; Sod 321 mg.
Nutritional information includes entire amount of vinaigrette.

Dietary Exchanges: Vegetable 11/2; Fat 2

Onion Salad

3 Vidalia or sweet onions, very thinly
    sliced
1 green bell pepper, thinly sliced
4 ounces feta cheese, crumbled
1/4 cup olive oil

2 tablespoons white wine vinegar
2 tablespoons fresh lemon juice
1/2 teaspoon oregano
Salt and pepper to taste

Combine onions, green pepper and cheese in bowl. Combine olive oil, vinegar, lemon juice, oregano, salt and pepper in small bowl; mix well. Add to onion mixture; toss to mix well. May add a small amount of sugar if desired. Yield: 8 servings.

Approx Per Serving: Cal 117; Prot 3 g; Carbo 5 g; Fiber 1 g;
    T Fat 10 g; 74% Calories from Fat; Chol 13 mg; Sod 159 mg.

Dietary Exchanges: Lean Meat 1/2; Vegetable 1/2; Fat 2

Italian Pasta Salad

7 ounces uncooked rotini
1 1/2 cups cubed Swiss cheese
6 ounces salami, cut into strips
1 cup thinly sliced cauliflower
1 cup thinly sliced zucchini
1/2 cup chopped green bell pepper
1 small onion, thinly sliced into rings
1/2 cup sliced black olives
1/4 cup grated Parmesan cheese

1/4 cup chopped parsley
1/2 cup olive oil
1/4 cup wine vinegar
2 cloves of garlic, minced
2 teaspoons dried basil, crushed
1 teaspoon dried oregano, crushed
1/2 teaspoon pepper
2 medium tomatoes, cut into wedges

Cook pasta using package directions; rinse with cold water and drain. Combine with Swiss cheese, salami, cauliflower, zucchini, green pepper, onion, olives, Parmesan cheese and parsley in large salad bowl. Combine olive oil, vinegar, garlic, basil, oregano and pepper in jar with tight lid; shake to mix well. Add to salad; toss gently. Chill, covered, for 4 to 24 hours. Add tomatoes at serving time; toss gently. Yield: 12 servings.

Approx Per Serving: Cal 266; Prot 10 g; Carbo 17 g; Fiber 1 g;
    T Fat 18 g; 60% Calories from Fat; Chol 26 mg; Sod 482 mg.

Dietary Exchanges: Bread 1; Lean Meat 1; Vegetable 1/2; Fat 3

Jill Hutchison, Antioch, Tennessee

Store tomatoes at room temperature for best flavor. Place them stem end down away from warm areas and direct sunlight. Do not wash them until ready to use.

Pasta and Shrimp Salad

1 7-ounce package pasta shells
4 ounces cooked small shrimp
1¹/₂ cups broccoli flowerets
1 cup coarsely shredded carrot
1¹/₂ cups sliced zucchini
¹/₄ cup chopped green onions

¹/₂ cup oil
¹/₂ cup lemon juice
1 teaspoon prepared horseradish
1 envelope Italian salad dressing mix
Hot sauce to taste

Cook pasta using package directions; rinse and drain. Combine with shrimp, broccoli, carrot, zucchini and green onions in large bowl. Combine oil, lemon juice, horseradish, salad dressing mix and hot sauce in jar with tight lid; shake to mix well. Add to salad; toss gently. Chill, covered, for several hours to overnight. Serve in lettuce-lined bowl. Yield: 8 servings.

Approx Per Serving: Cal 247; Prot 7 g; Carbo 24 g; Fiber 2 g;
   T Fat 14 g; 51% Calories from Fat; Chol 28 mg; Sod 165 mg.

Dietary Exchanges: Bread 1¹/₂; Lean Meat ¹/₂; Vegetable ¹/₂; Fat 2¹/₂

Jane Glenn, Antioch, Tennessee

When starting seedlings, avoid "damp off" by judging watering needs carefully. It is not caused by fungus but by keeping the planting medium excessively damp.

Marinated Peas and Carrots

16 ounces carrots, peeled, sliced
32 ounces black-eyed peas, cooked
1 large green bell pepper
1 medium onion

1 10-ounce can tomato soup
¹/₂ cup sugar
¹/₄ cup oil
¹/₂ cup cider vinegar

Cook carrots in a small amount of water in saucepan until tender; drain. Drain black-eyed peas. Combine carrots and black-eyed peas in large bowl. Cut green pepper into strips. Slice onion into rings. Add to carrot mixture. Pour mixture of soup, sugar, oil and vinegar over vegetables; mix well. Marinate in refrigerator for several hours to overnight. Yield: 15 servings.

Approx Per Serving: Cal 159; Prot 5 g; Carbo 26 g; Fiber 7 g;
   T Fat 4 g; 24% Calories from Fat; Chol 0 mg; Sod 145 mg.
   Nutritional information includes entire amount of marinade.

Dietary Exchanges: Bread ¹/₂; Lean Meat ¹/₂; Fruit ¹/₂; Vegetable ¹/₂; Fat 1

Purple Hull Pea Salad

6 cups drained cooked purple hull
  peas
1 large green bell pepper, chopped
1 large onion, sliced
3 tablespoons chopped pimento

1/2 cup oil
1/2 cup sugar
1/2 cup vinegar
1/2 cup tomato juice

Combine peas, green pepper, onion and pimento in large bowl. Mix oil, sugar, vinegar and tomato juice in small bowl. Add to pea mixture; mix gently. Chill, covered, overnight. Yield: 12 servings.

Approx Per Serving: Cal 202; Prot 3 g; Carbo 27 g; Fiber 7 g;
    T Fat 9 g; 41% Calories from Fat; Chol 0 mg; Sod 41 mg.

Dietary Exchanges: Bread 1; Fruit 1/2; Vegetable 1/2; Fat 2

Jean Gorrell, Lutts, Tennessee

Pickled Garden Salad

1 small head cauliflower, sliced into
  flowerets
2 carrots, cut into 2-inch strips
2 stalks celery, cut into 1-inch pieces
1 green bell pepper, cut into 2-inch
  strips
1 4-ounce jar pimentos, cut into strips
3/4 cup wine vinegar

1 3-ounce jar pitted green olives,
  drained
1/2 cup oil
2 tablespoons sugar
1 teaspoon salt
1/2 teaspoon dried oregano
1/4 teaspoon pepper

Combine cauliflower, carrots, celery, green pepper, pimentos, vinegar, olives, oil, sugar, salt, oregano and pepper in large skillet; mix well. Add a small amount of water if needed. Bring to a boil, stirring occasionally; reduce heat. Simmer for 5 minutes. Cool. Chill for 24 hours. Drain well before serving. Yield: 10 servings.

Approx Per Serving: Cal 138; Prot 1 g; Carbo 8 g; Fiber 2 g;
    T Fat 12 g; 75% Calories from Fat; Chol 0 mg; Sod 440 mg.
    Nutritional information includes entire amount of marinade.

Dietary Exchanges: Vegetable 1/2; Fat 2 1/2

Store leafy vegetables in the refrigerator as soon as possible; they can lose half of their vitamin B2 and C in half a day when kept in the light at room temperature.

Hot Dilled Potato Salad

1 tablespoon margarine
1 tablespoon flour
1 teaspoon salt
1/4 teaspoon dillweed
1/8 teaspoon pepper

1 cup low-fat milk
1/2 cup mayonnaise-type salad dressing
2 tablespoons finely chopped onion
5 hot boiled potatoes, cubed
Paprika to taste

Melt margarine in saucepan over low heat. Stir in flour, salt, dillweed and pepper. Add milk all at once. Cook until thickened, stirring constantly. Stir in salad dressing and onion. Pour over hot potatoes; toss to mix. Spoon into serving dish. Sprinkle with paprika. Yield: 6 servings.

Approx Per Serving: Cal 216; Prot 4 g; Carbo 30 g; Fiber 2 g;
    T Fat 9 g; 38% Calories from Fat; Chol 8 mg; Sod 543 mg.

Dietary Exchanges: Bread 11/2; Fat 11/2

Potato and Green Bean Salad

11/2 pounds small red potatoes, cut
    into halves
1 pound green beans, trimmed, cooked
1 sweet white onion, chopped
1 bunch scallions, chopped
1 pint cherry tomatoes, cut into halves

1/4 cup chopped fresh parsley
1 teaspoon dried dillweed
Onion powder, salt and pepper to taste
1 cup low-calorie Italian salad dressing
1/3 cup red wine vinegar

Boil potatoes in water to cover in saucepan until fork tender; drain. Combine with cooked green beans, onion, scallions, tomatoes, parsley, dillweed, onion powder, salt and pepper in large bowl; mix well. Mix salad dressing with vinegar in small bowl. Pour over vegetables; toss well to coat. Yield: 10 servings.

Approx Per Serving: Cal 112; Prot 3 g; Carbo 21 g; Fiber 3 g;
    T Fat 3 g; 20% Calories from Fat; Chol 0 mg; Sod 200 mg.

Dietary Exchanges: Bread 1; Vegetable 1; Fat 1

To keep boiled potatoes white, add a small amount of milk to the cooking water. The potatoes will taste better, too.

Garden Potato Salad

2 pounds red new potatoes
1 cup fresh green beans
1/2 cup corn kernels, cooked
1/2 cup shredded carrot
1/4 cup nonfat yogurt
1/4 cup nonfat cottage cheese

2 teaspoons milk
1/2 teaspoon cider vinegar
1/2 teaspoon onion powder
1/4 teaspoon tarragon
1/4 teaspoon salt
Pepper to taste

Cook potatoes in water to cover in saucepan until tender; drain. Rinse in cold water; drain. Cut potatoes into quarters. Steam green beans in saucepan for 2 to 3 minutes or until tender-crisp; drain. Combine potatoes, beans, corn and carrot in salad bowl. Combine yogurt, cottage cheese, milk, vinegar, onion powder, tarragon, salt and pepper in blender container. Process until smooth. Pour over salad; mix lightly. Chill, covered, for 2 hours or longer. Yield: 8 servings.

Approx Per Serving: Cal 137; Prot 7 g; Carbo 28 g; Fiber 3 g;
    T Fat <1 g; 2% Calories from Fat; Chol 1 mg; Sod 181 mg.

Dietary Exchanges: Bread 1 1/2

It is sunlight that causes potatoes to "light burn" and turn green, causing a bitter flavor. When digging potatoes, keep a dark covering (a gunny sack is good) over the unearthed harvest if it is not stored immediately.

Special Potato Salad

4 medium potatoes
1/2 cup chopped green bell pepper
3 tablespoons chopped onion
8 stuffed green olives, sliced
Whites of 3 hard-boiled eggs, chopped

1/4 teaspoon celery salt
1/4 teaspoon onion salt
1/4 cup plain low-fat yogurt
1 tablespoon Dijon mustard

Cook unpeeled potatoes in water to cover in saucepan until tender. Drain and chop potatoes. Combine with green pepper, onion, olives, egg whites, celery salt and onion salt in salad bowl; mix well. Add yogurt and mustard; mix gently. Serve immediately. Yield: 6 servings.

Approx Per Serving: Cal 125; Prot 5 g; Carbo 24 g; Fiber 3 g;
    T Fat 1 g; 9% Calories from Fat; Chol 1 mg; Sod 348 mg.

Dietary Exchanges: Bread 1

Hot Potato Salad

1 cup chopped onion
1 tablespoon butter
1/2 cup mayonnaise
1/3 cup cider vinegar
1 tablespoon sugar
1 teaspoon salt

1/4 teaspoon pepper
4 cups chopped cooked potatoes
1 tablespoon chopped parsley
1 tablespoon crumbled crisp-fried
   bacon

Sauté onion in butter in skillet over medium heat for 2 to 3 minutes or until tender. Add mayonnaise, vinegar, sugar, salt and pepper; mix well. Add potatoes. Cook for 2 minutes or until heated through, stirring constantly. Spoon into serving bowl; top with parsley and bacon. Yield: 6 servings.

Approx Per Serving: Cal 247; Prot 2 g; Carbo 24 g; Fiber 2 g;
    T Fat 17 g; 59% Calories from Fat; Chol 16 mg; Sod 493 mg.

Dietary Exchanges: Bread 1; Vegetable 1/2; Fat 3

Maurine Dement, Nashville, Tennessee

Red and Green Salad

1/4 cup vinegar
1/4 cup oil
1/4 cup sugar
2 cups chopped tomatoes

1 large onion, chopped
2 cups chopped green bell peppers
2 cups chopped cucumbers
Chopped hot pepper to taste

Mix vinegar, oil and sugar in large bowl. Add tomatoes, onion, green peppers, cucumbers and hot pepper; mix well. Chill until serving time. Yield: 8 servings.

Approx Per Serving: Cal 117; Prot 1 g; Carbo 14 g; Fiber 2 g;
    T Fat 7 g; 52% Calories from Fat; Chol 0 mg; Sod 7 mg.

Dietary Exchanges: Fruit 1/2; Vegetable 1; Fat 1 1/2

Garden "pets" will help control garden "pests." Encourage a healthy population of spiders, ladybugs, toads and other pest predators to call your garden home. Hay or dried mulch between rows attracts spider populations, and toads will love a cool moist corner with an upside-down broken flowerpot.

Garden Rice Salad

2 cups chopped celery
1 medium red onion, chopped
8 radishes, chopped
4 hard-boiled eggs, chopped
1¹/₂ cups light mayonnaise

4 teaspoons prepared mustard
¹/₂ teaspoon salt
1 cup rice, cooked, chilled
1 cucumber, chopped

Combine celery, onion, radishes and eggs in bowl; mix well. Add mayonnaise, mustard and salt; mix well. Fold in rice. Chill until serving time. Add cucumber just before serving. Yield: 10 servings.

Approx Per Serving: Cal 199; Prot 5 g; Carbo 24 g; Fiber 1 g;
      T Fat 10 g; 43% Calories from Fat; Chol 94 mg; Sod 367 mg.

Dietary Exchanges: Bread ¹/₂; Lean Meat ¹/₂; Vegetable ¹/₂; Fat 1¹/₂

Organic gardening is more than just "without insecticides." It is an ongoing plan that builds and rebuilds the soil and encourages populations of desirable insects and birds. Learn how to get the most from your labor with the least amount of damage to the environment.

Snow Pea Salad with Fruit

4 cups fresh snow peas, ends trimmed
1 cup red seedless grapes
Sections of 2 large oranges
Sections of 2 large grapefruit
1 green bell pepper, cut julienne-style
1 small red onion, sliced
¹/₂ cup sunflower seed

¹/₂ cup sugar
¹/₂ cup white vinegar
¹/₂ cup oil
2 teaspoons poppy seed
1 teaspoon onion flakes
¹/₂ teaspoon dry mustard

Combine peas, grapes, oranges, grapefruit, green pepper, onion and sunflower seed in large bowl; mix well. Combine sugar and vinegar in small deep bowl; whisk until blended. Whisk in oil. Add poppy seed, onion flakes and dry mustard; mix well. Pour over salad; toss well. May store dressing in refrigerator for up to 3 weeks. Yield: 10 servings.

Approx Per Serving: Cal 248; Prot 4 g; Carbo 27 g; Fiber 4 g;
      T Fat 15 g; 52% Calories from Fat; Chol 0 mg; Sod 4 mg.

Dietary Exchanges: Lean Meat ¹/₂; Fruit 2; Vegetable 1¹/₂; Fat 2¹/₂

Fresh Spinach Salad

2 tablespoons fresh lemon juice
3 tablespoons olive oil
1 teaspoon sugar
1/4 teaspoon grated lemon rind
3 drops of Tabasco sauce

3/4 teaspoon seasoned salt
4 cups torn spinach
8 ounces fresh mushrooms, sliced
1/4 cup chopped green onions
4 slices bacon, crisp-fried, crumbled

Combine lemon juice, olive oil, sugar, lemon rind, Tabasco sauce and seasoned salt in large bowl; beat until smooth. Add spinach, mushrooms, green onions and bacon; toss gently to mix well. Yield: 4 servings.

Approx Per Serving: Cal 161; Prot 5 g; Carbo 7 g; Fiber 2 g;
     T Fat 14 g; 73% Calories from Fat; Chol 5 mg; Sod 392 mg.

Dietary Exchanges: Lean Meat 1/2; Vegetable 1; Fat 2 1/2

Kay Dyer, Nashville, Tennessee

Spinach Salad with Special Dressing

6 ounces lettuce, torn
6 ounces spinach, torn
8 ounces bacon, crisp-fried, crumbled
2 tablespoons sugar
1 tablespoon grated onion

1/3 cup cider vinegar
1 tablespoon poppy seed
1 teaspoon dry mustard
1 teaspoon salt
1 1/2 cups large curd cottage cheese

Combine lettuce, spinach and bacon in bowl. Chill in refrigerator. Combine sugar, onion, vinegar, poppy seed, dry mustard and salt in small bowl; mix well. Stir in cottage cheese. Pour over salad; toss to mix well. Yield: 8 servings.

Approx Per Serving: Cal 121; Prot 9 g; Carbo 7 g; Fiber 1 g;
     T Fat 7 g; 50% Calories from Fat; Chol 14 mg; Sod 592 mg.

Dietary Exchanges: Lean Meat 1; Vegetable 1/2; Fat 1

When watering both vegetable and flower gardens, allow enough time to saturate the soil and encourage sturdy roots. Light sprinkling with a hand-held hose will only moisten the top of the soil and the foliage and may do more harm than good. An inch of water per week, whether from rain or watering, is a good rule of thumb.

Spinach and Pecan Salad

1/4 cup pecans
1 tablespoon margarine
2 12-ounce packages spinach, torn
4 ounces fresh mushrooms, sliced
1/2 cup sliced water chestnuts

1 cucumber, sliced
2 hard-boiled eggs, chopped
5 slices bacon, crisp-fried, crumbled
1 8-ounce bottle of low-fat creamy
   Caesar salad dressing

Sauté pecans in margarine in skillet. Combine with spinach, mushrooms, water chestnuts, cucumber, eggs and bacon in salad bowl. Add salad dressing; toss to mix well. Yield: 12 servings.

Approx Per Serving: Cal 95; Prot 4 g; Carbo 8 g; Fiber 2 g;
     T Fat 6 g; 52% Calories from Fat; Chol 38 mg; Sod 314 mg.

Dietary Exchanges: Lean Meat 1/2; Vegetable 1; Fat 1/2

Some foods are particularly rich in the carotene which protects against stroke, heart attack and oral and stomach cancer. Nutritionists recommend dark green leafy vegetables such as kale and spinach; orange-red vegetables such as carrots, sweet potatoes and pumpkin; and orange fruits such as apricots, cantaloupe and mango.

Strawberry and Spinach Salad

8 cups torn spinach
3 kiwifruit, peeled, sliced
1 cup sliced fresh strawberries
3/4 cup chopped macadamia nuts

2 tablespoons strawberry jam
2 tablespoons cider vinegar
1/3 cup oil

Combine spinach, half the kiwifruit, half the strawberries and half the macadamia nuts in large bowl; set aside. Process jam and vinegar in blender until blended. Add oil gradually, processing constantly. Pour over spinach mixture; toss gently. Place on individual salad plates. Top with remaining kiwifruit, strawberries and macadamia nuts. Yield: 8 servings.

Approx Per Serving: Cal 208; Prot 3 g; Carbo 13 g; Fiber 4 g;
     T Fat 18 g; 72% Calories from Fat; Chol 0 mg; Sod 47 mg.

Dietary Exchanges: Fruit 1/2; Vegetable 1/2; Fat 31/2

Layered Garden Tomato Salad

16 ounces mushrooms, sliced
1   8-ounce bottle of low-fat Italian
   salad dressing
1 medium head lettuce, torn

4 large tomatoes, chopped, drained
2 green onions, chopped
2 cups light mayonnaise
2 cups shredded Cheddar cheese

Combine mushrooms with salad dressing in bowl. Marinate for 1 hour or longer; drain. Layer lettuce, tomatoes, mushrooms and green onions in large salad bowl. Spread mayonnaise over layers, sealing to edge of bowl. Top with cheese. Chill for several hours. Garnish with crumbled crisp-fried bacon. Yield: 12 servings.

Approx Per Serving: Cal 216; Prot 6 g; Carbo 13 g; Fiber 1 g;
   T Fat 17 g; 66% Calories from Fat; Chol 30 mg; Sod 482 mg.
   Nutritional information includes entire amount of salad dressing marinade.

Dietary Exchanges: Lean Meat 1/2; Vegetable 1/2; Fat 3

Make-Ahead Tossed Salad

1/4 cup olive oil
Salt and pepper to taste
1 clove of garlic, minced
1 teaspoon Worcestershire sauce
1 1/2 tablespoons wine vinegar
1 clove of garlic
1 medium head romaine lettuce, torn
2 heads iceberg lettuce, torn
2 medium tomatoes, chopped

1 small cucumber, finely chopped
1 small onion, thinly sliced into rings
Sections of 1 navel orange
1/2 cup seedless grapes
4 radishes, sliced
1/2 avocado, finely chopped
2 tablespoons crumbled Roquefort
   cheese
1   2-ounce can rolled anchovies

Combine olive oil, salt, pepper, minced garlic, Worcestershire sauce and wine vinegar in covered container. Shake well. Chill in refrigerator. Rub salad bowl with garlic clove. Place lettuce in salad bowl. Cover with waxed paper. Layer tomatoes, cucumber, onion, orange, grapes, radishes, avocado, Roquefort cheese and anchovies with oil on waxed paper. Chill, covered with plastic wrap, until serving time. Remove plastic wrap; remove waxed paper. Toss salad. Add dressing to salad; toss to mix. May use other salad greens if desired. Yield: 8 servings.

Approx Per Serving: Cal 159; Prot 5 g; Carbo 13 g; Fiber 3 g;
   T Fat 11 g; 57% Calories from Fat; Chol 8 mg; Sod 325 mg.

Dietary Exchanges: Lean Meat 1/2; Fruit 1/2; Vegetable 1/2; Fat 2

Keep that summer lettuce crisp in the noonday sun by providing a shade cloth canopy. This durable fabric screen comes in varying sizes and light-reducing percentages to suit many needs.

Brazilian Vegetable Salad

3 potatoes
3 carrots
2 beets
1 chayote squash

1/2 onion, chopped
3/4 cup corn, cooked
1 cup light mayonnaise

Combine potatoes, carrots, beets and squash in water half the depth of vegetables in saucepan. Cook until tender, stirring occasionally. Peel vegetables; chop into small pieces. Combine with onion and corn in bowl. Add mayonnaise; toss to mix. Leave 1/2-inch stem on beets during cooking to prevent leaching of color. Yield: 10 servings.

Approx Per Serving: Cal 124; Prot 2 g; Carbo 19 g; Fiber 2 g;
      T Fat 5 g; 35% Calories from Fat; Chol 6 mg; Sod 143 mg.

Dietary Exchanges: Bread 1/2; Vegetable 1/2; Fat 1

Carolyn Hall makes her own **Thousand Island Salad Dressing** with 1/2 cup mayonnaise-type salad dressing, 3 tablespoons catsup, 1/4 cup pickle juice, 1 chopped dill pickle and a pinch of chili powder. She serves it on a fresh-from-the-garden tossed salad of 1 head lettuce, 1/2 head red cabbage, 2 thinly sliced carrots, a thinly sliced onion and wedges of 2 small tomatoes.

Cold Salad Soup

3 cups leftover salad with Italian salad
   dressing
3 cups tomato juice
1/4 cup chopped green bell pepper
1/4 cup chopped onion
1/4 cup chopped cucumber

1/2 cup chopped celery
2 cups chopped lettuce
1 tablespoon oil
1 tablespoon vinegar
2 teaspoons prepared mustard

Combine salad, tomato juice, green pepper, onion, cucumber, celery, lettuce, oil, vinegar and mustard in food processor container; process until smooth. Serve cold. Yield: 10 servings.

Approx Per Serving: Cal 54; Prot 1 g; Carbo 5 g; Fiber 1 g;
      T Fat 4 g; 57% Calories from Fat; Chol 0 mg; Sod 320 mg.

Dietary Exchanges: Vegetable 1/2; Fat 1/2

Pamela O'Neal, Nashville, Tennessee

Creamy Garlic Dressing

1 cup plain low-fat yogurt
1¹/₂ teaspoons Dijon mustard
¹/₂ teaspoon finely grated lemon rind

¹/₈ teaspoon cayenne pepper
2 tablespoons minced parsley
2 cloves of garlic, cut into halves

Whisk yogurt, mustard, lemon rind and cayenne pepper in medium bowl. Stir in parsley. Place garlic on wooden pick. Add to dressing. Chill, covered, for 6 hours to overnight. Discard garlic. Shake well before serving. Store leftover dressing in tightly covered jar in refrigerator. Yield: 16 (1-tablespoon) servings.

Approx Per Serving: Cal 11; Prot 1 g; Carbo 1 g; Fiber <1 g;
    T Fat <1 g; 22% Calories from Fat; Chol 1 mg; Sod 17 mg.

Dietary Exchanges: Free

Green Goddess Dressing

¹/₂ cup water
1 cup nonfat cottage cheese
2 sprigs of fresh parsley
1 teaspoon chopped chives
¹/₂ teaspoon sugar

1 clove of garlic, minced
1 teaspoon tarragon
¹/₂ teaspoon salt
Freshly ground pepper to taste

Combine water, cottage cheese, parsley, chives, sugar, garlic, tarragon, salt and pepper in bowl; beat until smooth. Let stand for 15 to 30 minutes.
Yield: 20 (1-tablespoon) servings.

Approx Per Serving: Cal 8; Prot 2 g; Carbo <1 g; Fiber <1 g;
    T Fat <1 g; <1% Calories from Fat; Chol <1 mg; Sod 95 mg.

Dietary Exchanges: Free

Ranch Salad Dressing

1 cup (or more) buttermilk
1 envelope original-recipe ranch salad
    dressing mix

2 cups low-fat cottage cheese
1 teaspoon Mrs. Dash seasoning

Process buttermilk and salad dressing mix in blender until well mixed. Add cottage cheese and seasoning. Blend at high speed for 2 minutes or until smooth. Add additional buttermilk if a thinner consistency is desired. Yield: 48 (1-tablespoon) servings.

Approx Per Serving: Cal 12; Prot 1 g; Carbo 1 g; Fiber 0 g;
    T Fat <1 g; 18% Calories from Fat; Chol 1 mg; Sod 84 mg.

Dietary Exchanges: Free

Herbed Dressing

1/2 cup wine vinegar
4 sage leaves, crushed
1/4 teaspoon tarragon
Savory to taste

1 tablespoon minced fresh parsley
1/2 clove of garlic, crushed
1/4 teaspoon dill
Freshly ground pepper to taste

Combine vinegar, sage, tarragon, savory, parsley, garlic, dill and pepper in covered jar. Shake well to mix. Yield: 8 (1-tablespoon) servings.

Approx Per Serving: Cal 3; Prot <1 g; Carbo 1 g; Fiber <1 g;
    T Fat <1 g; 1% Calories from Fat; Chol 0 mg; Sod <1 mg.

Dietary Exchanges: Free

Tom Maurie's Greek-Style Salad Dressing

2 large cloves of garlic, mashed
Juice of 1 lemon
1 teaspoon (heaping) oregano
1/2 teaspoon dry mustard
1/4 teaspoon paprika

2 teaspoons salt
2 teaspoons pepper
3/4 cup wine vinegar
1/2 cup water
1 1/2 cups (about) virgin olive oil

Combine garlic, lemon juice, seasonings, vinegar and water in jar or wine carafe. Add enough olive oil to fill jar; shake until well mixed. Store in refrigerator.
Yield: 40 (1-tablespoon) servings.

Demetria Kalodimos, Nashville, Tennessee

Approx Per Serving: Cal 73; Prot <1 g; Carbo <1 g; Fiber <1 g;
    T Fat 8 g; 98% Calories from Fat; Chol 0 mg; Sod 107 mg.

Dietary Exchanges: Fat 1 1/2

Herb Vinegar

1 cup chopped fresh herbs of choice
    such as tarragon, basil, oregano,
    dill, rosemary or chives

1 cup white wine vinegar

Place herbs in sterilized jar. Heat vinegar just to the simmering point in saucepan. Pour over herbs, covering completely. Seal with lid. Let stand for 1 to 4 weeks, shaking jar gently every day. Strain through several layers of cheesecloth into sterilized bottle. Store in dark cool place. Yield: 16 (1-tablespoon) servings.

Approx Per Serving: Cal 3; Prot <1 g; Carbo 1 g; Fiber <1 g;
    T Fat <1 g; 3% Calories from Fat; Chol 0 mg; Sod <1 mg.

Dietary Exchanges: Free

Asparagus Casserole

2 pounds asparagus, cooked
1 small onion, finely chopped
3 tablespoons chopped green bell
  pepper
1 tablespoon margarine

2 eggs, beaten
1 1/2 cups small curd nonfat cottage
  cheese
2 tablespoons chopped pimento
Salt and pepper to taste

Arrange cooked asparagus in greased shallow baking dish, reserving 3 or 4 spears. Sauté onion and green pepper in margarine in skillet. Spoon over asparagus. Combine eggs, cottage cheese, pimento, salt and pepper in bowl; mix well. Spread over top. Top with reserved asparagus. Bake at 350 degrees for 40 minutes or until set. Yield: 8 servings.

Approx Per Serving: Cal 89; Prot 10 g; Carbo 8 g; Fiber 2 g;
    T Fat 3 g; 27% Calories from Fat; Chol 55 mg; Sod 193 mg.

Dietary Exchanges: Lean Meat 1/2; Vegetable 1 1/2

Asparagus with Sesame Seed

1 1/2 pounds asparagus
1 1/2 teaspoons unsalted margarine
1 tablespoon sesame seed

1 teaspoon reduced-sodium soy sauce
1 teaspoon sesame oil
1/8 teaspoon pepper

Rinse asparagus, discarding tough stems. Cut into 1-inch lengths. Fill 10-inch skillet with 1 inch water. Bring to a boil. Add asparagus. Cook, covered, for 3 minutes or until tender-crisp. Drain and rinse under cold water. Drain and set aside. Melt margarine in skillet over medium heat. Add sesame seed. Sauté for 3 to 4 minutes or until golden brown. Return asparagus to skillet. Add soy sauce, sesame oil and pepper. Cook for 1 minute or until heated through, stirring constantly. Yield: 4 servings.

Approx Per Serving: Cal 76; Prot 5 g; Carbo 8 g; Fiber 3 g;
    T Fat 4 g; 43% Calories from Fat; Chol 0 mg; Sod 37 mg.

Dietary Exchanges: Vegetable 1 1/2; Fat 1

Asparagus Stir-Fry

1 pound fresh asparagus
2 cloves of garlic, chopped

1 tablespoon olive oil
Lemon pepper to taste

Trim asparagus; cut diagonally into 1 1/2-inch pieces. Stir-fry garlic in hot olive oil in wok until golden brown. Add asparagus. Stir-fry for 3 to 5 minutes or until tender-crisp. Sprinkle generously with lemon pepper. Yield: 4 servings.

Approx Per Serving: Cal 58; Prot 3 g; Carbo 6 g; Fiber 2 g;
    T Fat 4 g; 49% Calories from Fat; Chol 0 mg; Sod 3 mg.

Dietary Exchanges: Vegetable 1; Fat 1/2

Banana Pepper Pie

3 banana peppers, sliced
6 eggs, beaten

1 16-ounce can cream-style corn
1 cup shredded sharp Cheddar cheese

Line buttered 8x8-inch baking dish with peppers. Combine eggs, corn and cheese in bowl; mix well. Pour over peppers. Bake at 300 degrees for 45 minutes or until set. Yield: 8 servings.

Approx Per Serving: Cal 158; Prot 9 g; Carbo 12 g; Fiber 1 g;
T Fat 9 g; 48% Calories from Fat; Chol 174 mg; Sod 297 mg.

Dietary Exchanges: Bread 1/2; Lean Meat 1; Fat 1

Green Bean Casserole

2 cups cut fresh green beans
1 large onion, chopped
2 slices bacon, chopped
1/2 cup light mayonnaise
2 hard-boiled eggs, chopped
1 tablespoon horseradish

1 teaspoon Worcestershire sauce
1/2 teaspoon garlic salt
1/2 teaspoon celery salt
1 1/2 teaspoons parsley flakes
1 tablespoon lemon juice

Combine green beans, onion, bacon and a small amount of water in saucepan. Bring to a boil; reduce heat. Simmer, covered, for 1 hour; drain. Combine mayonnaise, eggs, horseradish, Worcestershire sauce, garlic salt, celery salt, parsley flakes and lemon juice in small bowl; mix well. Stir into beans. Spoon into baking dish. Bake at 350 degrees for 20 minutes. Yield: 4 servings.

Approx Per Serving: Cal 161; Prot 6 g; Carbo 13 g; Fiber 2 g;
T Fat 10 g; 56% Calories from Fat; Chol 116 mg; Sod 702 mg.

Dietary Exchanges: Lean Meat 1/2; Vegetable 1; Fat 1 1/2

Green Beans with Garlic Oil

2 pounds fresh green beans
1 small onion, thinly sliced into rings
2 cloves of garlic, minced
2 tablespoons olive oil

1/2 teaspoon cumin
1/4 teaspoon coriander
1/4 teaspoon salt
1/4 cup toasted slivered almonds

Cook green beans in a small amount of water in large saucepan for 10 to 12 minutes or until tender-crisp; drain. Cook onion and garlic in olive oil in skillet until tender. Stir in cumin, coriander and salt. Cook for 1 minute. Combine with green beans in bowl; mix well. Sprinkle with almonds. Yield: 12 servings.

Approx Per Serving: Cal 63; Prot 2 g; Carbo 7 g; Fiber 3 g;
T Fat 4 g; 50% Calories from Fat; Chol 0 mg; Sod 50 mg.

Dietary Exchanges: Vegetable 1; Fat 1/2

Baked Green Beans and Tomatoes

1¹/2 pounds fresh green beans
2 large white onions, cut into ¹/4-inch
  slices
5 medium tomatoes, cut into thick
  slices

Italian seasoning to taste
¹/4 cup olive oil
¹/2 cup water

Wash green beans; string and cut off tip ends. Layer beans, onion slices and tomatoes in shallow baking dish. Sprinkle with Italian seasoning; drizzle with olive oil. Add water. Bake, covered with foil, at 350 degrees for 1 hour. Yield: 10 servings.

Approx Per Serving: Cal 90; Prot 2 g; Carbo 10 g; Fiber 3 g;
    T Fat 6 g; 53% Calories from Fat; Chol 0 mg; Sod 10 mg.

Dietary Exchanges: Vegetable 1¹/2; Fat 1

Help your children learn to cook at an early age. At age 10, Jonathan Hall had already mastered opening a 28-ounce can of green beans, putting a tablespoon of margarine in a saucepan, adding the beans, heating for 15 minutes and sprinkling with salt and pepper to taste.

Harvest Beans

¹/4 cup chopped onion
¹/4 teaspoon cinnamon
1 tablespoon margarine
1¹/2 pounds fresh green beans, cut into
  1-inch pieces

¹/2 cup chicken broth
¹/8 teaspoon salt
Pepper to taste
2 tablespoons tomato paste

Sauté onion with cinnamon in margarine in medium saucepan or 10-inch skillet until onion is tender but not brown. Add beans, chicken broth, salt and pepper. Bring to a boil; reduce heat. Cook, covered, for 20 minutes or until beans are tender. Stir in tomato paste gently. Serve at once. May substitute two 10-ounce packages thawed frozen cut green beans for fresh beans. Yield: 6 servings.

Approx Per Serving: Cal 63; Prot 3 g; Carbo 10 g; Fiber 4 g;
    T Fat 2 g; 28% Calories from Fat; Chol 0 mg; Sod 182 mg.

Dietary Exchanges: Vegetable 1

Baked Fresh Lima Beans

2 cups fresh lima beans
2 slices bacon
1 tablespoon flour
2 tablespoons water
2 tablespoons chopped onion

1 tablespoon brown sugar
1/4 teaspoon salt
1/4 teaspoon celery salt
1/4 teaspoon paprika

Cook lima beans in water to cover in saucepan for 20 minutes or until tender; drain. Cook bacon in skillet until almost crisp; drain. Blend flour and 2 tablespoons water in large bowl. Add lima beans, onion, brown sugar, salt, celery salt and paprika; mix well. Spoon into 1-quart casserole; top with bacon. Bake at 375 degrees for 20 minutes. Yield: 4 servings.

Approx Per Serving: Cal 124; Prot 7 g; Carbo 20 g; Fiber <1 g;
T Fat 2 g; 16% Calories from Fat; Chol 3 mg; Sod 285 mg.

Dietary Exchanges: Fat 1/2

Hot and Cold Beans

1 1/2 cups mayonnaise
4 hard-boiled eggs, finely chopped
1 teaspoon Worcestershire sauce
Tabasco sauce to taste
1   7-ounce can sliced water chestnuts,
    drained
2 tablespoons finely minced onion

1 teaspoon dry mustard
1   16-ounce can French-style green
    beans, drained, chopped
1   8-ounce can lima beans
1   8-ounce can green peas
Salt to taste

Combine mayonnaise, eggs, Worcestershire sauce, Tabasco sauce, water chestnuts, onion and dry mustard in bowl; mix well. Chill in refrigerator. Combine green beans, lima beans, peas and salt in saucepan. Cook until heated through; drain. Spoon into serving dish. Spoon mayonnaise mixture over top. Serve immediately. Yield: 8 servings.

Approx Per Serving: Cal 399; Prot 7 g; Carbo 14 g; Fiber 4 g;
T Fat 36 g; 79% Calories from Fat; Chol 130 mg; Sod 590 mg.

Dietary Exchanges: Bread 1/2; Lean Meat 1/2; Vegetable 1; Fat 6 1/2

Nancy Evins, Lebanon, Tennessee

When cooking beets, leave 1 inch of stem to prevent "bleeding." Then peel and slice the beets.

Beets with Honey Sauce

2 tablespoons margarine
2 tablespoons flour
1 tablespoon honey

2 tablespoons light brown sugar
2 teaspoons lemon juice
3 cups cooked sliced beets

Melt margarine in saucepan. Stir in flour. Add honey, brown sugar and lemon juice. Simmer until thickened and clear, stirring constantly. Add beets. Cook until heated through. Yield: 6 servings.

Approx Per Serving: Cal 103; Prot 2 g; Carbo 17 g; Fiber 2 g;
T Fat 4 g; 33% Calories from Fat; Chol 0 mg; Sod 112 mg.

Dietary Exchanges: Fruit 1/2; Vegetable 1 1/2

Spicy Beets

1/4 cup vinegar
1 onion, chopped
1 teaspoon salt
1 teaspoon sugar

1/4 teaspoon dry mustard
1 teaspoon Worcestershire sauce
1 pound beets, sliced, cooked, drained

Combine vinegar, onion, salt, sugar, mustard and Worcestershire sauce in saucepan. Bring to a boil, stirring frequently. Add beets; mix gently. Cook until heated through. Serve hot or cold. Yield: 4 servings.

Approx Per Serving: Cal 67; Prot 2 g; Carbo 16 g; Fiber 4 g;
T Fat <1 g; 4% Calories from Fat; Chol 0 mg; Sod 636 mg.

Dietary Exchanges: Vegetable 2 1/2

Broccoli with Lemon Sauce

1 bunch fresh broccoli
2 tablespoons water
Salt to taste

1/2 cup lemon juice
1/4 cup margarine
1/2 cup slivered almonds

Cut flowerets from broccoli; peel and slice stems. Place stems in center of glass dish; arrange flowerets around outer edge. Add water. Microwave, covered with plastic wrap, on High for 8 minutes. Sprinkle with salt; let stand, covered, for several minutes. Combine lemon juice, margarine and almonds in glass measure. Microwave on High for 1 minute; mix well. Pour in a circle over broccoli. May add 1/2 teaspoon grated lemon rind if desired. Yield: 6 servings.

Approx Per Serving: Cal 156; Prot 4 g; Carbo 7 g; Fiber 3 g;
T Fat 14 g; 73% Calories from Fat; Chol 0 mg; Sod 107 mg.

Dietary Exchanges: Lean Meat 1/2; Vegetable 1/2; Fat 1

Theresa Robinson, Nashville, Tennessee

Broccoli and Pasta Casserole

8 ounces uncooked spaghetti
6 cups chicken broth
1 bunch fresh broccoli, chopped
8 green onions, chopped

2 tablespoons margarine
Salt and pepper to taste
12 ounces Cheddar cheese, sliced
³/₄ cup half and half

Cook spaghetti in chicken broth in saucepan until tender; drain. Cook broccoli in boiling water to cover in saucepan just until tender; drain. Sauté green onions in margarine in large skillet for 2 minutes. Add broccoli. Sauté for 3 minutes. Season with salt and pepper. Layer spaghetti and half the cheese in buttered 2-quart baking dish. Pour half and half over layers. Add broccoli and remaining cheese. Bake at 350 degrees for 40 minutes. Yield: 10 servings.

Approx Per Serving: Cal 301; Prot 16 g; Carbo 21 g; Fiber 2 g;
    T Fat 17 g; 50% Calories from Fat; Chol 43 mg; Sod 723 mg.

Dietary Exchanges: Bread 1¹/₂; Lean Meat 1; Vegetable ¹/₂; Fat 2

Broccoli Casserole

¹/₄ cup chopped onion
2 tablespoons flour
¹/₂ cup skim milk
8 ounces low-fat Cheddar cheese,
    shredded

3 cups chopped broccoli
6 egg whites, stiffly beaten
3 sheets phyllo dough, cut into halves

Coat shallow 1¹/₂-quart baking dish with nonstick cooking spray. Sauté onion in skillet sprayed with nonstick cooking spray. Blend flour and milk in small bowl. Add to onion. Cook until thickened, stirring constantly. Add cheese, stirring until melted. Add broccoli; mix well. Fold in egg whites gently. Spoon into prepared baking dish. Layer phyllo over top, spraying each sheet of dough with nonstick cooking spray. Bake at 325 degrees for 35 to 45 minutes or until golden brown. Yield: 9 servings.

Approx Per Serving: Cal 125; Prot 12 g; Carbo 9 g; Fiber 1 g;
    T Fat 5 g; 36% Calories from Fat; Chol 14 mg; Sod 221 mg.

Dietary Exchanges: Bread ¹/₂; Lean Meat 1¹/₂; Vegetable ¹/₂; Fat ¹/₂

Broccoli is America's favorite edible flower. The "flowerets" are actually blossoms and like most blossoms are fairly delicate. Eat them uncooked and crisp or cooked just until tender-crisp for best texture and flavor.

Broccoli and Ricotta Casserole

1¹/₂ pounds fresh broccoli
2 eggs, slightly beaten
³/₄ cup ricotta cheese
¹/₂ cup shredded Cheddar cheese
2 tablespoons chopped onion

1 tablespoon Worcestershire sauce
¹/₂ teaspoon salt
¹/₈ teaspoon pepper
¹/₄ cup dry bread crumbs
1 tablespoon margarine, melted

Rinse and trim broccoli; cut into spears. Cook, covered, in a small amount of water in saucepan for 10 minutes or until tender-crisp; drain. Combine eggs, ricotta cheese, Cheddar cheese, onion, Worcestershire sauce, salt and pepper in bowl; mix well. Place broccoli in shallow 1¹/₂-quart baking dish. Spread cheese mixture over top. Mix bread crumbs and margarine in bowl. Sprinkle over broccoli. Bake at 350 degrees for 15 minutes or until set. Yield: 6 servings.

Approx Per Serving: Cal 184; Prot 12 g; Carbo 11 g; Fiber 3 g;
T Fat 11 g; 53% Calories from Fat; Chol 96 mg; Sod 400 mg.

Dietary Exchanges: Lean Meat 1; Vegetable 1¹/₂; Fat 1

Place a heel of bread on cabbage, broccoli or Brussels sprouts before covering them to cook. It will not affect the flavor of the vegetable but will greatly reduce cooking odors.

Broccoli and Cheese Casserole

4 cups chopped fresh broccoli
¹/₂ teaspoon salt
1 tablespoon butter
1   10-ounce can cream of mushroom
  soup

1 egg, beaten
12 ounces extra-sharp Cheddar cheese,
  shredded
20 butter crackers, crushed

Cook broccoli with salt in water to cover in saucepan for 10 to 15 minutes or until tender; drain. Add butter. Combine soup, egg and ³/₄ of the Cheddar cheese in bowl. Add broccoli; mix gently. Spoon into 8x12-inch baking dish. Top with remaining cheese and cracker crumbs. Bake at 375 degrees for 30 to 40 minutes or until bubbly and brown. Yield: 8 servings.

Approx Per Serving: Cal 279; Prot 14 g; Carbo 10 g; Fiber 1 g;
T Fat 21 g; 66% Calories from Fat; Chol 76 mg; Sod 782 mg.

Dietary Exchanges: Bread ¹/₂; Lean Meat 1¹/₂; Vegetable ¹/₂; Fat 3

John and Jeanne Wright, Nashville, Tennessee

Light and Tasty Cabbage

1/2 teaspoon sugar
1/2 teaspoon salt

1 cup boiling water
3 cups coarsely shredded cabbage

Stir sugar and salt into boiling water in saucepan. Add cabbage gradually to saucepan. Cook for 10 to 15 minutes or just until tender; do not overcook. Yield: 4 servings.

Approx Per Serving: Cal 15; Prot 1 g; Carbo 3 g; Fiber 1 g;
T Fat <1 g; 7% Calories from Fat; Chol 0 mg; Sod 276 mg.

Dietary Exchanges: Vegetable 1/2

Eula Steele, Lutts, Tennessee

Pennsylvania Red Cabbage

2 tablespoons bacon drippings
4 cups shredded red cabbage
2 cups chopped unpeeled apples
1/4 cup vinegar
1/4 cup packed brown sugar

1 teaspoon salt
Pepper to taste
1/2 teaspoon caraway seed
1/4 cup water

Heat bacon drippings in large skillet. Add cabbage, apples, vinegar, brown sugar, salt, pepper, caraway seed and water; mix well. Cook, covered, over low heat for 15 minutes for tender-crisp cabbage or for 25 minutes for very tender cabbage, stirring occasionally. Yield: 4 servings.

Approx Per Serving: Cal 166; Prot 1 g; Carbo 26 g; Fiber 3 g;
T Fat 7 g; 38% Calories from Fat; Chol 7 mg; Sod 588 mg.

Dietary Exchanges: Fruit 1 1/2; Vegetable 1/2; Fat 1 1/2

Making your own sauerkraut is easier than you think. Shred or coarsely chop enough cabbage to pack tightly into a hot sterilized wide-mouth 1-quart jar (6 to 7 cups cabbage should be about right). Add 1 teaspoon sugar and 1 teaspoon salt. Fill jar with boiling water, leaving 1/2 inch headspace; seal jar with a standard 2-piece canning lid. Let sauerkraut stand for 3 weeks before opening.

Colcannon

4 baking potatoes
4 cups shredded cabbage
3 tablespoons margarine
1/2 cup lukewarm milk
4 green onions, finely chopped

1/2 teaspoon salt
1/2 teaspoon caraway seed
Freshly ground pepper to taste
1/4 cup finely chopped parsley

Scrub potatoes and pierce with fork. Bake at 400 degrees for 1 hour. Cool slightly. Combine cabbage and water to cover in saucepan. Boil, uncovered, for 8 minutes; drain and keep warm. Cut potatoes into halves. Scoop out pulp, reserving shells. Combine potato pulp with margarine in bowl; mash thoroughly. Add enough milk gradually to make creamy consistency. Add cabbage, green onions, salt, caraway seed and pepper; mix well. Spoon into potato shells. Sprinkle with parsley. Yield: 8 servings.

Approx Per Serving: Cal 169; Prot 4 g; Carbo 29 g; Fiber 3 g;
    T Fat 5 g; 26% Calories from Fat; Chol 2 mg; Sod 207 mg.

Dietary Exchanges: Bread 1^{1}/2; Vegetable 1/2

Customize your gardening tools for comfort and convenience. Be sure you keep all wooden parts smoothly sanded or padded to avoid blisters. Tung oil preserves the wood from moisture. Keep metal parts shiny and rust-free by wiping surfaces with an oiled rag after use.

Dilled Carrots

3 cups apple cider vinegar
9 cups water
1 cup coarse pickling salt
Carrots

Dill
Garlic
Red pepper

Combine vinegar, water and pickling salt in saucepan. Boil for 5 minutes; cool to room temperature. Pack carrots into jars; add 1 large head of dill, 2 large teaspoons minced garlic and 1/2 teaspoon red pepper to each jar. Pour cider mixture into jars, leaving 1/2 inch headspace; seal with 2-piece lids. Let stand for 10 days before serving. Yield: variable.

Nutritional information for this recipe is not available.

Jennifer Smith, Franklin, Tennessee

Maple Carrots and Apples

3 medium unpeeled tart apples
6 medium carrots, diagonally sliced
3 tablespoons margarine

1 large onion, sliced
2 tablespoons maple syrup
1/2 teaspoon salt

Cut apples into 1/4 to 1/2-inch wedges. Sauté carrots in margarine in skillet until partially done. Stir in onion, syrup and salt; reduce heat to low. Cook, covered, for 5 to 7 minutes. Add apples. Simmer just until carrots are tender, stirring occasionally. Yield: 6 servings.

Approx Per Serving: Cal 147; Prot 1 g; Carbo 24 g; Fiber 4 g;
     T Fat 6 g; 36% Calories from Fat; Chol 0 mg; Sod 271 mg.

Dietary Exchanges: Fruit 1; Vegetable 1

Cranberry Carrots

8 carrots, sliced
1 tablespoon water
1/4 cup margarine

1/4 cup cranberry sauce
Salt and pepper to taste

Steam carrots in water in covered saucepan until tender. Melt margarine in small saucepan. Add cranberry sauce, salt and pepper. Cook until cranberry sauce is melted. Place carrots in microwave-safe dish. Pour cranberry mixture over top. Microwave on High for 1 minute or until heated through. Yield: 4 servings.

Approx Per Serving: Cal 190; Prot 2 g; Carbo 21 g; Fiber 5 g;
     T Fat 12 g; 53% Calories from Fat; Chol 0 mg; Sod 189 mg.

Dietary Exchanges: Fruit 1/2; Vegetable 2

Honey-Dijon Carrots

3 tablespoons margarine
1 tablespoon honey

1 tablespoon Dijon mustard
2 cups steamed sliced carrots

Combine margarine, honey and mustard in saucepan. Heat for several minutes or until flavors are blended, stirring constantly. Pour over hot steamed carrots. Yield: 4 servings.

Approx Per Serving: Cal 129; Prot 1 g; Carbo 13 g; Fiber 3 g;
     T Fat 9 g; 59% Calories from Fat; Chol 0 mg; Sod 177 mg.

Dietary Exchanges: Fruit 1/2; Vegetable 1 1/2

Carrot and Rice Ring

3 cups cooked rice
2 cups grated carrots
1/4 cup grated onion
2 tablespoons flour
1 10-ounce can Cheddar cheese soup
1 egg, slightly beaten

1 teaspoon salt
1/4 teaspoon pepper
1 teaspoon Worcestershire sauce
Hot sauce to taste
1 10-ounce package frozen peas

Combine rice, carrots, onion and flour in large bowl. Add soup, egg, salt, pepper, Worcestershire sauce and hot sauce; mix well. Press mixture into greased 8-inch ring mold. Bake at 350 degrees for 30 minutes. Cook peas using package directions; drain. Invert rice ring onto platter; fill center with peas. Yield: 8 servings.

Approx Per Serving: Cal 201; Prot 7 g; Carbo 34 g; Fiber 3 g;
    T Fat 4 g; 18% Calories from Fat; Chol 35 mg; Sod 596 mg.

Dietary Exchanges: Bread 1 1/2; Lean Meat 1/2; Vegetable 1/2; Fat 1/2

Carrot Casserole

1 1/2 cups grated carrots
2 tablespoons chopped onion
1 cup cooked rice
1 cup shredded American cheese

2 eggs, beaten
1 tablespoon butter, softened
1/2 teaspoon salt
Pepper to taste

Combine carrots, onion, rice, cheese, eggs, butter, salt and pepper in bowl; mix well. Pour into greased 2-quart baking dish. Bake at 350 degrees for 45 minutes. Yield: 8 servings.

Approx Per Serving: Cal 127; Prot 6 g; Carbo 10 g; Fiber 1 g;
    T Fat 7 g; 51% Calories from Fat; Chol 70 mg; Sod 374 mg.

Dietary Exchanges: Bread 1/2; Lean Meat 1/2; Vegetable 1/2; Fat 1

To keep corn on the cob fresh, cut a piece off the base of each ear and stand it, in the husk, in a pan of water in the refrigerator.

Zesty Carrots

8 carrots, julienned
1 small onion, finely chopped
2 tablespoons prepared horseradish
1/2 cup mayonnaise
1 teaspoon salt

1/4 teaspoon pepper
1/8 teaspoon paprika
1/2 cup carrot juice
1/3 cup bread crumbs
1 tablespoon melted margarine

Cook carrots in boiling water in saucepan until tender; drain. Mix with onion, horse-radish, mayonnaise, salt, pepper, paprika and carrot juice in bowl. Pour into greased 1-quart baking dish. Toss bread crumbs with melted margarine in bowl. Sprinkle over carrots. Bake at 350 degrees for 15 to 20 minutes or until heated through. Yield: 8 servings.

Approx Per Serving: Cal 171; Prot 2 g; Carbo 13 g; Fiber 3 g;
    T Fat 13 g; 66% Calories from Fat; Chol 8 mg; Sod 431 mg.

Dietary Exchanges: Vegetable 1 1/2; Fat 2

If your garden only has room for a few corn stalks, be sure to plant in a compact square rather than 1 long row so that the pollen necessary to provide well-filled ears has a better chance of reaching the silks to fertilize the kernels-to-be.

Festive Corn Relish

1/2 cup sugar
1/2 cup light vinegar
1/2 teaspoon celery seed
1/8 teaspoon dry mustard
1/8 teaspoon Tabasco sauce

1/2 teaspoon salt
2 tablespoons chopped onion
1   12-ounce can whole kernel corn
    with peppers, drained

Combine sugar, vinegar, celery seed, dry mustard, Tabasco sauce and salt in 4-cup glass measure; mix well. Microwave on High for 3 to 4 minutes or until mixture boils for 1 minute. Stir in onion and corn. Cool to room temperature. Chill overnight before serving. May store in refrigerator for up to several weeks. Yield: 32 (1-tablespoon) servings.

Approx Per Serving: Cal 22; Prot <1 g; Carbo 5 g; Fiber <1 g;
    T Fat <1 g; 4% Calories from Fat; Chol 0 mg; Sod 68 mg.

Dietary Exchanges: Free

Sarah Wade, McEwen, Tennessee

Homemade Hominy

Dried kernels of 8 large ears of corn   **8 tablespoons baking soda**

Combine corn and baking soda in large stainless steel or enamel saucepan. Add cold water to cover. Simmer until skins slip from corn kernels. Drain and rinse several times, discarding skins. Combine corn with fresh cold water to cover in saucepan. Simmer until corn is tender, adding water as needed. My mama made hominy which she mashed with a wooden masher and seasoned with bacon drippings and salt. She also make a salad of 2 cups hominy, onion, celery, green pepper, salt and 1 tablespoon vinegar or lemon juice. Yield: 8 servings.

Approx Per Serving: Cal 133; Prot 4 g; Carbo 31 g; Fiber 6 g;
   T Fat 2 g; 9% Calories from Fat; Chol 0 mg; Sod 2484 mg.
   Nutritional information is for hominy only.

Dietary Exchanges: Bread 1¹/₂

Carrie Byrne Bartlett, Gallatin, Tennessee

Corn and Eggplant Casserole

1 medium eggplant
1 teaspoon salt
1 small onion, chopped
3 tablespoons chopped green bell
   pepper
2 tablespoons butter

1 cup cream-style corn
1 egg, beaten
¹/₄ cup (or less) milk
³/₄ cup cracker crumbs
¹/₂ cup shredded Cheddar cheese

Cook eggplant in salted boiling water in saucepan for 20 minutes or until tender; drain. Sauté onion and green pepper in butter in skillet. Combine with eggplant, corn and egg in bowl. Add enough milk to make of desired consistency. Spoon into 1¹/₂-quart baking dish; top with cracker crumbs and cheese. Bake at 350 degrees for 30 minutes or until brown. Yield: 6 servings.

Approx Per Serving: Cal 198; Prot 6 g; Carbo 23 g; Fiber 4 g;
   T Fat 10 g; 43% Calories from Fat; Chol 57 mg; Sod 729 mg.

Dietary Exchanges: Bread 1; Lean Meat ¹/₂; Vegetable 1; Fat 1¹/₂

Ruth C. Cook, White House, Tennessee

Female eggplant, with more seed, are more bitter than male eggplant. To select a male eggplant, look for a round dime-sized grayish indentation on the blossom end. The mark will be oval or oblong on a female eggplant.

Eggplant Parmigiana

3 tablespoons margarine
1/2 cup cornflake crumbs
1/4 cup grated Parmesan cheese
1/2 teaspoon salt
Pepper to taste
1 eggplant
1 egg, slightly beaten

1/2 teaspoon oregano
1 8-ounce can tomato sauce
1/4 teaspoon basil
1/2 teaspoon sugar
Onion salt to taste
1 cup shredded mozzarella cheese

Melt margarine in 8x10-inch baking dish. Combine cornflake crumbs, Parmesan cheese, salt and pepper in shallow dish; mix well and set aside. Peel eggplant and cut into 3/4-inch thick slices. Dip eggplant into egg; coat with crumb mixture. Arrange in baking dish. Bake at 400 degrees for 20 minutes. Turn slices over. Bake for 15 minutes longer. Combine oregano, tomato sauce, basil, sugar and onion salt in small saucepan. Bring to a boil, stirring occasionally. Spoon sauce over eggplant slices, turning to coat both sides. Sprinkle with mozzarella cheese. Bake for 3 minutes longer or until cheese melts. Yield: 8 servings.

Approx Per Serving: Cal 148; Prot 6 g; Carbo 11 g; Fiber 3 g;
 T Fat 9 g; 54% Calories from Fat; Chol 40 mg; Sod 523 mg.

Dietary Exchanges: Lean Meat 1/2; Vegetable 1; Fat 1/2

Chop onions and green peppers during their plentiful season and freeze them for later use in casseroles and soups.

Pisto

3 tablespoons oil
1 eggplant, peeled, chopped
2 tomatoes, chopped

2 cloves of garlic, chopped
3/4 teaspoon salt
3/4 teaspoon oregano

Heat oil in skillet. Add eggplant, tomatoes, garlic, salt and oregano. Simmer over low heat until eggplant is tender, stirring occasionally. Serve hot or cold. May add green or red bell peppers or substitute squash or beans for eggplant if preferred. Yield: 6 servings.

Approx Per Serving: Cal 96; Prot 1 g; Carbo 8 g; Fiber 3 g;
 T Fat 7 g; 63% Calories from Fat; Chol 0 mg; Sod 273 mg.

Dietary Exchanges: Vegetable 1; Fat 1 1/2

Vegetarian Eggplant

3 medium eggplant
8 ounces mushrooms, chopped
2 cloves of garlic, minced
1 cup chopped onion
Salt and pepper to taste
3 tablespoons margarine
1¹/₂ cups cottage cheese

1 cup cooked brown rice
1 cup shredded Cheddar cheese
¹/₂ teaspoon thyme
Several drops of Tabasco sauce
¹/₄ cup toasted sunflower seed
Paprika to taste
¹/₄ cup chopped fresh parsley

Slice eggplant into halves lengthwise. Scoop out pulp, reserving ¹/₄-inch shells. Chop pulp. Sauté eggplant pulp with mushrooms, garlic, onion, salt and pepper in margarine until onion is tender. Stir in cottage cheese, rice, cheese, thyme, Tabasco sauce and sunflower seed. Spoon into reserved eggplant shells; sprinkle with paprika and parsley. Arrange in buttered baking dish. Bake at 350 degrees for 40 minutes. Yield: 6 servings.

Approx Per Serving: Cal 349; Prot 17 g; Carbo 33 g; Fiber 11 g; T Fat 19 g; 46% Calories from Fat; Chol 28 mg; Sod 410 mg.

Dietary Exchanges: Bread ¹/₂; Lean Meat 2; Vegetable 3¹/₂; Fat 1¹/₂

Mushroom and Spinach Casserole

1 pound fresh spinach
1 pound fresh mushrooms, sliced
¹/₄ cup butter
¹/₂ onion, chopped
1 clove of garlic, minced

2 tablespoons lemon juice
2 tablespoons sherry
4 ounces cream cheese, softened
1¹/₂ cups sour cream
¹/₂ cup bread crumbs

Pour boiling water over spinach in colander; drain well, pressing out moisture. Chop and set aside. Sauté mushrooms in butter in large skillet over medium heat. Add onion, garlic, lemon juice and wine. Cook for 3 minutes. Stir in cream cheese until melted. Add sour cream and spinach gradually, stirring constantly. Spoon into baking dish; top with bread crumbs. Bake at 350 degrees for 30 minutes. May also serve as dip with chips. Yield: 6 servings.

Approx Per Serving: Cal 334; Prot 8 g; Carbo 17 g; Fiber 4 g; T Fat 27 g; 71% Calories from Fat; Chol 67 mg; Sod 300 mg.

Dietary Exchanges: Bread ¹/₂; Vegetable 1¹/₂; Fat 5

Tammy T. Algood, C.H.E., Food Marketing Agent
University of Tennessee Agricultural Extension Service
Nashville, Tennessee

Creole Okra

1 medium onion, sliced
1 medium green bell pepper, sliced
1 small clove of garlic, crushed
1/4 cup bacon drippings
2 pounds okra, sliced 1/2 inch thick

4 medium tomatoes, peeled, chopped
1 teaspoon Worcestershire sauce
1/4 cup sugar
Salt and pepper to taste
1 teaspoon gumbo filé

Sauté onion, green pepper and garlic in bacon drippings in heavy saucepan until onion is tender. Add okra, tomatoes, Worcestershire sauce, sugar, salt and pepper; mix well. Cook, covered, over medium heat for 20 minutes; remove from heat. Stir in filé. Serve over rice. Yield: 8 servings.

Approx Per Serving: Cal 145; Prot 3 g; Carbo 19 g; Fiber 4 g;
     T Fat 7 g; 19% Calories from Fat; Chol 7 mg; Sod 57 mg.
     Nutritional information does not include gumbo filé.

Dietary Exchanges: Fruit 1/2; Vegetable 2; Fat 1 1/2

Ann C. Frye, Antioch, Tennessee

Okra pods are best when they are 3 to 4 inches long; longer ones may be tough and stringy. Seed should be glossy rather dull.

Onion Pie

4 medium Vidalia onions, thinly
     sliced into rings
2 tablespoons margarine
1 unbaked 9-inch pie shell
1 cup shredded Swiss cheese

2 eggs, beaten
1 cup half and half
3/4 teaspoon salt
Pepper to taste
Paprika to taste

Sauté onions in margarine in skillet. Spread in pie shell. Sprinkle with cheese. Combine eggs, half and half, salt and pepper in mixer bowl. Beat until smooth. Pour over onions and cheese. Sprinkle with paprika. Bake at 425 degrees for 15 minutes; reduce temperature to 350 degrees. Bake for 30 minutes longer. Let stand for 15 minutes before serving. Yield: 6 servings.

Approx Per Serving: Cal 365; Prot 11 g; Carbo 23 g; Fiber 2 g;
     T Fat 26 g; 63% Calories from Fat; Chol 102 mg; Sod 560 mg.

Dietary Exchanges: Bread 1; Lean Meat 1; Vegetable 1; Fat 3 1/2

Onions Stuffed with Walnuts

6 large Bermuda onions
2 tablespoons margarine
1 cup packed coarse dry bread crumbs
1¹/₄ cups coarsely chopped walnuts
1 egg, beaten

¹/₄ teaspoon thyme
Salt and freshly ground pepper to taste
¹/₂ cup bread crumbs
1 tablespoon melted margarine

Peel onions, leaving root ends intact so onions will not separate. Cut thick slice from top of each. Boil onions and top slices in a large amount of water in saucepan for 30 minutes or just until tender; drain and cool. Scoop out centers to form cups, leaving ¹/₃ to ¹/₂-inch shells; reserve centers. Invert cups to drain. Chop tops and centers of onions. Sauté chopped onions in 2 tablespoons margarine in skillet until almost dry. Add dry bread crumbs, walnuts, egg, thyme, salt and pepper; mix well. Spoon stuffing into onion cups. Sprinkle tops with mixture of bread crumbs and 1 tablespoon melted margarine. Place onion cups in baking dish. Add enough water to barely cover bottom of dish. Bake at 375 degrees for 20 to 30 minutes or until crumbs are brown. May substitute filberts, pecans or Brazil nuts for walnuts. Yield: 6 servings.

Approx Per Serving: Cal 381; Prot 10 g; Carbo 35 g; Fiber 4 g;
    T Fat 24 g; 54% Calories from Fat; Chol 35 mg; Sod 335 mg.

Dietary Exchanges: Bread 1¹/₂; Vegetable 1¹/₂

Pea Pods and Almonds

¹/₂ cup water
1 tablespoon soy sauce
1¹/₂ teaspoons cornstarch
1 teaspoon instant chicken bouillon

2 tablespoons slivered almonds
2 tablespoons margarine
8 ounces pea pods
4 ounces mushrooms, sliced

Combine water, soy sauce, cornstarch and instant bouillon in small bowl; mix well. Stir-fry almonds in margarine in skillet for 2 minutes. Add pea pods. Stir-fry for 2 minutes longer. Stir in mushrooms and cornstarch mixture. Cook for 1 to 2 minutes longer or until thickened, stirring constantly. Yield: 4 servings.

Approx Per Serving: Cal 115; Prot 4 g; Carbo 8 g; Fiber 2 g;
    T Fat 8 g; 61% Calories from Fat; Chol <1 mg; Sod 616 mg.

Dietary Exchanges: Vegetable 1; Fat ¹/₂

Store onions in a cool dark place in a bag or basket that provides air circulation. Do not refrigerate until onion is cut.

Orange-Glazed Pea Pods

8 ounces fresh pea pods
1 teaspoon sugar
3/4 teaspoon cornstarch
Salt to taste

1/4 cup orange juice
1/2 teaspoon grated orange rind
2 teaspoons unsalted margarine
1/2 cup sliced almonds, toasted

Cook pea pods in a small amount of water in saucepan until tender-crisp; drain. Combine sugar, cornstarch and salt in double boiler. Add orange juice, blending until smooth. Add orange rind. Cook until mixture begins to thicken, stirring constantly. Add margarine, stirring until melted. Spoon over peas in serving dish; sprinkle with almonds. Yield: 4 servings.

Approx Per Serving: Cal 123; Prot 4 g; Carbo 10 g; Fiber 3 g;
T Fat 8 g; 57% Calories from Fat; Chol 0 mg; Sod 4 mg.

Dietary Exchanges: Lean Meat 1/2; Fruit 1/2; Vegetable 1; Fat 11/2

When it is necessary to use insecticide to debug your garden, get maximum coverage and effect from minimum amounts by sprinkling leaves and soil between rows with insecticide powder early in the morning when the dew still coats plant surfaces. A bath powder mitt or old sock filled with the powder will provide a fine dusting.

"Hoppin' Juan"

11/2 cups uncooked brown rice
1/2 cup dried black-eyed peas, cooked
1 large onion, chopped
3 jalapeño peppers, finely chopped
3 cloves of garlic, minced

Salt to taste
4 cups shredded part-skim mozzarella
cheese
4 ounces part-skim ricotta cheese
2 tablespoons 1% milk

Cook rice using package directions. Combine rice, cooked black-eyed peas, onion, jalapeño peppers, garlic and salt in large bowl; mix well. Mix 3 cups mozzarella cheese, ricotta cheese and milk in medium bowl. Alternate layers of rice mixture and cheese mixture in 9x13-inch baking dish until all ingredients are used, ending with rice mixture. Bake at 350 degrees for 25 minutes. Sprinkle remaining 1 cup mozzarella cheese over top. Bake for 5 minutes longer. Yield: 12 servings.

Approx Per Serving: Cal 225; Prot 14 g; Carbo 25 g; Fiber 3 g;
T Fat 8 g; 30% Calories from Fat; Chol 25 mg; Sod 191 mg.

Dietary Exchanges: Bread 11/2; Lean Meat 11/2; Fat 1/2

Poke Sallet Casserole

1 7-ounce package quick-cooking rice
2 tablespoons chopped onion
2 tablespoons butter
1 cup drained cooked poke sallet

1 10-ounce can cream of mushroom
  soup
2 cups plus 2 tablespoons water
1 8-ounce jar Cheez Whiz

Cook rice using package directions for 3 minutes. Sauté onion in butter in skillet. Add rice, poke sallet, soup, water and 3/4 of the Cheez Whiz; mix well. Spoon into baking dish; spread with remaining Cheez Whiz. Bake at 350 degrees until bubbly. Yield: 8 servings.

Approx Per Serving: Cal 243; Prot 8 g; Carbo 27 g; Fiber 1 g;
    T Fat 12 g; 43% Calories from Fat; Chol 24 mg; Sod 746 mg.

Dietary Exchanges: Bread 1; Lean Meat 1/2; Fat 2

Roberta J. Lee, Waverly, Tennessee

Potato and Apple Skillet

1/4 teaspoon salt
1/4 teaspoon pepper
3 potatoes, cut into strips
2 medium apples, chopped

1/2 cup chopped onion
1/4 cup chopped celery
2 tablespoons oil
1 cup shredded Cheddar cheese

Sprinkle salt and pepper over potatoes. Add potatoes, apples, onion and celery to hot oil in skillet, stirring to coat well. Cook, covered, for 20 minutes or until tender, stirring occasionally. Sprinkle with cheese. Serve hot. Yield: 4 servings.

Approx Per Serving: Cal 306; Prot 9 g; Carbo 32 g; Fiber 3 g;
    T Fat 17 g; 47% Calories from Fat; Chol 30 mg; Sod 321 mg.

Dietary Exchanges: Bread 1; Lean Meat 1; Fruit 1/2; Vegetable 1/2; Fat 2 1/2

Soil in a vegetable garden should be cultivated to be loose and airy so that roots develop properly, plant growth is not stunted and root crops can ⁀nd to optimum size.

Chili Salsa Potato Skins

5 large russet potatoes
1/3 cup melted margarine
3/4 cup shredded mild Cheddar cheese
3/4 cup shredded Monterey Jack cheese

1 8-ounce can tomato sauce
1 4-ounce can green chilies
1/4 cup chopped green onions

Pierce potatoes several times with fork. Bake at 400 degrees until tender. Cool. Cut potatoes into quarters lengthwise. Scoop out pulp, leaving 1/8-inch thick skins. Reserve pulp for another purpose if desired. Brush skins inside and out with margarine. Place skin side down on 12x15-inch baking sheet. Bake at 500 degrees for 12 minutes. Sprinkle with cheeses. Broil 4 inches from heat source for 2 minutes or until cheeses are melted. Combine tomato sauce, green chilies and green onions in bowl; mix well. Spoon over potato skins just before serving. Yield: 10 servings.

Approx Per Serving: Cal 187; Prot 6 g; Carbo 16 g; Fiber 2 g;
      T Fat 12 g; 54% Calories from Fat; Chol 17 mg; Sod 446 mg.

Dietary Exchanges: Bread 1; Lean Meat 1/2; Vegetable 1/2; Fat 1/2

Scoop a small cavity out of a potato and insert a baby onion before baking for a tasty surprise.

Grilled Cheesy Potatoes

11/2 pounds small red potatoes
1/2 cup chopped onion
1 large green bell pepper, julienned
1/2 teaspoon salt

1/4 teaspoon pepper
2 tablespoons margarine
8 ounces Cheddar cheese, shredded

Peel potatoes; slice 1/4 inch thick. Oil two 15-inch long strips of foil lightly. Combine potatoes, onion, green pepper, salt and pepper in bowl; mix well. Place half the mixture on 1 end of each strip of foil. Dot with margarine. Fold other end of foil over potatoes; seal. Grill 6 inches above hot coals for 15 minutes on each side. Fold back foil; sprinkle cheese over potatoes. Grill for 3 minutes longer or until cheese melts. Yield: 6 servings.

Approx Per Serving: Cal 299; Prot 12 g; Carbo 27 g; Fiber 2 g;
      T Fat 17 g; 49% Calories from Fat; Chol 40 mg; Sod 463 mg.

Dietary Exchanges: Bread 11/2; Lean Meat 11/2; Vegetable 1/2; Fat 2

Microwave New Potatoes

8 medium new potatoes
1 tablespoon butter
1 tablespoon chopped chives

1/2 cup shredded American cheese
1/2 cup nonfat sour cream
Salt and pepper to taste

Boil potatoes in water in saucepan until tender; drain and cool. Peel and slice potatoes. Place butter in shallow glass dish. Microwave on Medium until melted. Add chives. Microwave on High for 2 to 3 minutes. Add cheese. Microwave on Medium-High for 2 to 3 minutes or until melted. Add sour cream; mix well. Place potatoes in dish, stirring to coat with mixture. Sprinkle with salt and pepper. Microwave on High for 2 to 4 minutes or until mixture is bubbly. Yield: 8 servings.

Approx Per Serving: Cal 166; Prot 5 g; Carbo 29 g; Fiber 2 g;
    T Fat 4 g; 20% Calories from Fat; Chol 11 mg; Sod 131 mg.

Dietary Exchanges: Bread 11/2; Fat 1/2

Italian Potatoes

6 medium russet potatoes
1/2 cup toasted fine bread crumbs
1/2 cup grated Parmesan cheese
3 large tomatoes, thinly sliced
2 large red onions, thinly sliced into
    rings

11/2 teaspoons oregano
1 teaspoon salt
Pepper to taste
1/4 cup olive oil

Peel potatoes; cut into wedges lengthwise. Place in bowl of cold water. Combine bread crumbs and Parmesan cheese in plastic bag. Drain potatoes; do not dry. Coat potatoes with crumb mixture. Arrange in shallow 9x13-inch baking dish; sprinkle with any remaining crumb mixture. Place tomato slices and onion rings over potatoes. Sprinkle with oregano, salt and pepper. Drizzle with olive oil. Bake at 350 degrees for 1 hour and 10 minutes or just until potatoes are brown. Yield: 6 servings.

Approx Per Serving: Cal 289; Prot 8 g; Carbo 38 g; Fiber 4 g;
    T Fat 12 g; 38% Calories from Fat; Chol 7 mg; Sod 595 mg.

Dietary Exchanges: Bread 2; Lean Meat 1/2; Vegetable 1; Fat 2

Plant herbs around the house and among the vegetables to help control bugs and add zest to your cooking.

Mashed Potatoes Deluxe

3 cups nonfat cottage cheese
4 cups mashed cooked potatoes
3/4 cup nonfat sour cream
1 1/2 tablespoons finely grated onion

1 teaspoon salt
1/8 teaspoon white pepper
1 tablespoon melted margarine
1/2 cup chopped almonds

Press cottage cheese through sieve until smooth. Combine with mashed potatoes. Add sour cream, onion, salt and pepper; mix well. Spoon into greased 2-quart casserole. Brush top with melted margarine. Bake at 350 degrees for 30 minutes. Place under broiler to brown top. Sprinkle with almonds before serving. Yield: 8 servings.

Approx Per Serving: Cal 208; Prot 17 g; Carbo 25 g; Fiber 3 g;
T Fat 6 g; 26% Calories from Fat; Chol 6 mg; Sod 932 mg.

Dietary Exchanges: Bread 1; Lean Meat 1; Milk 1/2; Fat 1/2

Oven-Browned Potatoes

6 potatoes
1/4 cup flour
3/4 teaspoon salt

1/8 teaspoon pepper
1/4 cup grated Parmesan cheese
1/3 cup margarine

Cut potatoes into quarters; do not peel. Combine flour, salt, pepper and Parmesan cheese in plastic bag. Shake potatoes in bag until thoroughly coated. Melt margarine in 9x13-inch baking pan. Add potatoes, turning to coat well. Bake at 370 degrees for 1 hour, turning potatoes occasionally to brown evenly. Yield: 6 servings.

Approx Per Serving: Cal 261; Prot 5 g; Carbo 35 g; Fiber 3 g;
T Fat 12 g; 39% Calories from Fat; Chol 3 mg; Sod 473 mg.

Dietary Exchanges: Bread 2

Quick Microwave Potatoes

1 tablespoon parsley flakes
1/4 cup grated Parmesan cheese
1/2 teaspoon salt

1/4 teaspoon pepper
2 tablespoons butter
4 medium potatoes, cut into halves

Mix parsley flakes, Parmesan cheese, salt and pepper in dish. Place butter in glass dish. Microwave on High for 30 seconds or until melted. Dip potatoes into butter; coat with cheese mixture. Arrange in dish. Microwave on High for 10 minutes or until tender. Yield: 8 servings.

Approx Per Serving: Cal 106; Prot 3 g; Carbo 16 g; Fiber 1 g;
T Fat 4 g; 32% Calories from Fat; Chol 10 mg; Sod 226 mg.

Dietary Exchanges: Bread 1; Fat 1/2

Theresa Robinson, Nashville, Tennessee

Picnic Potatoes

6 large onions
7 pounds potatoes
Salt and pepper to taste

6 tablespoons oil
1 cup water
1¹/₂ pounds Cheddar cheese, sliced

Slice onions and potatoes ¹/₈ inch thick. Cover bottom of Dutch oven with onions. Place 1-inch layer of potatoes on top. Repeat layers until Dutch oven is filled, seasoning layers with salt and pepper to taste. Pour oil down sides of Dutch oven. Add water; cover. Place over medium-hot coals. Cook for 45 minutes or until potatoes are tender. Top with cheese. Cook just until cheese melts. Yield: 20 servings.

Approx Per Serving: Cal 332; Prot 12 g; Carbo 37 g; Fiber 3 g;
    T Fat 16 g; 42% Calories from Fat; Chol 36 mg; Sod 220 mg.

Dietary Exchanges: Bread 2; Lean Meat 1; Vegetable ¹/₂; Fat 2¹/₂

Starchy foods such as potatoes are valuable sources of fiber, complex carbohydrates, protein, vitamins and minerals and should not be excluded from any diet. Dieters should, however, avoid the butter and sauces which frequently go with starchy foods.

Potato Skillet

1 medium onion, chopped
1 small clove of garlic, crushed
2 tablespoons olive oil
³/₄ cup chopped parsley
¹/₄ cup chopped pimento

1 cup chicken broth
Freshly ground pepper to taste
6 medium potatoes, peeled, thinly
    sliced

Sauté onion and garlic in olive oil in skillet until tender. Stir in parsley, pimento, broth and pepper; remove from heat. Layer potatoes in skillet. Bring to a boil; reduce heat. Simmer, covered, for 20 minutes or until potatoes are tender. Remove to serving bowl with slotted spoon. Drizzle pan juices over top. Yield: 8 servings.

Approx Per Serving: Cal 129; Prot 3 g; Carbo 22 g; Fiber 2 g;
    T Fat 4 g; 25% Calories from Fat; Chol 0 mg; Sod 106 mg.

Dietary Exchanges: Bread 1; Vegetable ¹/₂; Fat ¹/₂

Creamy Radishes

12 ounces red radishes, sliced
3 tablespoons margarine
1 tablespoon flour

1/2 teaspoon salt
Pepper to taste
1/4 cup milk

Bring radishes to a boil in water to cover in 2-quart saucepan; reduce heat. Simmer for 5 to 7 minutes or until tender-crisp. Drain, reserving 1/2 cup liquid. Melt margarine in skillet over low heat. Blend in flour, salt and pepper. Cook over low heat until mixture is thick and bubbly, stirring constantly. Remove from heat; stir in milk and reserved 1/2 cup cooking liquid. Simmer for 1 minute, stirring constantly. Add radishes. Cook for 5 minutes longer or until heated through. Pour into serving dish; garnish with chives or parsley. Yield: 6 servings.

Approx Per Serving: Cal 72; Prot 1 g; Carbo 4 g; Fiber 1 g;
T Fat 6 g; 76% Calories from Fat; Chol 1 mg; Sod 263 mg.

Dietary Exchanges: Vegetable 1/2

Spinach Lover's Quiches

6 eggs, beaten
3 cups small curd nonfat cottage
cheese
8 ounces Swiss cheese, shredded

3 10-ounce packages frozen chopped
spinach, thawed
Salt and pepper to taste
2 9-inch deep-dish pie shells

Combine eggs, cottage cheese, Swiss cheese, spinach, salt and pepper in large bowl; mix well. Pour into pie shells. Bake at 450 degrees for 15 minutes. Reduce oven temperature to 375 degrees. Bake for 45 minutes longer or until golden brown. Yield: 12 servings.

Approx Per Serving: Cal 325; Prot 20 g; Carbo 20 g; Fiber 2 g;
T Fat 19 g; 52% Calories from Fat; Chol 126 mg; Sod 545 mg.

Dietary Exchanges: Bread 1; Lean Meat 1 1/2; Vegetable 1/2; Fat 3

Gingered Acorn Squash

2 small acorn squash
1/4 cup fresh orange juice

1/2 teaspoon ground ginger
1/2 teaspoon nutmeg

Cut squash into halves; remove and discard seed. Cut a thin slice from bottom of squash so each will stand straight. Arrange squash in shallow baking pan. Spoon orange juice into cavities; sprinkle with ginger and nutmeg. Cover with foil. Bake at 375 degrees for 1 to 1 1/2 hours or until tender. Let stand for 5 minutes before serving. Yield: 4 servings.

Approx Per Serving: Cal 92; Prot 2 g; Carbo 24 g; Fiber 7 g;
T Fat <1 g; 2% Calories from Fat; Chol 0 mg; Sod 6 mg.

Dietary Exchanges: Bread 1 1/2

Squash and Apple Casserole

1 medium acorn squash
3 cups sliced apples
Brown sugar substitute to equal 1/2
  cup packed brown sugar
1/4 cup melted margarine

1 tablespoon flour
1/2 teaspoon nutmeg
1/2 teaspoon salt
1/4 cup chopped walnuts

Cut squash into halves lengthwise, discarding seed. Cut into small pieces. Alternate layers of squash and apples in baking dish. Combine brown sugar substitute, margarine, flour, nutmeg, salt and walnuts in bowl; mix well. Sprinkle over layers. Bake, covered with foil, at 350 degrees for 50 minutes or until squash is tender. May bake squash halves at 350 degrees for 35 minutes, fill centers with apples, sprinkle with brown sugar mixture and walnuts and bake until squash is tender. Yield: 8 servings.

Approx Per Serving: Cal 135; Prot 1 g; Carbo 16 g; Fiber 3 g;
    T Fat 8 g; 51% Calories from Fat; Chol 0 mg; Sod 210 mg.

Dietary Exchanges: Bread 1/2; Fruit 1/2

Stuffed Squash

14 uniform yellow squash
6 slices bacon
3 onions, chopped
6 tablespoons butter

1/3 cup cracker meal
1/2 teaspoon sugar
1/8 teaspoon each salt and pepper

Cook squash in water to cover in large saucepan for 20 minutes; drain. Cool to room temperature. Cut a thin slice from side of each squash; scoop pulp into bowl, reserving shells. Microwave bacon in microwave-safe dish until crisp; drain, reserving 6 tablespoons drippings. Sauté onions in reserved drippings and butter in skillet until tender. Add to reserved squash pulp with cracker meal, crumbled bacon, sugar, salt and pepper; mix well. Spoon into squash shells; arrange in greased 9x13-inch baking dish. Bake at 325 degrees for 20 minutes. Garnish with paprika and parsley or celery leaves. Yield: 14 servings.

Approx Per Serving: Cal 130; Prot 4 g; Carbo 16 g; Fiber 4 g;
    T Fat 7 g; 43% Calories from Fat; Chol 16 mg; Sod 118 mg.

Dietary Exchanges: Vegetable 2 1/2; Fat 1

Lois Sissom, Manchester, Tennessee

Yellow squash is best when it is 4 to 6 inches long and smooth skinned; zucchini should be 6 to 8 inches long and shiny skinned; pattypan should be 4 to 6 inches in diameter and shiny white.

Cheesy Spaghetti Squash

1 medium spaghetti squash	2 green onions, chopped
2 tablespoons water	8 slices Cheddar cheese
2 tablespoons butter	Salt and pepper to taste

Cut squash into halves lengthwise. Discard seed. Pierce with fork several times. Place cut side down in microwave-safe dish with 2 tablespoons water. Cover with plastic wrap. Microwave on High for 8 to 10 minutes or until squash is tender. Cool for 10 minutes. Scoop out strands into bowl. Microwave butter in medium glass dish until melted. Add green onions. Microwave on High for 3 minutes. Place cheese over green onions. Microwave on Medium for 3 minutes or until melted. Stir in spaghetti squash. Sprinkle with salt and pepper to taste. Microwave on High for 4 to 5 minutes or until bubbly. Yield: 8 servings.

Approx Per Serving: Cal 157; Prot 8 g; Carbo 4 g; Fiber 2 g;
T Fat 12 g; 70% Calories from Fat; Chol 38 mg; Sod 216 mg.

Dietary Exchanges: Lean Meat 1; Fat 2

Plant marigolds among your tomatoes and other vegetables. The roots produce a chemical that discourages nematodes.

Fried Green Tomatoes

1 teaspoon salt	4 firm green tomatoes
2/3 cup cornmeal	Oil for frying
Pepper to taste	

Sift salt, cornmeal and pepper into shallow bowl. Slice tomatoes ¼ inch thick. Dip each tomato slice into meal, coating both sides. Fry in oil in skillet until brown and tomatoes are tender. Yield: 6 servings.

Approx Per Serving: Cal 76; Prot 2 g; Carbo 16 g; Fiber 2 g;
T Fat <1 g; 5% Calories from Fat; Chol 0 mg; Sod 366 mg.
Nutritional information does not include oil for frying.

Dietary Exchanges: Bread ½; Vegetable 1

Tomatoes Florentine

12 ounces spinach, cooked, drained,
   chopped
1/2 cup soft bread crumbs
1/2 cup seasoned dry bread crumbs
1/2 cup finely chopped green onions
3 eggs, slightly beaten

1/4 cup melted margarine
1/3 cup grated Parmesan cheese
4 slices crisp-fried bacon, crumbled
Pepper to taste
8 thick tomato slices

Combine spinach with bread crumbs, green onions, eggs, margarine, cheese, bacon and pepper in bowl; mix well. Arrange tomato slices in greased 9x9-inch baking dish. Spoon spinach mixture onto slices. Bake at 350 degrees for 15 minutes or until light brown. Yield: 8 servings.

Approx Per Serving: Cal 162; Prot 8 g; Carbo 9 g; Fiber 2 g;
   T Fat 11 g; 59% Calories from Fat; Chol 86 mg; Sod 435 mg.

Dietary Exchanges: Bread 1/2; Lean Meat 1/2; Vegetable 1/2; Fat 1/2

Turnip and Apple Casserole

2 medium turnips, peeled, sliced
1 cup applesauce
2 eggs
3 tablespoons margarine
1 teaspoon (or more) sugar

Salt to taste
1/4 teaspoon pepper
2 apples, chopped
1 3/4 cups bread crumbs
2 tablespoons melted margarine

Cook turnips in water in saucepan until tender; drain. Mash with applesauce, eggs, 3 tablespoons margarine, sugar, salt and pepper in bowl. Stir in apples and half the crumbs. Spoon into greased 2-quart baking dish. Top with mixture of remaining crumbs and melted margarine. Bake at 350 degrees for 30 minutes. Yield: 8 servings.

Approx Per Serving: Cal 222; Prot 5 g; Carbo 30 g; Fiber 2 g;
   T Fat 10 g; 39% Calories from Fat; Chol 53 mg; Sod 311 mg.

Dietary Exchanges: Bread 1; Lean Meat 1/2; Fruit 1/2; Vegetable 1/2

Try something different: look for spaghetti squash, jicama, radicchio, enoki mushrooms, chayote and other new produce at your grocery market. If you like them, try adding a few rows to your next season's garden to see how they grow.

Turnip Casserole

1 pound white turnips, peeled, cubed
1 cup milk
1 tablespoon sugar

Salt to taste
1/2 cup margarine
1/4 cup cracker crumbs

Cook turnips in water to cover in saucepan for 1 hour or until turnips are tender; drain. Mash turnips with milk, sugar, salt and margarine in bowl until smooth. Spoon into lightly greased 1-quart baking dish. Top with cracker crumbs. Bake at 300 degrees for 20 minutes or until brown. Yield: 4 servings.

Approx Per Serving: Cal 307; Prot 4 g; Carbo 17 g; Fiber 2 g;
    T Fat 26 g; 73% Calories from Fat; Chol 8 mg; Sod 442 mg.

Dietary Exchanges: Bread 1/2; Vegetable 1; Milk 1/2; Fat 1/2

Where do those rambling squash and melon vines start? Whether searching to pull them up or to feed a dose of fertilizer, it makes life easier if you marked the main stem with a 2 or 3-foot stake when the plant was small.

Cheese-Stuffed Zucchini

4 medium zucchini
2 tablespoons nonfat sour cream
2 tablespoons melted margarine

2 tablespoons nonfat cottage cheese
Salt and pepper to taste
2 tablespoons grated Parmesan cheese

Cook whole zucchini in boiling water in saucepan until nearly tender. Cut off thin lengthwise slice from each zucchini. Scoop out pulp, reserving shells. Strain pulp to remove water. Combine pulp with sour cream, margarine, cottage cheese, salt and pepper in bowl; mix well. Spoon into zucchini shells. Arrange in baking dish. Sprinkle with Parmesan cheese. Bake at 350 degrees until heated through. Yield: 4 servings.

Approx Per Serving: Cal 110; Prot 6 g; Carbo 9 g; Fiber 3 g;
    T Fat 7 g; 52% Calories from Fat; Chol 3 mg; Sod 164 mg.

Dietary Exchanges: Vegetable 2

Corn Bread-Zucchini Bake

2 medium zucchini
8 ounces sausage
1/4 cup chopped onion

1 8-ounce package corn bread mix
1/2 cup shredded Cheddar cheese

Shred enough zucchini coarsely to measure 1/3 cup; reserve. Cut remaining zucchini into 1/4-inch slices. Brown sausage in skillet, stirring until crumbly. Remove with slotted spoon. Drain skillet, reserving 1 tablespoon pan drippings. Add zucchini slices and onion to reserved pan drippings in skillet, stirring to coat. Cook over medium-low heat for 3 to 5 minutes or until zucchini is tender, stirring occasionally. Arrange zucchini slices in circles in greased 8-inch round casserole. Prepare corn bread mix using package directions. Stir shredded zucchini, sausage and cheese into batter. Spread over sliced zucchini. Bake at 350 degrees for 25 to 30 minutes or until brown. Loosen edge with spatula; invert onto serving dish. Cut into wedges. Yield: 8 servings.

Approx Per Serving: Cal 213; Prot 8 g; Carbo 22 g; Fiber 2 g;
    T Fat 11 g; 44% Calories from Fat; Chol 43 mg; Sod 527 mg.

Dietary Exchanges: Bread 1 1/2; Lean Meat 1/2; Vegetable 1/2; Fat 1 1/2

Zucchini in Dill Cream Sauce

2 1/4 pounds unpeeled zucchini, cut
    into strips
1/4 cup finely chopped onion
1/2 cup water
1 teaspoon instant chicken bouillon
1/2 teaspoon dillweed

1 teaspoon salt
2 tablespoons melted butter
1 teaspoon lemon juice
2 tablespoons flour
1/2 cup nonfat sour cream

Combine zucchini, onion, water, bouillon, dillweed and salt in saucepan. Bring to a boil; reduce heat. Simmer, covered, for 5 minutes or until tender-crisp; do not drain. Add butter and lemon juice; remove from heat. Blend flour and sour cream in bowl. Stir half the hot liquid from zucchini into sour cream mixture; stir sour cream mixture into saucepan. Cook until thickened, stirring constantly. Yield: 8 servings.

Approx Per Serving: Cal 63; Prot 3 g; Carbo 7 g; Fiber 2 g;
    T Fat 3 g; 41% Calories from Fat; Chol 8 mg; Sod 454 mg.

Dietary Exchanges: Vegetable 1; Fat 1/2

To keep vegetables fresh longer, line the refrigerator food crisper with 2 layers of paper towels to absorb the moisture.

Zucchini Genovese

¹/₂ cup sliced green onions
1 cup green bell pepper strips
1 cup red bell pepper strips
1¹/₂ tablespoons olive oil
1 pound zucchini, cut into thin strips

Basil, salt and freshly ground pepper
  to taste
2 cloves of garlic, crushed
¹/₂ cup pitted black olives

Sauté green onions and peppers in olive oil in skillet for 5 minutes. Add zucchini. Cook for 5 minutes or until tender-crisp. Add basil, salt and pepper. Stir in garlic and olives. Yield: 4 servings.

Approx Per Serving: Cal 89; Prot 2 g; Carbo 8 g; Fiber 3 g;
    T Fat 6 g; 60% Calories from Fat; Chol 0 mg; Sod 75 mg.

Dietary Exchanges: Vegetable 1¹/₂; Fat 1

Cajun Vegetables

8 ounces bacon
2¹/₂ pounds potatoes, peeled, sliced
1 pound yellow squash, sliced
1 pound zucchini, sliced
8 ounces whole okra

1 large onion, sliced into rings
2 large tomatoes, sliced
Cajun seasoning to taste
Lemon pepper to taste
¹/₂ cup margarine

Layer bacon, potatoes, squash, zucchini, okra, onion and tomatoes in 9x13-inch greased baking dish, sprinkling each layer with Cajun seasoning and lemon pepper. Dot with margarine. Bake, covered with foil, at 275 degrees for 3 to 4 hours or until vegetables are tender. Yield: 10 servings.

Approx Per Serving: Cal 258; Prot 6 g; Carbo 32 g; Fiber 4 g;
    T Fat 13 g; 43% Calories from Fat; Chol 6 mg; Sod 227 mg.

Dietary Exchanges: Bread 1¹/₂; Lean Meat ¹/₂; Vegetable 1¹/₂; Fat ¹/₂

A Trip Through the Garden

¹/₂ cup butter
6 potatoes, thinly sliced
2 cups thinly sliced carrots

2 cups fresh green beans
2 large onions, thinly sliced into rings
Salt and pepper to taste

Melt butter in 9x13-inch baking pan. Arrange potatoes, carrots, beans and onions in pan. Sprinkle with salt and pepper. Cover with metal lid or foil. Place on grill over hot coals. Grill for 1¹/₂ hours or until vegetables are tender, stirring every 30 minutes. Yield: 8 servings.

Approx Per Serving: Cal 222; Prot 3 g; Carbo 28 g; Fiber 4 g;
    T Fat 12 g; 46% Calories from Fat; Chol 31 mg; Sod 138 mg.

Dietary Exchanges: Bread 1; Vegetable 1¹/₂; Fat 2¹/₂

Crustless Garden-Fresh Quiche

1 small eggplant, peeled, chopped
1 cup chopped onion
1 large clove of garlic, minced
3 tablespoons oil
1 small zucchini, sliced
1 teaspoon oregano

1/2 teaspoon salt
1/8 teaspoon pepper
3 tomatoes, chopped
3 eggs, beaten
1 cup shredded mozzarella cheese
1/4 cup grated Parmesan cheese

Sauté eggplant, onion and garlic in oil in large heavy skillet for 10 minutes or until tender. Stir in zucchini, oregano, salt, pepper and tomatoes. Cook over medium heat for 20 minutes or until all liquid has evaporated, stirring frequently. Cool slightly. Stir eggs and half the mozzarella cheese into vegetable mixture. Spoon into buttered 9-inch pie plate or quiche pan. Top with remaining mozzarella cheese and Parmesan cheese. Bake at 375 degrees for 25 minutes or until golden brown. Let stand for 25 minutes. Cut into wedges. Yield: 8 servings.

Approx Per Serving: Cal 162; Prot 8 g; Carbo 9 g; Fiber 3 g;
    T Fat 11 g; 61% Calories from Fat; Chol 93 mg; Sod 274 mg.

Dietary Exchanges: Lean Meat 1; Vegetable 1 1/2; Fat 1 1/2

Summer Vegetable Bowl

4 slices bacon
12 small white onions
2 green bell peppers, chopped
2 cups hot water
1 1/2 pounds green beans

8 ears of corn, cut into thirds
Salt and pepper to taste
6 zucchini, chopped
2 large stalks celery, chopped
2 tomatoes, cut into wedges

Fry bacon in 6-quart saucepan until crisp. Remove bacon to paper towel to drain, reserving drippings. Sauté onions and green peppers in bacon drippings until golden brown. Add hot water, green beans, corn, salt and pepper. Bring to a boil. Simmer, covered, for 10 minutes. Add zucchini and celery. Simmer, covered, for 10 minutes longer or until all vegetables are tender. Drain vegetables; arrange on large serving platter. Crumble bacon over vegetables; top with tomato wedges. Yield: 10 servings.

Approx Per Serving: Cal 172; Prot 7 g; Carbo 36 g; Fiber 9 g;
    T Fat 3 g; 12% Calories from Fat; Chol 2 mg; Sod 72 mg.

Dietary Exchanges: Bread 1; Vegetable 3 1/2

Fare Game

I remember as if it were yesterday that, as a boy, I had to account for every shotgun shell. If I missed, we didn't eat.

Barbecued Venison

5 pounds venison loin, trimmed
1 cup minced onion
1 tablespoon margarine
3 tablespoons brown sugar

1/3 cup water
Crushed dried red peppers to taste
1   32-ounce bottle of catsup
1 cup apple cider vinegar

Cook venison in a small amount of water in covered saucepan until very tender. Drain and cool. Chop into small pieces. Place in large baking pan. Sauté onion in margarine in skillet until tender. Add brown sugar, water and red peppers. Cook over high heat for 1 to 2 minutes, stirring constantly. Reduce heat to low. Add catsup; mix well. Remove from heat. Stir in vinegar. Add venison; mix well. Spoon into baking pan. Bake at 300 degrees until heated through. Serve on sandwich buns. Yield: 20 servings.

Approx Per Serving: Cal 168; Prot 21 g; Carbo 15 g; Fiber 1 g;
    T Fat 3 g; 15% Calories from Fat; Chol 75 mg; Sod 581 mg.

Dietary Exchanges: Lean Meat 2; Fruit 1; Vegetable 1/2

Barbecued Venison Roast

1   3-pound venison roast
1 tablespoon oil
1/4 cup vinegar
1 cup catsup
1 onion, thinly sliced

1 clove of garlic, minced
1 lemon, sliced
2 tablespoons Worcerstershire sauce
Salt to taste
Cinnamon and nutmeg to taste

Brown venison in oil in skillet; remove venison to roasting pan. Add vinegar, catsup, onion, garlic, lemon slices, Worcestershire sauce, salt, cinnamon and nutmeg to skillet; mix well. Simmer for 10 minutes, stirring constantly. Pour over venison. Roast at 350 degrees for 11/2 to 2 hours or until tender, turning occasionally. Yield: 8 servings.

Approx Per Serving: Cal 217; Prot 31 g; Carbo 12 g; Fiber 1 g;
    T Fat 5 g; 21% Calories from Fat; Chol 112 mg; Sod 459 mg.

Dietary Exchanges: Lean Meat 3; Fruit 1/2; Vegetable 1/2; Fat 1/2

Venison usually refers to the meat from deer but is also a reference to that from elk, antelope and other four-footed game. Venison recipes work well with beef but not all beef recipes work with venison because venison is frequently leaner, tougher and stronger flavored and may benefit from special handling and seasoning.

Venison and Broccoli Stir-Fry

1 pound venison roast or steak
3 tablespoons olive oil
Flowerets of 1 pound fresh broccoli
2 teaspoons cornstarch

2 tablespoons reduced-sodium soy
  sauce
1   14-ounce can chicken broth

Slice venison diagonally cross grain into ¼x2-inch strips. Stir-fry in 1 tablespoon olive oil in wok for 2 minutes. Remove to bowl. Add remaining 2 tablespoons olive oil and broccoli to wok. Stir-fry for 2 to 3 minutes. Remove to bowl. Add mixture of cornstarch, soy sauce and broth. Cook over medium heat until thickened, stirring constantly. Add venison and broccoli. Cook for 2 minutes. Serve over rice. Yield: 4 servings.

Approx Per Serving: Cal 250; Prot 26 g; Carbo 6 g; Fiber 2 g;
    T Fat 14 g; 49% Calories from Fat; Chol 76 mg; Sod 868 mg.

Dietary Exchanges: Lean Meat 2½; Vegetable ½; Fat 2

Enjoy the outdoor experience and the thrill of the hunt but kill only the game that you intend to eat or share with others.

Venison Burgundy

2 pounds venison, cut into strips
½ cup flour
Salt and black pepper to taste
2 tablespoons olive oil
1 teaspoon reduced-sodium soy sauce
Tabasco sauce to taste
Oregano, garlic salt and cayenne
  pepper to taste

4 carrots, sliced
1 green pepper, sliced
3 stalks celery, sliced
4 small potatoes, thinly sliced
½ cup Burgundy

Coat venison with mixture of flour, salt and black pepper. Brown venison in hot olive oil in skillet. Add soy sauce, Tabasco sauce, oregano, garlic salt and cayenne pepper. Cook over low heat for 5 minutes. Add carrots, green pepper, celery and potatoes. Cook, covered, for 20 minutes. Stir in Burgundy. Cook for 3 minutes longer, stirring constantly. Yield: 6 servings.

Approx Per Serving: Cal 318; Prot 30 g; Carbo 28 g; Fiber 3 g;
    T Fat 8 g; 22% Calories from Fat; Chol 100 mg; Sod 109 mg.

Dietary Exchanges: Bread 1; Lean Meat 2½; Vegetable 1; Fat 1

Venison Cutlets

8 venison loin cutlets
3 tablespoons grated Parmesan cheese
1 egg, beaten
1 teaspoon minced parsley
Salt and pepper to taste

1/4 teaspoon nutmeg
1/2 cup milk
6 tablespoons margarine
Juice of 1 lemon

Pound venison with meat mallet until very thin. Combine cheese, egg, parsley, salt, pepper, nutmeg and milk in bowl; mix well. Dip cutlets into batter. Brown on both sides in 4 tablespoons margarine in skillet over low heat. Remove to heated platter. Add remaining 2 tablespoons margarine to skillet. Cook until margarine browns. Add lemon juice, stirring to deglaze skillet. Pour over cutlets. Yield: 4 servings.

Approx Per Serving: Cal 320; Prot 25 g; Carbo 3 g; Fiber <1 g;
     T Fat 23 g; 65% Calories from Fat; Chol 136 mg; Sod 355 mg.

Dietary Exchanges: Lean Meat 2 1/2; Fat 1/2

When outdoors camping, hunting or fishing, keep an eye on the weather for the safety of yourself and others.

Venison Goulash

2 pounds 1-inch venison cubes
1 onion, sliced
1/8 teaspoon garlic powder
2 tablespoons margarine
1 1/2 cups water
3/4 cup catsup
2 tablespoons Worcestershire sauce

1 tablespoon brown sugar
2 teaspoons paprika
1/2 teaspoon dry mustard
Hot sauce to taste
1/4 cup cold water
2 tablespoons flour

Brown venison with onion and garlic powder in margarine in deep skillet. Stir in 1 1/2 cups water, catsup, Worcestershire sauce, brown sugar, paprika, dry mustard and hot sauce. Bring to a boil; reduce heat. Simmer, covered, for 2 to 2 1/2 hours or until venison is tender. Combine 1/4 cup water and flour in covered container; shake to mix well. Stir into goulash. Cook until thickened, stirring constantly. Cook for 1 minute longer, stirring constantly. Serve over egg noodles. Yield: 6 servings.

Approx Per Serving: Cal 234; Prot 28 g; Carbo 15 g; Fiber 1 g;
     T Fat 7 g; 27% Calories from Fat; Chol 100 mg; Sod 512 mg.

Dietary Exchanges: Lean Meat 2 1/2; Fruit 1/2; Vegetable 1/2

Grilled Venison

2 pounds venison
1 16-ounce bottle of fat-free Italian
   dressing
3 large green bell peppers, coarsely
   chopped

1 cup cherry tomatoes
2 cups mushrooms
4 small onions, cut into chunks

Cut venison into 1-inch cubes. Combine with salad dressing in bowl. Marinate in refrigerator for 24 hours; drain. Place venison, green peppers, tomatoes, mushrooms and onions on foil. Place on grill. Grill over hot coals for 45 minutes, stirring 4 or 5 times. Yield: 6 servings.

Approx Per Serving: Cal 204; Prot 29 g; Carbo 15 g; Fiber 2 g;
     T Fat 3 g; 14% Calories from Fat; Chol 100 mg; Sod 809 mg.
     Nutritional information includes entire amount of marinade.

Dietary Exchanges: Lean Meat 2^{1}/$_{2}$; Fruit ^{1}/$_{2}$; Vegetable 1^{1}/$_{2}$

Venison Roast

1 4-pound venison roast
^{1}/$_{4}$ cup cider vinegar
1 clove of garlic, cut into 8 slivers
2 slices bacon, cut into quarters

1 16-ounce bottle of fat-free Italian
   salad dressing
1 16-ounce bottle of fat-free Russian
   salad dressing

Drizzle roast with vinegar. Insert 1 piece of garlic and 1 piece of bacon into each of 8 slits in roast. Place in roasting pan. Pour salad dressings over top. Roast at 325 degrees for 25 minutes per pound, basting occasionally. Remove to serving plate. Serve sliced with gravy. Yield: 8 servings.

Approx Per Serving: Cal 372; Prot 51 g; Carbo 25 g; Fiber <1 g;
     T Fat 6 g; 15% Calories from Fat; Chol 189 mg; Sod 1452 mg.
     Nutritional information includes entire amount of salad dressing.

Dietary Exchanges: Lean Meat 5; Fruit 1^{1}/$_{2}$

Add a portable pantry to your camping equipment. Keep a supply of dry milk powder, dry buttermilk powder, spices, sauce and gravy mixes and other nonperishable staples ready to go. Be sure to replenish as necessary so only fresh groceries need to be added at the last minute.

Sautéed Venison

2 pounds venison
Meat tenderizer to taste
Garlic powder and onion powder to
  taste
Juice of 1 lemon
1/2 cup Worcestershire sauce

1/4 cup melted margarine
1/4 teaspoon cayenne pepper
1/2 teaspoon salt
Black pepper to taste
2 tablespoons oil

Cut venison into serving pieces 1/2 inch thick. Sprinkle with meat tenderizer. Let stand for 1 hour. Sprinkle with garlic powder and onion powder. Pound lightly with meat mallet. Combine lemon juice, Worcestershire sauce, margarine, cayenne pepper, salt and black pepper in bowl; mix well. Set temperature of large electric skillet at 350 degrees. Sauté venison in oil in skillet until light brown on both sides. Add sauce. Simmer, covered, for 15 to 20 minutes or until sauce is thickened to desired consistency. Yield: 6 servings.

Approx Per Serving: Cal 266; Prot 27 g; Carbo 5 g; Fiber <1 g;
  T Fat 15 g; 52% Calories from Fat; Chol 100 mg; Sod 537 mg.

Dietary Exchanges: Lean Meat 2½; Fruit ½; Fat 1

Venison Stew

2 pounds venison stew meat
2 tablespoons oil
3 large onions, coarsely chopped
2 cloves of garlic, crushed
1 tablespoon Worcestershire sauce
1 bay leaf
1 teaspoon oregano

1 tablespoon salt
1 teaspoon pepper
3 cups water
7 potatoes, peeled, cut into quarters
1 pound carrots, cut into 1-inch pieces
1/4 cup flour
1/4 cup cold water

Brown stew meat in oil in heavy saucepan; drain. Add onions, garlic, Worcestershire sauce, bay leaf, oregano, salt, pepper and 3 cups water; mix well. Simmer, uncovered, for 1½ to 2 hours or until venison is tender. Add potatoes and carrots. Simmer for 30 to 45 minutes or until vegetables are tender. Stir in mixture of flour and 1/4 cup water. Cook until thickened, stirring constantly. Discard bay leaf. May add browning sauce if desired. Yield: 10 servings.

Approx Per Serving: Cal 235; Prot 19 g; Carbo 29 g; Fiber 4 g;
  T Fat 5 g; 18% Calories from Fat; Chol 60 mg; Sod 707 mg.

Dietary Exchanges: Bread 1; Lean Meat 1½; Vegetable 1; Fat ½

Angela Russell, Lewisburg, Tennessee

Tipsy Tenderloin Kabobs

2 2-pound venison tenderloins	2 cloves of garlic, chopped
1/4 cup whiskey	1 green bell pepper, cut into 8 pieces
1/4 cup olive oil	1 red bell pepper, cut into 8 pieces
1/4 teaspoon pepper	2 medium onions, cut into 8 pieces
1/4 cup Worcestershire sauce	8 mushrooms
1/4 teaspoon thyme	

Marinate venison in mixture of whiskey, olive oil, pepper, Worcestershire sauce, thyme and garlic in bowl in refrigerator for 4 to 8 hours. Drain, reserving marinade. Cut venison into cubes. Thread onto skewers alternately with bell peppers, onions, and mushrooms. Grill over low to medium coals until done to taste, basting frequently with reserved marinade. Serve over rice. Yield: 4 servings.

Approx Per Serving: Cal 627; Prot 83 g; Carbo 12 g; Fiber 2 g;
    T Fat 22 g; 33% Calories from Fat; Chol 300 mg; Sod 315 mg.
    Nutritional information includes entire amount of marinade.

Dietary Exchanges: Lean Meat 7 1/2; Vegetable 1 1/2; Fat 3 1/2

Try some well-soaked hickory chips, some liquid smoke or smoke-seasoned salt to enhance the flavor of grilled or broiled food.

Venison Marinade

1/2 cup oil	1 1/2 teaspoons parsley flakes
1/2 cup Worcestershire sauce	2 cloves of garlic, crushed
2 tablespoons dry mustard	1/3 cup lemon juice
Salt and pepper to taste	1/2 cup reduced-sodium soy sauce
1/2 cup wine vinegar	

Combine oil, Worcestershire sauce, mustard, salt, pepper, vinegar, parsley flakes, garlic, lemon juice and soy sauce in bowl; mix well. Store in refrigerator or freezer. Use to marinate venison steaks for 24 hours before broiling or grilling.
Yield: 2 2/3 cups (1/3 cup per serving).

Approx Per Serving: Cal 275; Prot 1 g; Carbo 7 g; Fiber <1 g;
    T Fat 28 g; 89% Calories from Fat; Chol 0 mg; Sod 557 mg.

Dietary Exchanges: Fruit 1/2; Fat 5 1/2

Venison Burgers

1 pound ground venison
1 medium onion, chopped
1 green bell pepper, chopped
1   16-ounce can tomatoes with green
    chilies

1¹/₂ tablespoons flour
Salt and pepper to taste
4 slices American cheese

Shape venison into 4 patties. Brown on both sides in skillet. Reduce temperature. Add onion and green pepper. Cook for 20 minutes. Add tomatoes. Bring to a boil. Blend flour with a small amount of water in bowl; stir into sauce. Season with salt and pepper. Cook until thickened, stirring constantly. Top each patty with cheese slice. Heat until cheese is melted. Yield: 4 servings.

Approx Per Serving: Cal 246; Prot 31 g; Carbo 11 g; Fiber 3 g;
    T Fat 8 g; 30% Calories from Fat; Chol 109 mg; Sod 751 mg.

Dietary Exchanges: Lean Meat 3; Vegetable 1; Fat 1

Deer Burger Pie

7 slices peppered bacon
1 pound ground venison
2 cups shredded Cheddar cheese
1 unbaked pie shell

4 eggs
3 tablespoons chopped onion
¹/₂ cup chopped green bell pepper

Fry bacon in skillet until crisp. Remove bacon and crumble 4 slices. Add venison to drippings in skillet. Cook until venison is brown and crumbly; drain. Add crumbled bacon and 1¹/₂ cups cheese; mix well. Spoon into pie shell. Combine eggs with onion and green pepper in bowl; mix well. Spoon over venison mixture. Bake at 400 degrees for 30 minutes. Crumble remaining 3 slices bacon over top; sprinkle with remaining ¹/₂ cup cheese. Bake for 5 minutes longer. Yield: 6 servings.

Approx Per Serving: Cal 495; Prot 35 g; Carbo 16 g; Fiber 1 g;
    T Fat 32 g; 58% Calories from Fat; Chol 251 mg; Sod 587 mg.

Dietary Exchanges: Bread 1; Lean Meat 4; Fat 4¹/₂

Sarah Wade, McEwen, Tennessee

To store cast-iron cookware, rub interior with light film of oil. Wipe and rinse before using. A griddle or frying pan is properly preheated when a few drops of water spatter and sizzle when they hit the surface. Heat the pan before adding butter or oil to keep food from sticking to the pan.

Venison Chili

1 pound ground venison
1 onion, chopped
1 tablespoon (or more) chili powder
Salt and pepper to taste

2 16-ounce cans tomatoes
³/₄ cup chili sauce
1 16-ounce can dark red kidney beans

Brown ground venison with onion in large saucepan, stirring until venison is crumbly; drain. Stir in chili powder, salt and pepper. Add tomatoes, chili sauce and beans; mix well. Simmer for 1 hour or until of desired consistency, stirring occasionally. Garnish servings with cheese. May add cooked macaroni is desired. Yield: 4 servings.

Approx Per Serving: Cal 345; Prot 36 g; Carbo 44 g; Fiber 11 g;
    T Fat 4 g; 11% Calories from Fat; Chol 95 mg; Sod 1506 mg.

Dietary Exchanges: Bread 1; Lean Meat 2¹/₂; Fruit 1; Vegetable 2¹/₂

Whenever it rains or there is thunder and lightning in nearby hills, be ready to move out quickly if you see or hear water increasing in speed or depth. Even if you just suspect a flood is coming, move to high ground immediately! Be careful when moving to high ground during flooding. Climb high enough to get away from the flood but stay off hilltops and don't get under tall trees. Lightning may strike.

Venison Meatballs

1¹/₂ pounds ground venison
¹/₂ cup dry bread crumbs
1 egg, beaten
¹/₂ cup mashed cooked potatoes

¹/₂ teaspoon brown sugar
Salt, pepper, allspice, nutmeg, cloves
    and ginger to taste
2 tablespoons melted margarine

Combine venison with bread crumbs, egg, potatoes, brown sugar, salt, pepper, allspice, nutmeg, cloves and ginger in bowl; mix well. Shape into 1-inch balls. Brown in margarine in skillet, turning to brown evenly. Simmer, covered, for 15 minutes. Serve over rice or noodles or as appetizer. Yield: 6 servings.

Approx Per Serving: Cal 228; Prot 28 g; Carbo 10 g; Fiber 1 g;
    T Fat 8 g; 32% Calories from Fat; Chol 131 mg; Sod 226 mg.

Dietary Exchanges: Bread ¹/₂; Lean Meat 2¹/₂

Venison Pie

1 pound ground venison
1 cup chopped onion
1 cup chopped green bell pepper
2 8-ounce cans tomato sauce
1 12-ounce can corn, drained
1 clove of garlic

1 teaspoon salt
2 teaspoons chili powder
6 ounces sharp Cheddar cheese,
 chopped
1 6-ounce package corn muffin mix

Brown venison with onion and green pepper in 2-quart cast-iron skillet, stirring frequently. Add tomato sauce, corn, garlic, salt and chili powder; mix well. Simmer for 20 to 25 minutes or until thickened, stirring frequently. Add cheese, stirring until melted. Prepare corn muffin mix using package directions. Spoon over top. Bake at 375 degrees for 40 minutes or until corn bread tests done. Yield: 8 servings.

Approx Per Serving: Cal 319; Prot 23 g; Carbo 31 g; Fiber 4 g;
 T Fat 12 g; 34% Calories from Fat; Chol 90 mg; Sod 1161 mg.

Dietary Exchanges: Bread 1 1/2; Lean Meat 2; Vegetable 1; Fat 1 1/2

Venison Sausage

2 pounds ground venison
1/2 teaspoon garlic powder
1/4 teaspoon onion powder

1 1/2 teaspoons liquid smoke
Salt to taste
2 tablespoons Tender Quick

Combine venison, garlic powder, onion powder, liquid smoke, salt and Tender Quick in bowl; mix well. Shape into 4 rolls. Wrap in plastic wrap. Chill for 24 hours. Slice and fry in skillet sprayed with nonstick cooking spray or bake rolls on rack in baking pan at 300 degrees for 1 hour. Yield: 12 servings.

Approx Per Serving: Cal 90; Prot 17 g; Carbo <1 g; Fiber 0 g;
 T Fat 2 g; 19% Calories from Fat; Chol 64 mg; Sod 911 mg.
 Nutritional information does not include liquid smoke.

Dietary Exchanges: Lean Meat 1 1/2

Bill Hall's LaGoota

1 goat shoulder
Garlic, sliced

Favorite barbecue sauce

Combine goat shoulder with equal parts of vinegar and water to cover in large saucepan for 3 hours; drain. Cut slits in shoulder. Stuff garlic into slits. Place on grill over preheated charcoal to which hickory chips or green hickory sapling have been added. Grill for 3 hours or longer, basting 3 times with barbecue sauce. Yield: variable.

Nutritional information for this recipe is not available.

Bill Hall, Nashville, Tennessee

Hill "Billy" Lasagna

1 large onion, chopped
2 cloves of garlic, crushed
1/4 cup oil
2 green peppers, chopped
4 zucchini, chopped
1 1/2 pounds ground goat
1 16-ounce can tomatoes
1 6-ounce can tomato sauce

1 tablespoon brown sugar
1/4 cup water
1/4 cup white wine
1 teaspoon each oregano and basil
Salt and pepper to taste
9 lasagna noodles, cooked
2 cups shredded mozzarella cheese

Sauté onion and garlic in oil in saucepan until onion is tender. Add green peppers and zucchini. Cook until vegetables are tender. Add ground goat. Cook until goat is brown, stirring until crumbly; drain. Add undrained tomatoes, tomato sauce, brown sugar, water, wine, oregano, basil, salt and pepper; mix well. Simmer for 15 minutes. Layer noodles, meat sauce and cheese 1/2 at a time in shallow baking dish. Bake at 400 degrees for 20 minutes or until bubbly. Yield: 6 servings.

Approx Per Serving: Cal 542; Prot 40 g; Carbo 48 g; Fiber 4 g;
    T Fat 21 g; 35% Calories from Fat; Chol 93 mg; Sod 517 mg.

Dietary Exchanges: Bread 2; Lean Meat 3; Vegetable 3; Fat 3

Roast 'Possum

1 opossum
Salt and pepper to taste
1 onion, chopped
1 tablespoon bacon drippings
1 cup bread crumbs

1/4 teaspoon Worcestershire sauce
1 egg, beaten
1 teaspoon salt
4 slices bacon
4 cups water

Clean but do not skin opossum; reserve liver. Hang opossum in cool place for 48 hours. Skin opossum. Rub with salt and pepper to taste. Cook onion in bacon drippings in skillet until light brown. Add liver. Cook until tender. Add bread crumbs, Worcestershire sauce, egg and 1 teaspoon salt; mix well. Stuff mixture into opossum; truss like turkey. Place back side up in roasting pan; arrange bacon over back. Pour water into roasting pan. Roast, uncovered, at 350 degrees for 2 1/2 to 3 hours or until tender. Serve with baked or candied sweet potatoes. Yield: 4 servings.

Approx Per Serving: Cal 196; Prot 7 g; Carbo 21 g; Fiber 1 g;
    T Fat 9 g; 43% Calories from Fat; Chol 62 mg; Sod 888 mg.

Dietary Exchanges: Bread 1; Lean Meat 1/2; Vegetable 1/2; Fat 1 1/2

Roberta J. Lee, Waverly, Tennessee

Barbecued Rabbit

1 rabbit, cut up
1 onion, chopped
1 green bell pepper, chopped
1/4 cup chili sauce
2 tablespoons lemon juice

2 tablespoons Worcestershire sauce
Garlic powder to taste
1/2 cup catsup
1/2 cup vinegar
1 tablespoon brown sugar

Wash rabbit; pat dry. Place in baking dish. Bake at 325 degrees for 30 minutes. Combine onion, green pepper, chili sauce, lemon juice, Worcestershire sauce, garlic powder, catsup, vinegar and brown sugar in saucepan. Heat until bubbly. Pour over rabbit. Bake for 35 minutes longer or until rabbit is tender, basting every 15 minutes.
Yield: 4 servings.

Approx Per Serving: Cal 420; Prot 51 g; Carbo 22 g; Fiber 1 g;
    T Fat 14 g; 30% Calories from Fat; Chol 139 mg; Sod 757 mg.

Dietary Exchanges: Lean Meat 6; Fruit 1; Vegetable 1

Fiesta Rabbit

2 rabbits, cut up
Salt, red pepper, black pepper, onion
    powder and garlic powder to taste
1/4 cup oil
2 onions, chopped
1 green bell pepper, chopped

1 10-ounce can tomatoes with green
    chilies
1 14-ounce can chicken broth
1 pound mushrooms, sliced
2 tablespoons margarine

Sprinkle rabbit with salt, red pepper, black pepper, onion powder and garlic powder. Brown in oil in skillet. Add onions, green pepper, tomatoes and half the broth. Simmer, covered, until rabbit and vegetables are tender and gravy is thickened, adding remaining broth as needed. Sauté mushrooms in margarine in skillet. Stir into skillet. Serve over steamed rice. Yield: 6 servings.

Approx Per Serving: Cal 625; Prot 71 g; Carbo 10 g; Fiber 3 g;
    T Fat 32 g; 47% Calories from Fat; Chol 187 mg; Sod 759 mg.

Dietary Exchanges: Lean Meat 8 1/2; Vegetable 1 1/2; Fat 2

Hasenpfeffer

3 cups water
1 cup vinegar
1/4 cup (or more) sugar
1 onion, sliced
1 teaspoon mixed pickling spices

Salt and pepper to taste
1   2-pound rabbit
2 tablespoons flour
2 tablespoons oil

Combine water, vinegar, sugar, onion, pickling spices, salt and pepper in large bowl; mix well. Cut rabbit into serving pieces. Add to marinade. Marinate, covered, in refrigerator for 2 days. Remove rabbit and pat dry, reserving 1 cup marinade. Place flour in plastic bag. Add rabbit; shake to coat. Brown rabbit on both sides in hot oil in skillet. Add reserved marinade. Simmer, covered, over low heat for 45 to 60 minutes or until rabbit is tender. May thicken pan drippings for gravy. Yield: 2 servings.

Approx Per Serving: Cal 730; Prot 67 g; Carbo 43 g; Fiber 1 g;
T Fat 32 g; 40% Calories from Fat; Chol 186 mg; Sod 110 mg.
Nutritional information includes entire amount of marinade.

Dietary Exchanges: Bread 1/2; Lean Meat 8; Fruit 2; Vegetable 1/2; Fat 21/2

Santa Fe Spanish Rabbit

1   3-pound rabbit, cleaned
Salt to taste
1/4 cup flour
Freshly ground pepper to taste
4 to 6 tablespoons olive oil
1 small onion, chopped
1 stalk celery, chopped
2 cloves of garlic, minced

4 tomatoes, coarsely chopped
1 to 2 tablespoons chopped fresh
  oregano
1 cup white wine
2 cups beef stock
10 black olives, cut into halves
10 green olives, cut into halves

Cut rabbit into pieces, discarding, fat, sinew and larger bones. Soak rabbit in salted water to cover in bowl; drain. Coat lightly with mixture of flour and pepper. Brown lightly on both sides in hot olive oil in skillet; drain. Add onion, celery and garlic to drippings in skillet. Sauté for 3 minutes or until tender. Add tomatoes and oregano. Cook for 3 to 5 minutes or until tomatoes are tender. Add wine. Cook for 2 minutes or until liquid is reduced by 1/2. Stir in beef stock and olives. Bring to a boil; add rabbit. Simmer for 30 minutes or until rabbit is tender. Garnish with freshly roasted slices of red bell pepper. Serve with black beans and rice. Yield: 6 servings.

Approx Per Serving: Cal 435; Prot 36 g; Carbo 10 g; Fiber 2 g;
T Fat 25 g; 52% Calories from Fat; Chol 93 mg; Sod 534 mg.

Dietary Exchanges: Lean Meat 4; Vegetable 1; Fat 31/2

Deana Reed, Brentwood, Tennessee

Dove Braised in Red Wine

1 onion, chopped
1/4 cup margarine
16 dove breasts
Salt and pepper to taste
2 teaspoons Worcestershire sauce
1/4 teaspoon thyme

2 teaspoons chopped parsley
1 cup red wine
1 cup beef bouillon
2 tablespoons flour
2 tablespoons water

Sauté onion in margarine in skillet until tender. Add dove breasts. Cook until brown on both sides; turn meaty side up. Add salt, pepper, Worcestershire sauce, thyme, parsley and wine. Cook until reduced by 1/2. Add bouillon. Simmer, covered, for 45 minutes or until tender. Remove dove from skillet; place on heated platter. Mix flour and 2 tablespoons water in small bowl. Stir into skillet. Cook until thickened, stirring constantly. Serve with dove. Yield: 8 servings.

Approx Per Serving: Cal 256; Prot 38 g; Carbo 4 g; Fiber <1 g;
   T Fat 8 g; 28% Calories from Fat; Chol 109 mg; Sod 181 mg.

Dietary Exchanges: Lean Meat 3; Fat 1/2

Be alert to possible flooding due to releasing water into the rivers through the dams on many of Tennessee's man-made lakes. Park your car or truck on high ground and be prepared to retreat at short notice.

Dove Breasts with Rice

2 cups uncooked brown and wild rice
   mix
4 cups boiling water
1 bunch green onions, sliced

8 ounces mushrooms, sliced
12 dove breasts
1/4 cup margarine

Stir rice into boiling water in saucepan. Cook, covered, over low heat for 20 minutes. Spoon into large casserole. Sauté green onions, mushrooms and dove breasts in margarine in skillet. Remove dove breasts. Fold sautéed vegetables into rice. Place dove breasts on top. Bake, loosely covered, at 300 degrees for 30 minutes.
Yield: 6 servings.

Approx Per Serving: Cal 459; Prot 45 g; Carbo 47 g; Fiber 2 g;
   T Fat 11 g; 21% Calories from Fat; Chol 109 mg; Sod 98 mg.

Dietary Exchanges: Bread 2 1/2; Lean Meat 3; Vegetable 1/2

Fruited Dove Olé

12 dove breasts
1 cup orange juice
1¹/₂ cups white wine
¹/₂ teaspoon each rosemary, sage, thyme, garlic powder and salt

1 teaspoon freshly ground pepper
¹/₄ cup melted margarine
1 cup honey
Juice and slivered rind of 2 limes and 2 oranges

Wash dove and pat dry. Combine with orange juice and wine in bowl. Marinate in refrigerator overnight; drain. Sprinkle with rosemary, sage, thyme, garlic powder, salt and pepper; place in baking dish. Blend margarine, honey, lime juice and orange juice in saucepan. Stir in lime and orange rind. Cook until bubbly, stirring constantly. Spoon over dove. Bake at 350 degrees for 40 minutes. Serve with rice. Yield: 6 servings.

Approx Per Serving: Cal 485; Prot 38 g; Carbo 56 g; Fiber <1 g;
    T Fat 10 g; 18% Calories from Fat; Chol 109 mg; Sod 95 mg.
    Nutritional information includes entire amount of marinade.

Dietary Exchanges: Lean Meat 3; Fruit 3¹/₂; Fat 1

Dove with Rice and Sausage Dressing

12 dove breasts
1 cup flour
Salt, pepper and paprika to taste
2 tablespoons oil
4 ounces sausage

1 onion, chopped
¹/₂ teaspoon sage
¹/₂ cup wild rice, cooked
¹/₂ cup red wine
³/₄ cup water

Coat dove breasts with mixture of flour, salt, pepper and paprika. Brown in oil in skillet. Arrange in circle in baking dish. Brown sausage with onion and sage in skillet; drain. Add rice; mix well. Spoon into center of baking dish. Pour mixture of wine and water over top. Bake, covered, at 350 degrees for 1 hour or until dove breasts are tender. Yield: 6 servings.

Approx Per Serving: Cal 385; Prot 43 g; Carbo 28 g; Fiber 1 g;
    T Fat 10 g; 23% Calories from Fat; Chol 116 mg; Sod 118 mg.

Dietary Exchanges: Bread 1¹/₂; Lean Meat 3; Fat 1¹/₂

Be sure that campfire coals are cold when leaving a campsite by touching them with your bare hand. Then scatter the remains and cover the spot with wet leaves or pine needles.

Skillet Barbecued Duck

6 duck breast filets
2 medium onions
1 pound mushrooms, sliced

1 cup barbecue sauce
2 tablespoons honey

Cut duck into strips. Combine with onions, mushrooms and a small amount of water in skillet. Simmer, covered, until duck is no longer pink; drain. Blend barbecue sauce and honey in bowl. Brush over duck. Simmer for 30 to 45 minutes or until tender. Serve over rice. Yield: 6 servings.

Approx Per Serving: Cal 190; Prot 20 g; Carbo 18 g; Fiber 2 g;
    T Fat 5 g; 22% Calories from Fat; Chol 66 mg; Sod 392 mg.

Dietary Exchanges: Lean Meat 2; Fruit 1/2; Vegetable 2

Be sure that other hunters can distinguish you from the game they seek. Wear your bright hunting clothes and take no chances. Be careful when shooting, too. Do not fire blindly into brush or field.

Duck Stir-Fry

6 duck breast filets
Garlic powder and lemon pepper to
   taste
2 tablespoons oil
2 medium onions, sliced

1 green bell pepper, sliced
1 small bunch broccoli, chopped
8 ounces mushrooms, sliced
1/2 cup dry white wine
1/2 cup orange marmalade

Rinse duck and pat dry. Slice into 1/2-inch strips. Sprinkle with garlic powder and lemon pepper. Stir-fry duck in oil in skillet until brown; remove from skillet. Add vegetables. Stir-fry for 2 minutes. Cook, covered, for several minutes or until broccoli is tender-crisp. Add duck, wine and marmalade. Simmer, covered, for 10 minutes or until heated through. Serve over rice. Yield: 6 servings.

Approx Per Serving: Cal 262; Prot 20 g; Carbo 26 g; Fiber 3 g;
    T Fat 9 g; 28% Calories from Fat; Chol 66 mg; Sod 79 mg.

Dietary Exchanges: Lean Meat 2; Fruit 1; Vegetable 1 1/2; Fat 1

Honey-Glazed Wild Duck

4 wild ducks
1/4 cup margarine, softened
Salt and pepper to taste

3 tablespoons honey
2 teaspoons reduced-sodium soy sauce

Cut ducks into halves. Wash and pat dry inside and out. Rub with margarine. Sprinkle with salt and pepper. Place skin side up on rack in roasting pan. Roast at 350 degrees for 1 to 1½ hours or until tender. Brush with mixture of honey and soy sauce. Roast for 15 minutes longer. Brush with remaining honey mixture. Serve with wild rice. Yield: 8 servings.

Approx Per Serving: Cal 345; Prot 22 g; Carbo 7 g; Fiber 0 g;
       T Fat 25 g; 66% Calories from Fat; Chol 102 mg; Sod 224 mg.

Dietary Exchanges: Lean Meat 3; Fruit ½; Fat 2

Duck with Orange Sauce

3 wild ducks
1½ teaspoons garlic powder
1½ teaspoons onion powder
1½ teaspoons pepper
6 lemons
6 oranges

1/4 cup margarine
1/4 cup thawed frozen orange juice
  concentrate
1/4 cup packed light brown sugar
2 tablespoons grated orange rind

Rinse ducks; pat dry. Sprinkle each with 1/4 teaspoon garlic powder, onion powder and pepper. Place each breast side up on 3 layers of foil. Squeeze juice of ½ lemon and ½ orange over each. Place half of each remaining lemon and orange in duck cavity. Wrap in foil, sealing well. Grill for 1 hour. Combine margarine, orange juice concentrate, brown sugar and orange rind in saucepan. Cook until thickened, stirring constantly. Place ducks on serving plate lined with greens. Spoon sauce over top. Yield: 6 servings.

Approx Per Serving: Cal 467; Prot 25 g; Carbo 34 g; Fiber 5 g;
       T Fat 27 g; 51% Calories from Fat; Chol 102 mg; Sod 166 mg.

Dietary Exchanges: Lean Meat 3; Fruit 2½; Fat 2

Duck, goose and other wild fowl are a special culinary treat, but be aware that what the bird eats will drastically affect the flavor. Fish-eating fowl have a much stronger, gamier flavor than grain and vegetation feeders.

Stuffed Roasted Wild Duck

1 5-pound wild duck
3 cups bread cubes, toasted
1/2 cup hot water
Sections of 1 orange, chopped
2 cups chopped celery
1/4 cup melted margarine

1 egg, beaten
Salt and pepper to taste
1/4 teaspoon poultry seasoning
2 teaspoons grated orange rind
2 tablespoons oil
1/2 cup hot water

Wash duck; pat dry inside and out. Soak bread in 1/2 cup hot water in bowl for 15 minutes. Add orange, celery, margarine, egg, salt, pepper, poultry seasoning and orange rind; mix lightly. Stuff into duck. Place in roasting pan. Roast at 325 degrees for 2 to 3 hours or until tender, basting occasionally with mixture of oil and 1/2 cup hot water. Yield: 6 servings.

Approx Per Serving: Cal 581; Prot 36 g; Carbo 13 g; Fiber 2 g;
     T Fat 42 g; 66% Calories from Fat; Chol 187 mg; Sod 316 mg.

Dietary Exchanges: Bread 1/2; Lean Meat 41/2; Fat 4

Slow-Cooker Oriental Duck

1 5-pound duck, cut up
1/2 cup reduced-sodium soy sauce
1/4 cup honey
1 clove of garlic, minced

1/4 teaspoon ginger
1/2 teaspoon dry mustard
1/2 cup thinly sliced green onions

Combine duck, soy sauce, honey, garlic, ginger, dry mustard and green onions in slow cooker. Cook on Low for 6 hours or until tender. Yield: 8 servings.

Approx Per Serving: Cal 519; Prot 27 g; Carbo 11 g; Fiber <1 g;
     T Fat 40 g; 70% Calories from Fat; Chol 119 mg; Sod 475 mg.

Dietary Exchanges: Lean Meat 5; Fruit 1/2; Fat 41/2

Duck and Sauerkraut

1 5-pound duck
Salt and pepper to taste

1 32-ounce package sauerkraut, drained
2 tablespoons caraway seed

Rinse duck. Sprinkle duck inside and out with salt and pepper. Place in roasting pan. Bake at 325 degrees for 31/2 to 4 hours or until duck tests done. Drain. Sauté sauerkraut with caraway seed in skillet until lightly browned, stirring frequently. Spoon sauerkraut around duck. Bake at 250 degrees for 1 hour longer. Yield: 8 servings.

Approx Per Serving: Cal 505; Prot 28 g; Carbo 6 g; Fiber 3 g;
     T Fat 41 g; 73% Calories from Fat; Chol 119 mg; Sod 833 mg.

Dietary Exchanges: Lean Meat 5; Vegetable 1; Fat 41/2

Smothered Wild Duck Breast

8 wild duck breast halves, skinned	Salt and pepper to taste
1/2 cup flour	1 8-ounce can mushroom pieces

Coat duck breast halves with flour. Brown on both sides in oil in skillet; drain. Sprinkle with salt and pepper; add undrained mushrooms. Simmer, covered, for 1 hour and 20 minutes. Serve with wild rice. Yield: 8 servings.

Approx Per Serving: Cal 140; Prot 18 g; Carbo 7 g; Fiber 1 g;
    T Fat 4 g; 25% Calories from Fat; Chol 66 mg; Sod 169 mg.

Dietary Exchanges: Bread 1/2; Lean Meat 2; Vegetable 1/2

Roast Wild Goose

6 cups toasted bread crumbs	Sections of 3 oranges, chopped
1 onion, chopped	1/4 cup margarine
1 cup raisins	Salt and pepper to taste
1 cup chopped celery	1 wild goose
1 cup chopped walnuts	

Mix bread crumbs, onion, raisins, celery, walnuts and oranges in bowl. Melt margarine with salt and pepper in saucepan. Stir into crumb mixture. Add enough water to moisten. Rinse goose; pat dry. Stuff with bread mixture, spooning any remaining stuffing into greased baking dish. Place goose in roasting pan. Roast goose at 350 degrees for 3 1/2 hours or until tender. Bake remaining stuffing for 1 hour. Yield: 8 servings.

Approx Per Serving: Cal 708; Prot 27 g; Carbo 81 g; Fiber 7 g;
    T Fat 32 g; 40% Calories from Fat; Chol 52 mg; Sod 771 mg.

Dietary Exchanges: Bread 4; Lean Meat 2; Fruit 1 1/2; Vegetable 1/2; Fat 1

Cooking over a charcoal fire—on a grill or in a Dutch oven or skillet—is fun, easy, and adaptable to many recipes you normally bake, broil, or fry. Charcoal should be preheated for about 30 minutes for all types of cooking. The temperature may be gauged by how long you can hold your hand 4 inches above the coals: 2 seconds equals hot (400 degrees); 4 seconds equals medium (350 degrees); 5 seconds equals low (300 degrees). For **grilling**, use hot coals and greased grill rack. For added flavor, add mesquite, hickory or apple chips soaked in cold water to hot coals. **Pan frying** is done in a heavy skillet on rack over hot coals. Breads as well as meats may be prepared in this manner. For **Dutch oven cooking**, use enough coals to equal twice the diameter of the Dutch oven for medium heat or 3 times the diameter for high heat. Place half the coals underneath and half on the lid toward the edge. Cooking time will be about the same as for stove or oven.

Smothered Grouse with Wild Rice

²/₃ cup wild rice
8 grouse breast filets
1 egg, beaten
¹/₂ cup buttermilk
¹/₂ cup flour
Garlic powder, oregano and basil to
    taste

1 teaspoon freshly ground pepper
¹/₄ cup margarine
1¹/₂ cups chicken broth
8 ounces mushrooms, sliced

Cook rice using package directions until tender; keep warm. Rinse grouse and pat dry; pound until flattened and tender. Combine with mixture of egg and buttermilk in bowl. Let stand for 1 hour. Shake with mixture of flour, garlic powder, oregano, basil and pepper in bag, coating well. Brown on both sides in margarine in skillet. Add broth and mushrooms. Simmer, covered, for 20 minutes. Spoon rice onto serving plates. Place grouse over rice; spoon sauce over top. Yield: 4 servings.

Approx Per Serving: Cal 519; Prot 60 g; Carbo 37 g; Fiber 1 g;
    T Fat 15 g; 26% Calories from Fat; Chol 54 mg; Sod 477 mg.

Dietary Exchanges: Bread 2; Lean Meat 4; Vegetable ¹/₂

Braised Pheasant Marsala

1 pheasant, cleaned
1 pheasant liver
1 tangerine, peeled
¹/₄ cup lard
12 mushrooms
3 tablespoons butter
4 shallots, finely chopped

1 clove of garlic, sliced
1 tablespoon flour
2 tablespoons dry Marsala
¹/₄ cup chicken broth
¹/₂ teaspoon crushed fennel seed
6 juniper berries, crushed

Rinse pheasant inside and out and pat dry. Stuff with liver and tangerine; truss tightly. Brown on all sides in melted lard in deep skillet for 15 minutes, turning to brown evenly, and basting constantly. Remove to warm baking dish. Sauté mushrooms in pan drippings and butter in skillet until moisture has nearly evaporated. Remove to baking dish with slotted spoon. Sauté shallots and garlic in remaining pan drippings. Stir in flour. Cook for several minutes, stirring constantly; do not brown. Remove from heat. Stir in wine and broth. Cook until thickened, stirring constantly. Stir in fennel seed and juniper berries. Add to baking dish. Bake at 450 degrees for 40 to 50 minutes or until done to taste. Yield: 4 servings.

Approx Per Serving: Cal 494; Prot 29 g; Carbo 21 g; Fiber 2 g;
    T Fat 32 g; 58% Calories from Fat; Chol 142 mg; Sod 194 mg.

Dietary Exchanges: Lean Meat 3¹/₂; Vegetable 3; Fat 4¹/₂

Emily B. King, Nashville, Tennessee

Southwest Pheasant

8 pheasant breast filets
8 canned green chili peppers
8 strips pepper cheese
1/2 cup bread crumbs
1/4 cup grated Parmesan cheese
1 tablespoon chili powder

1/4 teaspoon cumin
1/4 teaspoon garlic powder
Salt and pepper to taste
1/2 cup melted margarine
1   12-ounce jar salsa

Rinse pheasant and pat dry; pound to 1/4-inch thickness. Place 1 green chili and 1 strip pepper cheese on each filet. Roll filets to enclose filling, secure with wooden picks. Mix bread crumbs, Parmesan cheese, chili powder, cumin, garlic powder, salt and pepper in dish. Dip pheasant rolls in margarine; coat with bread crumb mixture. Place in baking dish. Drizzle with any remaining margarine. Bake at 400 degrees for 20 to 30 minutes or until cooked through. Warm salsa in saucepan until heated through. Spoon over pheasant. Garnish with sliced green onions. Yield: 8 servings.

Approx Per Serving: Cal 392; Prot 40 g; Carbo 13 g; Fiber 2 g;
      T Fat 21 g; 47% Calories from Fat; Chol 91 mg; Sod 1363 mg.

Dietary Exchanges: Bread 1/2; Lean Meat 5; Vegetable 1; Fat 1/2

Pheasant Chop Suey

2 pheasants
1 bunch celery, chopped
2 onions, chopped
1/4 cup margarine
2   4-ounce cans sliced mushrooms
4   16-ounce cans chop suey vegetables

2   8-ounce cans sliced water chestnuts
1   46-ounce can tomato juice
Garlic powder, onion powder, celery
   salt, salt and pepper to taste
2   5-ounce cans chow mein noodles

Rinse pheasants well. Cook in pressure cooker using manufacturer's directions. Chop into bite-sized pieces, discarding skin and bones. Sauté celery and onions in margarine in large saucepan. Add pheasant, mushrooms, chop suey vegetables, water chestnuts, tomato juice, garlic powder, onion powder, celery salt, salt and pepper; mix well. Simmer until of desired consistency. Serve over chow mein noodles. Serve with soy sauce. Yield: 12 servings.

Approx Per Serving: Cal 349; Prot 21 g; Carbo 30 g; Fiber 4 g;
      T Fat 18 g; 44% Calories from Fat; Chol 50 mg; Sod 1035 mg.

Dietary Exchanges: Bread 1;
      Lean meat 2 1/2; Vegetable 2 1/2; Fat 1 1/2

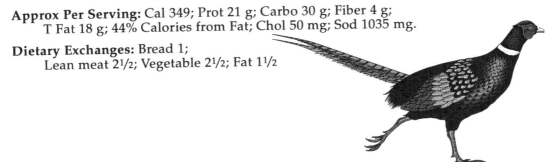

Pheasant with Poached Pears

1/2 cup fresh cranberries	2 pheasant
1 tablespoon egg white	1/4 cup margarine
2 tablespoons sugar	1 medium onion, sliced
1 cup cranberry juice cocktail	Parsley sprigs
1/4 cup sugar	1 pound baby carrots, cooked
4 Bartlett pears, peeled	1 pound Brussels sprouts, cooked

Coat cranberries with egg white. Place in bag with 2 tablespoons sugar; shake to coat. Spread in shallow dish. Let stand until dry. Combine cranberry juice cocktail and remaining 1/4 cup sugar in saucepan. Bring to a boil. Cut pears into halves lengthwise. Add to boiling liquid. Cook until almost tender. Chill in refrigerator, turning occasionally. Rinse pheasant; pat dry inside and out. Brown in margarine in skillet. Place breast side up on rack in roasting pan. Stuff with onion and parsley. Roast at 450 degrees for 20 minutes or until tender. Arrange on serving platter with vegetables and pears. Spoon cranberries into pears. Yield: 8 servings.

Approx Per Serving: Cal 405; Prot 27 g; Carbo 39 g; Fiber 7 g;
    T Fat 16 g; 35% Calories from Fat; Chol 76 mg; Sod 148 mg.

Dietary Exchanges: Lean Meat 3 1/2; Fruit 1 1/2; Vegetable 1 1/2

Pheasant Pie

1 3 to 4-pound pheasant	1 2-ounce jar chopped pimento
1 bay leaf	1/2 cup margarine
1 stalk celery	1/2 cup flour
6 peppercorns	1 cup half and half
8 ounces fresh pearl onions	1/2 teaspoon salt
4 ounces fresh mushrooms, sliced	1/2 teaspoon pepper
1 10-ounce package frozen peas	1 recipe 1-crust pie pastry

Rinse pheasant inside and out. Combine with bay leaf, celery, peppercorns and water to cover in large saucepan. Simmer, covered, for 2 hours or until tender. Drain, reserving 2 cups broth. Chop pheasant; strain broth. Combine pheasant, onions, mushrooms, peas and pimento in 2-quart baking dish. Melt margarine in medium saucepan. Stir in flour. Add reserved broth gradually, stirring constantly. Stir in half and half, salt and pepper. Cook until thickened, stirring constantly. Pour over pheasant mixture. Top with pastry, sealing to edge; cut vents. Bake at 450 degrees for 25 minutes or until pastry is golden brown. Yield: 8 servings.

Approx Per Serving: Cal 607; Prot 32 g; Carbo 33 g; Fiber 4 g;
    T Fat 38 g; 57% Calories from Fat; Chol 92 mg; Sod 564 mg.

Dietary Exchanges: Bread 1 1/2; Lean Meat 3 1/2; Fruit 1/2; Vegetable 1/2; Fat 3

Pheasant Potpie

1 pheasant
1 small onion
3 cloves
1 stalk celery with leaves, sliced
8 peppercorns
1/2 teaspoon thyme
1 bay leaf
2 1/2 cups wine
2 1/2 cups water
2 potatoes, chopped
3 medium onions, chopped

2 carrots, sliced
1 stalk celery, sliced
1/4 cup butter
3 tablespoons flour
Saffron to taste
1/4 teaspoon cinnamon
1/4 teaspoon nutmeg
1/2 tablespoon Worcestershire sauce
1/2 cup (about) cream
1 recipe 1-crust pastry

Rinse pheasant inside and out. Combine with 1 onion studded with cloves, 1 stalk celery with leaves, peppercorns, thyme, bay leaf, wine and water in saucepan. Simmer for 1 to 1 1/2 hours or until pheasant is tender. Remove pheasant from saucepan. Add potatoes to saucepan. Cook until tender; drain, reserving 3 cups strained stock. Chop pheasant, discarding skin and bones. Sauté 3 onions, carrots and 1 stalk celery in butter in saucepan until carrots are tender. Stir in flour. Cook for several minutes, stirring constantly; remove from heat. Stir in reserved broth, saffron, cinnamon, nutmeg and Worcestershire sauce. Simmer for 3 to 4 minutes, adding cream as needed for desired thickness. Add pheasant and potatoes; mix lightly. Spoon into baking dish. Top with pastry. Bake at 500 degrees for 15 minutes or until top is brown. Yield: 6 servings.

Approx Per Serving: Cal 673; Prot 22 g; Carbo 45 g; Fiber 4 g;
    T Fat 38 g; 51% Calories from Fat; Chol 98 mg; Sod 413 mg.

Dietary Exchanges: Bread 1 1/2; Lean Meat 2 1/2; Fruit 1/2; Vegetable 1 1/2; Fat 7 1/2

Emily B. King, Nashville, Tennessee

Quail Amandine

4 quail
1/4 cup lemon juice
Salt and pepper to taste
1/2 cup flour
1/4 cup margarine

1/2 cup dry white wine
1/4 cup chicken broth
1 teaspoon grated lemon rind
1/2 cup seedless green grape halves
1/4 cup toasted sliced almonds

Rinse quail and pat dry inside and out. Drizzle with lemon juice in bowl; sprinkle with salt and pepper. Marinate in refrigerator for 1 hour. Coat with flour. Brown on all sides in margarine in saucepan. Add wine, chicken broth and lemon rind. Simmer, covered, for 20 minutes. Stir in grapes and almonds. Simmer until heated through.
Yield: 2 servings.

Approx Per Serving: Cal 900; Prot 50 g; Carbo 41 g; Fiber 3 g;
    T Fat 56 g; 56% Calories from Fat; Chol 166 mg; Sod 487 mg.

Dietary Exchanges: Bread 1 1/2; Lean Meat 6 1/2; Fruit 1; Fat 4

Quail au Vin

6 quail, skinned
1 8-ounce can mushrooms
1 cup white wine

1 tablespoon teriyaki sauce
1 envelope dry onion soup mix

Wash quail and pat dry inside and out. Place in foil-lined baking pan. Pour mixture of undrained mushrooms, wine and teriyaki sauce over quail. Sprinkle with soup mix. Seal foil loosely. Bake at 350 degrees for 1 hour. Yield: 6 servings.

Approx Per Serving: Cal 250; Prot 23 g; Carbo 3 g; Fiber 1 g;
     T Fat 13 g; 48% Calories from Fat; Chol 83 mg; Sod 441 mg.

Dietary Exchanges: Lean Meat 3; Vegetable 1/2; Fat 11/2

Baked Quail Supreme

6 quail
6 slices bacon
Salt and pepper to taste
8 ounces mushrooms
1 bunch green onions, chopped

2 tablespoons melted margarine
2 tablespoons prepared mustard
1/2 teaspoon ginger
1 cup orange marmalade

Wash quail; pat dry inside and out. Wrap with bacon. Arrange on large piece of foil. Sprinkle with salt and pepper. Sauté mushrooms and green onions in margarine in skillet. Spoon over quail; seal foil. Place on baking sheet. Bake at 325 degrees for 1 hour or until quail are tender. Combine mustard, ginger and marmalade in saucepan. Heat to serving temperature, stirring frequently. Serve with quail. Yield: 6 servings.

Approx Per Serving: Cal 429; Prot 25 g; Carbo 39 g; Fiber 2 g;
     T Fat 21 g; 42% Calories from Fat; Chol 88 mg; Sod 303 mg.

Dietary Exchanges: Lean Meat 31/2; Fruit 2; Vegetable 1/2; Fat 11/2

Being struck by lightning is not necessarily fatal. Administer first aid—mouth-to-mouth resuscitation if victim is not breathing, cardiopulmonary resuscitation if victim has no pulse or both. Burns and shock may also need special attention. Be prepared. Take a Red Cross first aid course before you need it.

California Quail

1 large onion, coarsely chopped
3 cloves of garlic, minced
2 tablespoons oil
1 28-ounce can tomatoes, drained,
    coarsely chopped

2/3 cup picante sauce
1/4 cup sliced green olives
6 quail
1/4 cup coarsely chopped cilantro

Sauté onion and garlic in oil in skillet for 4 minutes. Add tomatoes, picante sauce and olives. Bring to a boil. Add quail, spooning sauce over top. Simmer, covered, for 30 to 45 minutes or until quail are tender. Remove to serving platter. Cook sauce over high heat until thickened to desired consistency. Sprinkle with cilantro. Serve with quail. Serve with additional picante sauce. Yield: 6 servings.

Approx Per Serving: Cal 305; Prot 23 g; Carbo 10 g; Fiber 3 g;
    T Fat 19 g; 56% Calories from Fat; Chol 83 mg; Sod 587 mg.

Dietary Exchanges: Lean Meat 3; Vegetable 2; Fat 2

Be sure that you do your part to keep your favorite outdoor areas intact. Leave a site cleaner than you found it—carry away your own trash and that of litterbugs before you for proper disposal. Be especially careful to remove all plastic, cigarette filters and other non-biodegradable materials.

Quail Dijon

1 envelope Italian salad dressing mix
1/4 cup red wine vinegar
2 tablespoons water

2/3 cup vegetable oil
2 tablespoons Dijon mustard
4 quail

Prepare salad dressing mix with vinegar, water and oil in covered container, using package directions. Add mustard; shake to mix well. Rinse quail and pat dry. Combine with marinade in airtight container; mix well. Marinate, covered, in refrigerator overnight, shaking container several times. Drain, reserving marinade. Place quail in shallow roasting pan. Drizzle with reserved marinade. Roast at 350 degrees for 1 hour. Yield: 4 servings.

Approx Per Serving: Cal 549; Prot 22 g; Carbo 2 g; Fiber 0 g;
    T Fat 51 g; 82% Calories from Fat; Chol 83 mg; Sod 498 mg.
    Nutritional information includes entire amount of marinade.

Dietary Exchanges: Lean Meat 3; Fat 8 1/2

Quail with Lemon Sauce

4 ounces smoked bacon, chopped
3 carrots, sliced
2 large onions, sliced
7 peppercorns
Breasts and drumsticks of 16 quail
1 cup (or more) chicken broth

2 tablespoons margarine
1 tablespoon flour
Juice and grated rind of 1 lemon
3 tablespoons nonfat sour cream
Salt to taste

Combine bacon, carrots, onions and peppercorns in skillet. Cook for 10 minutes. Wash quail and pat dry. Add to skillet. Simmer, covered, until tender, stirring occasionally. Add a small amount of broth if necessary for desired consistency. Remove quail to platter; keep warm. Strain broth, reserving vegetables; discard peppercorns. Purée vegetables in blender container. Blend margarine and flour in skillet. Add strained broth. Cook until thickened, stirring constantly. Add lemon juice and rind. Simmer for 10 minutes. Stir in puréed vegetables and sour cream. Bring to a boil; add salt. Pour over quail. Yield: 8 servings.

Approx Per Serving: Cal 637; Prot 59 g; Carbo 7 g; Fiber 1 g;
    T Fat 40 g; 58% Calories from Fat; Chol 221 mg; Sod 362 mg.

Dietary Exchanges: Lean Meat 8; Vegetable 1/2; Fat 3

Oriental Quail

3 quail
2 tablespoons oil
1 cup sliced mushrooms
1 cup sliced water chestnuts
1 cup snow peas

1 cup (or more) chicken broth
1/4 cup sherry
2 tablespoons reduced-sodium soy
  sauce
2 tablespoons cornstarch

Wash quail; pat dry inside and out. Cut into 2-inch pieces with poultry shears. Brown in oil in skillet until tender. Add mushrooms, water chestnuts, snow peas and broth. Cook for 4 minutes. Remove quail and vegetables to hot serving dish. Add enough additional broth to pan juices to measure 1 1/2 cups. Stir in sherry and mixture of soy sauce and cornstarch. Cook until thickened, stirring constantly. Pour over quail and vegetables. Yield: 3 servings.

Approx Per Serving: Cal 390; Prot 25 g; Carbo 17 g; Fiber 3 g;
    T Fat 23 g; 53% Calories from Fat; Chol 83 mg; Sod 585 mg.

Dietary Exchanges: Bread 1/2; Lean Meat 3; Vegetable 2; Fat 3

Stuffed Quail

1 cup cracker crumbs
2 slices bacon, crisp-fried, crumbled
2 tablespoons chopped celery
1/2 cup chicken broth

8 quail
8 slices bacon
1/2 cup white wine

Mix cracker crumbs, crumbled bacon, celery and chicken broth in bowl; mix gently. Rinse quail and pat dry. Stuff with cracker crumb mixture. Wrap each quail with 1 slice bacon; secure with wooden picks. Arrange in greased baking dish. Add wine. Roast at 350 degrees for 30 minutes, adding additional broth as needed. Yield: 4 servings.

Approx Per Serving: Cal 625; Prot 50 g; Carbo 16 g; Fiber 1 g;
    T Fat 37 g; 54% Calories from Fat; Chol 179 mg; Sod 743 mg.

Dietary Exchanges: Bread 1; Lean Meat 6½; Fat 4

Emily B. King, Nashville, Tennessee

A quick accompaniment for all types of game is canned applesauce mixed with a generous amount of horseradish.

Spinach-Stuffed Quail

1   10-ounce package frozen chopped
    spinach
1 cup low-fat cottage cheese
1/4 cup grated Parmesan cheese
1 egg
1 clove of garlic, crushed
1/4 cup chopped walnuts

Salt and pepper to taste
2 quail
1 lemon, cut into halves
2 tablespoons olive oil
1/4 teaspoon each crushed oregano,
    rosemary and basil

Cook spinach using package directions; drain and press to remove moisture. Combine with cottage cheese, Parmesan cheese, egg, garlic, walnuts, salt and pepper in bowl; mix well. Rinse quail inside and out; sprinkle cavities with juice of 1/2 lemon and pepper. Separate skin gently from tops of breasts, thighs and legs. Spoon stuffing evenly between skin and quail. Place in roasting pan. Brush with olive oil; sprinkle with crushed oregano, rosemary and basil. Drizzle with juice of remaining 1/2 lemon. Roast at 350 degrees for 45 to 60 minutes or until done to taste. Serve with risotto or wild rice, broiled tomato halves and fresh broccoli. Yield: 2 servings.

Approx Per Serving: Cal 665; Prot 52 g; Carbo 17 g; Fiber 5 g;
    T Fat 45 g; 59% Calories from Fat; Chol 208 mg; Sod 888 mg.

Dietary Exchanges: Lean Meat 6; Fruit 1/2; Vegetable 1½; Fat 4

Texas-Style Grilled Quail

1 quail, dressed and cleaned
1/4 onion

2 jalapeño peppers
1 slice bacon

Rinse quail; pat dry inside and out. Place onion and jalapeño peppers inside cavity. Wrap with bacon; secure with wooden pick. Grill over hot coals for 4 to 8 minutes or until tender. Yield: 1 serving.

Approx Per Serving: Cal 271; Prot 25 g; Carbo 6 g; Fiber <1 g;
    T Fat 16 g; 55% Calories from Fat; Chol 88 mg; Sod 160 mg.

Dietary Exchanges: Lean Meat 3½; Vegetable 1; Fat 1½

Wild Turkey Casserole

1½ cups chopped cooked wild turkey
Salt and pepper to taste
1/4 cup oil
1/2 cup chopped onion
1 15-ounce can tomato sauce
2 cups water

1 cup uncooked rice
1 teaspoon salt
1/4 teaspoon pepper
1 10-ounce package frozen peas
1/2 cup sliced black olives

Sprinkle turkey with salt and pepper to taste. Brown lightly in oil in large skillet. Add onion. Sauté for several minutes. Stir in tomato sauce, water, rice, 1 teaspoon salt and 1/4 teaspoon pepper. Bring to a boil; reduce heat. Simmer for 25 minutes or until turkey is tender. Add peas and olives. Simmer for 15 minutes longer. Yield: 4 servings.

Approx Per Serving: Cal 497; Prot 24 g; Carbo 57 g; Fiber 7 g;
    T Fat 19 g; 35% Calories from Fat; Chol 40 mg; Sod 1433 mg.

Dietary Exchanges: Bread 2½; Lean Meat 1½; Vegetable 1½; Fat 3

Roberta J. Lee, Waverly, Tennessee

Your camping pantry can supply first aid relief, too. A dusting or paste of baking soda relieves the itch of rashes and poisin ivy. Cayenne pepper sprinkled in socks can help with cold feet. Tannic acid in tea bags acts as an astringent for mouth sores and small wounds.

Fried Wild Turkey Breast

1 wild turkey breast, boned
Salt to taste
1 teaspoon baking powder
1 teaspoon paprika

1 cup flour
1 cup buttermilk
Oil for deep frying

Cut turkey breast into bite-sized pieces; season with salt. Combine baking powder, paprika and flour in bowl; mix well. Dip turkey pieces into buttermilk; coat with flour mixture. Deep-fry in hot oil in deep skillet until golden brown. Yield: 4 servings.

Approx Per Serving: Cal 437; Prot 70 g; Carbo 27 g; Fiber 1 g;
T Fat 3 g; 7% Calories from Fat; Chol 184 mg; Sod 266 mg.
Nutritional information does not include oil for deep frying.

Dietary Exchanges: Bread 1¹/₂; Lean Meat 5¹/₂; Milk ¹/₂

Ground Wild Turkey Sausage

1 pound ground wild turkey
¹/₈ teaspoon savory
¹/₂ teaspoon crushed fennel seed
¹/₄ teaspoon sage

¹/₄ teaspoon thyme
¹/₄ teaspoon marjoram
¹/₄ teaspoon salt
¹/₄ teaspoon pepper

Combine ground turkey, savory, fennel seed, sage, thyme, marjoram, salt and pepper in bowl; mix well. Shape into 4 patties. Cook in nonstick skillet until brown on both sides. Yield: 4 servings.

Approx Per Serving: Cal 200; Prot 23 g; Carbo 0 g; Fiber 0 g;
T Fat 11 g; 52% Calories from Fat; Chol 87 mg; Sod 224 mg.

Dietary Exchanges: Lean Meat 3¹/₂

Smoked Wild Turkey

3 stalks celery, chopped
1 onion, chopped
1 bay leaf, crushed

1 wild turkey
¹/₄ cup melted margarine
2 tablespoons Cajun seasoning

Mix celery, onion and bay leaf in bowl. Rinse turkey; pat dry. Rub inside and outside generously with margarine and Cajun seasoning. Stuff turkey with celery mixture. Arrange charcoal briquets in smoker. Arrange wet mesquite chips over briquets. Pour 1 gallon water into water pan. Place turkey on smoker grill. Smoke, covered, at 170 degrees for 10 to 12 hours, checking occasionally and adding additional water if necessary. Yield: 8 servings.

Approx Per Serving: Cal 637; Prot 100 g; Carbo 2 g; Fiber <1 g;
T Fat 23 g; 33% Calories from Fat; Chol 258 mg; Sod 319 mg.

Dietary Exchanges: Lean Meat 10¹/₂; Vegetable ¹/₂

Marinades

Barbecue Marinade

½ cup packed brown sugar
½ cup garlic-flavored barbecue sauce
½ cup vermouth

¼ cup soy sauce
¼ cup wine vinegar
⅛ teaspoon ginger

Cranberry Marinade

½ cup cranberry juice cocktail
½ cup dry red wine
¼ cup oil

1 tablespoon rosemary
1 teaspoon black peppercorns
½ teaspoon salt

Lemon Yogurt Marinade

8 ounces lemon yogurt
1 teaspoon ginger
½ teaspoon garlic powder

½ teaspoon paprika
½ teaspoon coriander

Sweet and Hot Marinade

2 tablespoons olive oil
2 tablespoons soy sauce
2 tablespoons honey
1 tablespoon vinegar
1 teaspoon freshly ground black pepper

½ teaspoon cayenne pepper
½ teaspoon thyme
½ teaspoon paprika
½ teaspoon allspice

The Easiest Marinade

8 to 16 ounces of your favorite vinegar
    and oil or fat-free Italian salad
    dressing

Here are a bevy of marinades suitable for game, steak or chicken. Just mix up the ingredients, pour over the meat or baste and turn the meat occasionally to be sure the marinade reaches all surfaces to promote flavor and tenderizing. Grill or broil in your favorite mode and prepare for rave reviews. A little experimenting will determine whether just an hour of marinating or overnight produces the results that suit your tastes. Be sure that marinating which takes more than an hour is done in the refrigerator.

Carry a supply of sealable plastic bags with pre-mixed marinades sealed inside. Add meat up to 1 hour before cooking.

Go Fish

Carl Brasil and I outta Sligo Boat Dock. I guess we showed
those fellas outta New York the true meaning of night fishing.

Bass Amandine

¹/2 cup thinly sliced almonds
1 tablespoon margarine
6 bass filets
1 cup milk

1 teaspoon dry mustard
¹/2 cup flour
Salt and pepper to taste
¹/4 cup oil

Sauté almonds in margarine in skillet; set aside. Combine fish with mixture of milk and dry mustard in bowl. Marinate for 10 minutes; drain. Coat with mixture of flour, salt and pepper. Brown on both sides in oil in skillet; drain. Serve with almonds. Yield: 3 servings.

Approx Per Serving: Cal 598; Prot 38 g; Carbo 23 g; Fiber 2 g;
T Fat 39 g; 59% Calories from Fat; Chol 119 mg; Sod 198 mg.

Dietary Exchanges: Bread 1; Lean Meat 4; Milk 1/2; Fat 51/2

Take the family fishing or boating. Nothing beats the heat like the cooling waters of lake or stream. Tennessee Wildlife Resources Agency counts 29 major lakes, 100,000 farm ponds and more than 20,000 miles of streams for lots of water in Tennessee. See page 7 for a few location tips.

Baked Bass

4 pounds bass
Juice of 1 lemon
Salt to taste
1 cup bread crumbs
4 ounces mushrooms, sliced
¹/2 cup chopped onion

¹/4 cup chopped celery
¹/4 cup melted margarine
1 tablespoon brandy
1 tablespoon milk
Thyme and pepper to taste

Rub fish inside and out with mixture of lemon juice and salt; place in baking dish. Mix bread crumbs, mushrooms, onion, celery and margarine in bowl. Add brandy, milk, thyme and pepper; mix well. Spread over fish. Bake at 350 degrees for 45 minutes. Yield: 6 servings.

Approx Per Serving: Cal 506; Prot 61 g; Carbo 15 g; Fiber 1 g;
T Fat 20 g; 37% Calories from Fat; Chol 211 mg; Sod 458 mg.

Dietary Exchanges: Bread 1; Lean Meat 61/2; Vegetable 1/2

Bass Chowder

6 medium bass filets
4 cups water
3 large carrots, peeled, chopped
3 medium white onions, chopped
1 medium green bell pepper, chopped
2 tablespoons chopped parsley

3 tablespoons oil
1   16-ounce can tomatoes
3 potatoes, peeled, chopped
1/2 teaspoon thyme
2 small bay leaves
Salt and pepper to taste

Cook bass in water in saucepan just until fish flakes easily; drain, flake and set aside. Sauté carrots, onions, green pepper and parsley in oil in saucepan over medium heat for 5 minutes. Add tomatoes, potatoes, fish, thyme and bay leaves. Simmer for 40 minutes, adding water if needed for desired consistency. Discard bay leaves; season with salt and pepper. May sauté vegetables in bacon drippings or rendered salt pork if preferred. Yield: 6 servings.

Approx Per Serving: Cal 306; Prot 25 g; Carbo 26 g; Fiber 4 g;
      T Fat 12 g; 34% Calories from Fat; Chol 79 mg; Sod 223 mg.

Dietary Exchanges: Bread 1; Lean Meat 2½; Vegetable 2; Fat 1½

Bass Milano

2 pounds bass filets
1 medium onion, chopped
1 tablespoon olive oil
1   14-ounce can tomatoes
1/4 cup dry white wine

1 bay leaf, crumbled
1 tablespoon minced parsley
Salt and pepper to taste
1/4 cup bread crumbs

Cut filets into serving pieces; arrange in buttered baking dish. Sauté onion in olive oil in skillet over medium heat for 7 minutes. Add tomatoes, wine, bay leaf, parsley, salt and pepper. Cook over high heat for 10 to 15 minutes or until liquid is reduced. Spoon over filets; sprinkle with crumbs. Bake at 400 degrees for 25 to 30 minutes or until fish flakes easily. Garnish with lemon wedges. Yield: 4 servings.

Approx Per Serving: Cal 308; Prot 46 g; Carbo 11 g; Fiber 2 g;
      T Fat 7 g; 20% Calories from Fat; Chol 123 mg; Sod 408 mg.

Dietary Exchanges: Bread ½; Lean Meat 4½; Vegetable 1; Fat 1

Pickled Bass

3 pounds bass filets	1 cup white port
2 cups salt	1/2 cup sugar
1 gallon water	4 cups white vinegar
2 onions, thinly sliced into rings	1 tablespoon mixed pickling spices

Cut fish into 1-inch pieces. Soak in mixture of salt and water in refrigerator for 12 to 24 hours; drain and rinse in cold water. Pack into jars with onion rings. Combine wine, sugar, vinegar and pickling spices in saucepan; mix well. Bring to a simmer over medium heat. Pour over fish, leaving 1/2 inch headspace; seal with 2-piece lids. Store in refrigerator. Yield: 8 servings.

Approx Per Serving: Cal 320; Prot 33 g; Carbo 25 g; Fiber <1 g;
    T Fat 7 g; 18% Calories from Fat; Chol 118 mg; Sod 25703 mg.
    Nutritional information includes entire amount of soaking solution.

Dietary Exchanges: Lean Meat 3 1/2; Fruit 1 1/2; Vegetable 1/2; Fat 1/2

Make up your own special **Seafood Seasoning** for home or lakeside cooking. Start with 1 1/2 to 2 cups paprika and add 1/2 cup garlic powder or granulated garlic, 1/4 cup each chili powder, oregano and onion powder, 2 to 3 teaspoons each cayenne and black pepper and salt to taste. Use when broiling or baking fish or add to flour for coating fish.

Steamed Bass

1 3-pound bass	1 1/2 tablespoons margarine
2 cups water	1 tablespoon flour
1 tablespoon lemon juice	Salt and pepper to taste
Seasoned salt to taste	1 cup milk
3 tablespoons chopped green bell pepper	1/4 cup shredded Cheddar cheese

Clean bass, leaving head intact. Place on rack in fish poacher. Add mixture of water, lemon juice and seasoned salt. Poach for 8 to 10 minutes or until fish flakes easily; keep warm. Sauté green pepper in margarine in saucepan. Stir in flour, salt and pepper. Cook for several minutes. Stir in milk. Cook until thickened, stirring constantly. Add cheese, stirring until melted. Drain fish; serve with sauce. Yield: 4 servings.

Approx Per Serving: Cal 167; Prot 13 g; Carbo 5 g; Fiber <1 g;
    T Fat 10 g; 56% Calories from Fat; Chol 48 mg; Sod 157 mg.

Dietary Exchanges: Lean Meat 1 1/2; Milk 1/2; Fat 1/2

Buttermilk Bream

3 cups self-rising flour
2 eggs
4 cups buttermilk
Juice of 1 lemon

Salt and pepper to taste
12 bream
Oil for frying

Combine flour, eggs, buttermilk, lemon juice, salt and pepper in bowl; mix well. Add fish; let stand for 20 minutes. Fry in hot oil in skillet on both sides until brown. Substitute all-purpose flour for self-rising flour for lighter crust. Yield: 12 servings.

Approx Per Serving: Cal 410; Prot 62 g; Carbo 28 g; Fiber 1 g;
    T Fat 4 g; 9% Calories from Fat; Chol 228 mg; Sod 719 mg.
    Nutritional information does not include oil for frying.

Dietary Exchanges: Bread 1½; Lean Meat 5; Milk ½

Grilled Bream

20 small bream
¼ cup melted margarine
½ teaspoon Worcestershire sauce
1 teaspoon vinegar

Juice of 1 lemon
Garlic salt, onion salt and pepper to
    taste
1 large onion, chopped

Arrange bream in greased pan; place on grill over hot coals. Combine next 7 ingredients in bowl; mix well. Spoon over fish. Grill for 30 minutes, basting occasionally. Add onion. Grill for 15 minutes longer. Yield: 10 servings.

Approx Per Serving: Cal 426; Prot 83 g; Carbo 1 g; Fiber <1 g;
    T Fat 8 g; 17% Calories from Fat; Chol 285 mg; Sod 397 mg.

Dietary Exchanges: Lean Meat 7

Oven-Fried Bream

2 tablespoons flour
1 teaspoon oil
1 teaspoon reduced-sodium soy sauce
2 eggs, beaten
4 bream, cleaned

1 cup bread crumbs
2 onions, sliced
1 tablespoon olive oil
Paprika to taste

Combine flour, 1 teaspoon oil, soy sauce and eggs in bowl; mix well. Dip fish into mixture; coat with bread crumbs. Arrange on onion slices in baking dish. Drizzle with olive oil; sprinkle with paprika. Bake at 425 degrees for 20 minutes or until fish flakes easily and coating is crisp. Yield: 4 servings.

Approx Per Serving: Cal 465; Prot 62 g; Carbo 26 g; Fiber 2 g;
    T Fat 11 g; 21% Calories from Fat; Chol 296 mg; Sod 508 mg.

Dietary Exchanges: Bread 1½; Lean Meat 5; Vegetable ½; Fat 1

Saucy Baked Bream

1 onion, chopped
1 clove of garlic, chopped
1 tablespoon oil
1   10-ounce can tomato-basil soup
1 soup can low-fat milk

2 carrots, finely chopped
1/2 cup chopped green bell pepper
Basil to taste
6 bream
1 tablespoon margarine

Sauté onion and garlic in oil in skillet until golden brown. Combine with soup, milk, carrots, green pepper and basil in bowl; mix well. Arrange fish in greased baking pan. Pour sauce over top; dot with margarine. Bake at 350 to 375 degrees for 1 hour. Yield: 6 servings.

Approx Per Serving: Cal 368; Prot 58 g; Carbo 14 g; Fiber 1 g;
    T Fat 8 g; 20% Calories from Fat; Chol 193 mg; Sod 635 mg.

Dietary Exchanges: Lean Meat 4 1/2; Vegetable 1; Fat 1

Cheesy Catfish Filets

2 pounds catfish filets
1   10-ounce can tomato soup
2 tablespoons chopped onion

Salt and pepper to taste
1 cup shredded Cheddar cheese

Cut fish into 6 serving pieces; place in 8x12-inch baking dish. Combine soup, onion, salt and pepper in bowl; spoon over fish. Sprinkle with cheese. Bake at 350 degrees for 25 to 30 minutes or until fish flakes easily. Yield: 6 servings.

Approx Per Serving: Cal 284; Prot 33 g; Carbo 7 g; Fiber <1 g;
    T Fat 13 g; 43% Calories from Fat; Chol 108 mg; Sod 531 mg.

Dietary Exchanges: Lean Meat 4; Vegetable 1/2; Fat 1

Grilled Marinated Catfish

1/2 cup red wine
Juice of 1 lemon
1 tablespoon Worcestershire sauce
1/2 cup reduced-sodium soy sauce

2 cloves of garlic, minced
1 1/2 pounds catfish filets
Salt and pepper to taste

Mix wine, lemon juice, Worcestershire sauce, soy sauce and garlic in shallow dish. Add catfish. Marinate in refrigerator for 8 hours; drain. Place fish in grilling baskets sprayed with nonstick cooking spray. Grill over medium coals for 10 minutes on each side or until fish flakes easily. Sprinkle with salt and pepper. Yield: 4 servings.

Approx Per Serving: Cal 238; Prot 31 g; Carbo 6 g; Fiber <1 g;
    T Fat 7 g; 28% Calories from Fat; Chol 99 mg; Sod 920 mg.

Dietary Exchanges: Lean Meat 3 1/2; Fat 1/2

Catfish Parmesan

1/2 cup grated Parmesan cheese
1/4 cup flour
1 teaspoon paprika
Salt and pepper to taste
1 egg

1/4 cup milk
6 catfish filets
1/4 cup melted margarine
1/3 cup toasted sliced almonds

Mix Parmesan cheese, flour, paprika, salt and pepper in shallow dish. Beat egg with milk in bowl. Dip catfish into egg mixture; coat with cheese mixture. Arrange in lightly greased 9x13-inch baking dish. Drizzle with margarine; sprinkle with almonds. Place in 400-degree oven; reduce oven temperature to 350 degrees. Bake for 35 to 40 minutes or until fish flakes easily. Yield: 6 servings.

Approx Per Serving: Cal 306; Prot 27 g; Carbo 6 g; Fiber 1 g;
T Fat 19 g; 56% Calories from Fat; Chol 109 mg; Sod 325 mg.

Dietary Exchanges: Lean Meat 3; Fat 1

Catfish Potato Cakes

1 pound catfish filets, chopped
2 cups grated potatoes
3 eggs, beaten
2 tablespoons flour

2 tablespoons grated onion
1 tablespoon chopped parsley
Nutmeg, salt and pepper to taste

Combine fish, potatoes, eggs, flour, onion, parsley, nutmeg, salt and pepper in bowl; mix well. Ladle by 1/3 cupfuls onto heated greased griddle or skillet; flatten slightly with spatula. Bake for 6 to 8 minutes or until brown on both sides, turning once; drain. Yield: 4 servings.

Approx Per Serving: Cal 320; Prot 28 g; Carbo 31 g; Fiber 2 g;
T Fat 9 g; 25% Calories from Fat; Chol 225 mg; Sod 119 mg.

Dietary Exchanges: Bread 1 1/2; Lean Meat 3; Fat 1/2

Southern-Fried Catfish

2 pounds catfish filets
1 cup mustard

3 cups cornmeal
3 cups canola oil for frying

Clean and rinse filets, discarding excess skin and fat. Coat well with mustard. Roll in cornmeal, coating well. Fry in 1/2 inch or more oil in deep skillet until golden brown. Yield: 4 servings.

Approx Per Serving: Cal 688; Prot 53 g; Carbo 84 g; Fiber 7 g;
T Fat 14 g; 19% Calories from Fat; Chol 132 mg; Sod 914 mg.
Nutritional information does not include oil for frying.

Dietary Exchanges: Bread 4 1/2; Lean Meat 5; Vegetable 1; Fat 1/2

Smoked Catfish

1 cup reduced-sodium soy sauce
1 cup Worcestershire sauce

10 drops of liquid smoke
3 pounds catfish filets

Combine soy sauce, Worcestershire sauce and liquid smoke in bowl. Add catfish. Marinate in refrigerator for 2 hours; drain. Heat coals and hickory chips in smoker. Place fish in smoker. Smoke for 2 hours or until fish flakes easily; do not overcook. Yield: 6 servings.

Approx Per Serving: Cal 309; Prot 41 g; Carbo 12 g; Fiber 0 g;
    T Fat 10 g; 29% Calories from Fat; Chol 132 mg; Sod 1613 mg.

Dietary Exchanges: Lean Meat 5; Fruit 1/2

Catfish and Pasta Casserole

1 4-ounce can sliced mushrooms
2 tablespoons flour
Salt and pepper to taste
2 tablespoons melted margarine
1 1/4 cups milk
1 cup grated Parmesan cheese

2 tablespoons chopped pimento
2 cups flaked cooked catfish
3 cups cooked spaghetti
1/2 cup bread crumbs
2 tablespoons melted margarine

Drain mushrooms, reserving liquid. Blend flour, salt and pepper into 2 tablespoons melted margarine in saucepan. Cook until bubbly, stirring constantly. Add milk and reserved liquid gradually. Cook until thickened, stirring constantly. Stir in cheese, pimento, mushrooms and fish. Layer spaghetti and fish sauce 1/2 at a time in greased 1 1/2-quart baking dish. Top with mixture of bread crumbs and 2 tablespoons margarine. Bake at 350 degrees for 30 to 35 minutes or until bubbly. Yield: 6 servings.

Approx Per Serving: Cal 418; Prot 29 g; Carbo 32 g; Fiber 2 g;
    T Fat 19 g; 41% Calories from Fat; Chol 68 mg; Sod 625 mg.

Dietary Exchanges: Bread 1 1/2; Lean Meat 3; Vegetable 1/2; Fat 1

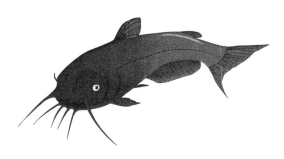

Catfish Stew

1 cup chopped onion
1 tablespoon oil
1 29-ounce can tomatoes
2 cups chopped potatoes
Salt and pepper to taste

1¹/₂ cups water
1 pound catfish filets, chopped
1 10-ounce package frozen mixed
  vegetables
¹/₂ cup mixed vegetable juice cocktail

Sauté onion in oil in 3-quart saucepan until tender. Add tomatoes, potatoes, salt, pepper and water; mix well. Simmer, covered, for 30 minutes. Add fish, mixed vegetables and mixed vegetable juice cocktail. Simmer, covered, for 15 minutes longer or until done to taste. Yield: 4 servings.

Approx Per Serving: Cal 323; Prot 26 g; Carbo 36 g; Fiber 7 g;
     T Fat 9 g; 24% Calories from Fat; Chol 66 mg; Sod 539 mg.

Dietary Exchanges: Bread 1; Lean Meat 2¹/₂; Vegetable 4; Fat ¹/₂

Store your fresh catch for later enjoyment by freezing in a carton of water to preserve the fresh flavor. Clean paper milk cartons work well and can be sealed tightly with freezer tape. For optimum flavor use within 3 months.

Stuffed Catfish

8 fresh mushrooms, sliced
¹/₂ onion, chopped
2 shallots, chopped
2 tablespoons margarine
8 catfish filets
1 green bell pepper, finely chopped
1 pimento, finely chopped

1 egg
¹/₂ cup light mayonnaise
1 tablespoon English mustard
Salt and white pepper to taste
1 pound lump crab meat
5 ounces white wine

Sauté mushrooms, onion and shallots in margarine in skillet. Spoon into shallow baking dish. Arrange fish in prepared dish. Mix green pepper, pimento, egg, mayonnaise, mustard, salt and white pepper in bowl. Stir in crab meat gently. Spoon into mound on filets. Add wine. Bake at 400 degrees for 15 to 20 minutes or until fish flakes easily. Yield: 8 servings.

Approx Per Serving: Cal 298; Prot 34 g; Carbo 9 g; Fiber 1 g;
     T Fat 13 g; 38% Calories from Fat; Chol 153 mg; Sod 371 mg.

Dietary Exchanges: Lean Meat 4; Vegetable 1; Fat 1

Crappie Amandine

2 eggs
1 cup low-fat milk
2 pounds crappie filets
1 cup flour
Seasoned salt, salt and pepper to taste
Oil for frying

¹/₂ cup sliced almonds
¹/₄ cup melted margarine
1 teaspoon (or more) Worcestershire
  sauce
1 teaspoon lemon juice

Beat eggs with milk in bowl. Dip fish into egg mixture; coat with mixture of flour and seasonings. Fry in oil in skillet on both sides until golden brown; drain. Place on ovenproof platter; sprinkle with almonds. Combine margarine, Worcestershire sauce and lemon juice in small bowl; drizzle over fish. Broil for 1 to 2 minutes. Yield: 6 servings.

Approx Per Serving: Cal 444; Prot 37 g; Carbo 20 g; Fiber 1 g;
  T Fat 24 g; 48% Calories from Fat; Chol 167 mg; Sod 220 mg.
  Nutritional information for this recipe does not include oil for frying.

Dietary Exchanges: Bread 1; Lean Meat 5; Fat 1

Baked Crappie

4 crappie
Salt and lemon pepper to taste
¹/₂ cup nonfat Italian salad dressing

¹/₄ cup melted margarine
¹/₄ cup lemon juice

Sprinkle fish with salt and lemon pepper; place in baking dish. Pour salad dressing over fish. Marinate in refrigerator for 30 minutes or longer; drain. Combine margarine and lemon juice in small bowl. Bake fish at 375 degrees for 20 minutes. Brush with lemon-margarine mixture. Bake for 8 to 10 minutes longer or until fish flakes easily, basting several times. Yield: 4 servings.

Approx Per Serving: Cal 602; Prot 70 g; Carbo 3 g; Fiber <1 g;
  T Fat 33 g; 50% Calories from Fat; Chol 219 mg; Sod 598 mg.

Dietary Exchanges: Lean Meat 10

The best protection from weather-related injuries is to be aware of possible dangerous weather and know how to react. Your local television and radio stations stand ready with updates and special bulletins to provide you with information supplied by the U.S. Commerce Department's National Oceanic and Atmospheric Administration's (NOAA) National Weather Service.

Beer-Batter Crappie

1¹/₂ cups baking mix
1 egg, beaten
1¹/₂ cups beer

1 teaspoon salt
8 crappie filets
Oil for deep frying

Combine baking mix, egg, beer and salt in bowl; mix until smooth. Dip crappie into batter. Deep-fry in 375-degree oil for 2 to 3 minutes or until golden brown; drain well. Yield: 8 servings.

Approx Per Serving: Cal 286; Prot 25 g; Carbo 18 g; Fiber <1 g;
    T Fat 11 g; 35% Calories from Fat; Chol 97 mg; Sod 633 mg.
    Nutritional information for this recipe does not include oil for deep frying.

Dietary Exchanges: Bread 1; Lean Meat 3¹/₂; Fat 1

Crappie Chowder

1 onion, chopped
¹/₄ cup margarine
2 potatoes, chopped
8 crappie filets, chopped

Salt and pepper to taste
2 cups low-fat milk
1 cup cooked corn kernels

Sauté onion in margarine in saucepan. Add potatoes and water to cover. Cook until potatoes are nearly tender. Add fish, salt and pepper. Cook until fish flakes easily. Add milk and corn; reduce heat. Simmer for 3 to 5 minutes; do not boil. May thicken with mixture of 1 tablespoon cornstarch and a small amount of cold water. Yield: 8 servings.

Approx Per Serving: Cal 294; Prot 26 g; Carbo 16 g; Fiber 2 g;
    T Fat 14 g; 43% Calories from Fat; Chol 75 mg; Sod 162 mg.

Dietary Exchanges: Bread ¹/₂; Lean Meat 3; Milk ¹/₂; Fat ¹/₂

Grilled Crappie

¹/₂ cup melted margarine
¹/₃ cup lemon juice
3 tablespoons Cajun-Quick blackened
    fish seasoning

3 tablespoons paprika
Salt and pepper to taste
8 crappie filets

Combine first 6 ingredients in bowl. Place fish on grill sprayed with nonstick cooking spray. Grill over low to medium coals for 15 to 20 minutes or until fish flakes easily, brushing frequently with lemon juice mixture. Yield: 8 servings.

Approx Per Serving: Cal 268; Prot 23 g; Carbo 2 g; Fiber 1 g;
    T Fat 19 g; 62% Calories from Fat; Chol 70 mg; Sod 194 mg.

Dietary Exchanges: Lean Meat 3

Carolyn Sullivan, Fairview, Tennessee

Crappie Parmesan

¹/₄ cup margarine
1¹/₂ pounds crappie
Salt and pepper to taste
¹/₂ cup lemon juice

¹/₂ cup white wine
¹/₄ cup grated Parmesan cheese
Paprika to taste

Melt margarine in 9x13-inch baking dish in 400-degree oven. Season fish with salt and pepper. Place in margarine in prepared dish, turning to coat well. Bake at 400 degrees for 10 to 15 minutes or until fish flakes easily, reducing oven temperature to 350 to 375 degrees if margarine browns too quickly. Pour mixture of lemon juice and wine over fish. Sprinkle with cheese and paprika. Broil for 5 minutes. Yield: 4 servings.

Approx Per Serving: Cal 392; Prot 36 g; Carbo 3 g; Fiber <1 g;
T Fat 24 g; 55% Calories from Fat; Chol 110 mg; Sod 340 mg.

Dietary Exchanges: Lean Meat 5; Fat ¹/₂

Smoked Crappie Appetizers

1 pound smoked crappie
8 ounces cream cheese, softened
1 tablespoon lemon juice
1 tablespoon Worcestershire sauce

¹/₄ cup grated onion
¹/₂ cup finely chopped pecans
2 tablespoons parsley flakes

Flake fish into bowl. Add cream cheese, lemon juice, Worcestershire sauce and onion; mix well. Shape into small balls. Roll in mixture of pecans and parsley flakes, coating well. Serve as appetizers. Yield: 12 servings.

Approx Per Serving: Cal 143; Prot 11 g; Carbo 2 g; Fiber <1 g;
T Fat 10 g; 64% Calories from Fat; Chol 33 mg; Sod 455 mg.

Dietary Exchanges: Lean Meat 1; Fat 2

Fried Crawfish Tails

2 eggs
2 cups milk
2 pounds crawfish tails

1¹/₂ cups self-rising flour
Salt and pepper to taste
Oil for frying

Beat eggs with milk in bowl. Dip crawfish tails into egg mixture; coat with mixture of flour, salt and pepper. Fry in hot oil in deep skillet until golden brown. Yield: 4 servings.

Approx Per Serving: Cal 438; Prot 42 g; Carbo 41 g; Fiber 1 g;
T Fat 9 g; 20% Calories from Fat; Chol 364 mg; Sod 856 mg.
Nutritional information for this recipe does not include oil for frying.

Dietary Exchanges: Bread 2; Lean Meat 3¹/₂; Milk ¹/₂; Fat 1

Crawfish Pie

1/2 cup oil
1/3 cup flour
1 tablespoon catsup
1/2 cup chopped green onion tops
1 1/2 cups water

1 1/2 pounds crawfish tails
1/2 cup chopped parsley
Salt and pepper to taste
Garlic powder to taste
1 recipe 2-crust pie pastry

Heat oil in cast-iron saucepan. Add flour gradually, stirring until smooth. Cook over medium-high heat until golden brown, stirring constantly; remove from heat. Add catsup, green onion tops and water; mix well. Add crawfish. Cook over medium heat for 30 minutes. Stir in parsley, salt, pepper and garlic powder. Cook until thickened, stirring constantly. Pour into pastry-lined pie plate. Top with remaining pastry, sealing edge and cutting vents. Bake at 400 degrees for 45 minutes. Yield: 6 servings.

Approx Per Serving: Cal 554; Prot 20 g; Carbo 32 g; Fiber 2 g;
     T Fat 38 g; 62% Calories from Fat; Chol 121 mg; Sod 408 mg.

Dietary Exchanges: Bread 2; Lean Meat 1 1/2; Fat 7

Tomato and Basil Baked Perch

3 plum tomatoes, chopped
2 tablespoons chopped fresh basil
1 pound perch filets

2 tablespoons chopped green onions
Salt and pepper to taste
2 tablespoons olive oil

Combine tomatoes and basil in bowl; mix well. Arrange fish filets in single layer in baking dish; sprinkle with green onions, salt and pepper. Spoon tomato mixture over top; drizzle with olive oil. Bake at 450 degrees for 10 minutes or until fish flakes easily. Yield: 2 servings.

Approx Per Serving: Cal 361; Prot 44 g; Carbo 5 g; Fiber 1 g;
     T Fat 18 g; 45% Calories from Fat; Chol 98 mg; Sod 184 mg.

Dietary Exchanges: Lean Meat 4 1/2; Vegetable 1; Fat 2 1/2

Do not wash clothes or dishes, or bathe, in lakes or streams. Dip the water into a large container, use only biodegradable soap and be sure to dump the used water far away from the water source so it has time and distance to filter and cleanse on the way back to its source.

Stir-Fried Pike

1/3 cup plain nonfat yogurt
2 teaspoons flour
1/4 cup low-fat milk
1 teaspoon instant chicken bouillon
1/2 teaspoon dillweed

1 carrot, sliced diagonally
2 cups pea pods
1 tablespoon oil
8 pike filets, chopped

Blend yogurt and flour in small bowl. Add milk, chicken bouillon and dillweed; set aside. Stir-fry carrot in wok or skillet sprayed with nonstick cooking spray for 2 minutes. Add pea pods. Stir-fry for 2 to 3 minutes or until tender-crisp; remove carrot and pea pods to warm bowl. Add oil and fish to wok. Stir-fry gently for 3 to 6 minutes or until cooked through; remove to warm bowl. Reduce heat; stir in yogurt mixture. Cook until thickened, stirring constantly. Add vegetables and fish; mix gently. Heat to serving temperature. Yield: 4 servings.

Approx Per Serving: Cal 794; Prot 157 g; Carbo 11 g; Fiber 3 g;
T Fat 9 g; 11% Calories from Fat; Chol 312 mg; Sod 624 mg.

Dietary Exchanges: Lean Meat 12 1/2; Vegetable 1 1/2; Fat 1/2

Do not overcook fish. Whether baking, grilling or poaching, a good rule of thumb is to cook for 10 minutes per inch of thickness or just until the fish flakes easily.

Baked Pike and Rice Casserole

1 1/2 pounds pike filets
3 cups cooked rice
1/2 cup chopped onion
1/2 cup chopped celery
1/2 cup chopped green bell pepper
2 tablespoons margarine

1 28-ounce can Italian-style tomato
   sauce
1 teaspoon basil
Garlic powder, salt and pepper to taste
2 cups shredded mozzarella cheese

Layer fish and rice in 9x13-inch baking dish. Sauté onion, celery and green pepper in margarine in skillet. Stir in tomato sauce, basil, garlic powder, salt and pepper. Spoon over casserole; sprinkle with cheese. Bake at 350 degrees for 45 minutes or until fish flakes easily. Yield: 6 servings.

Approx Per Serving: Cal 430; Prot 34 g; Carbo 41 g; Fiber 3 g;
T Fat 14 g; 29% Calories from Fat; Chol 129 mg; Sod 1054 mg.

Dietary Exchanges: Bread 1 1/2; Lean Meat 3; Vegetable 2; Fat 1

Salmon Pie

1 green bell pepper, chopped	2 cups milk
2 small onions, chopped	2 cups flaked cooked salmon
3 tablespoons margarine	1 cup cooked peas
1/4 cup flour	1 tablespoon lemon juice
Salt to taste	1 recipe biscuit dough

Sauté green pepper and onions in margarine in saucepan over low heat for 5 minutes or until tender. Stir in flour and salt. Cook until bubbly. Add milk gradually. Cook until thickened, stirring constantly. Stir in salmon, peas and lemon juice. Spoon into greased baking dish. Cut biscuit dough with biscuit cutter. Arrange over salmon mixture. Bake at 425 degrees for 20 to 25 minutes or until biscuits are golden brown. Yield: 6 servings.

Approx Per Serving: Cal 435; Prot 26 g; Carbo 32 g; Fiber 3 g;
T Fat 22 g; 46% Calories from Fat; Chol 70 mg; Sod 373 mg.

Dietary Exchanges: Bread 1 1/2; Lean Meat 2 1/2; Vegetable 1/2; Milk 1/2; Fat 1 1/2

Poached Salmon

1 1/2 pounds salmon filets	Dill and lemon pepper to taste
Juice of 1 lemon	1 onion, thinly sliced into rings
Garlic powder and parsley to taste	

Place salmon on large sheet of heavy-duty foil. Drizzle with lemon juice; sprinkle with garlic powder, parsley, dill and lemon pepper. Top with onion rings; seal foil tightly. Place in skillet with 1/2 inch water. Poach, covered, for 15 minutes or until fish flakes easily. Yield: 3 servings.

Approx Per Serving: Cal 410; Prot 50 g; Carbo 4 g; Fiber 1 g;
T Fat 20 g; 45% Calories from Fat; Chol 158 mg; Sod 121 mg.

Dietary Exchanges: Lean Meat 7 1/2; Vegetable 1/2

Smoking is a great way to preserve fish. You can use almost any closed grill (read your instruction manual) for smoking. With a little patience and practice you'll have a delicacy to savor. Soak the fish for 5 to 6 hours in a brine of 1 cup sugar and 1 cup salt dissolved in 4 to 6 cups water or enough to cover fish. Drain fish; rinse and pat dry. Rub with favorite seasonings such as garlic, dill, thyme or tarragon and place on rack over smoking hickory, mesquite or other aromatic wood. Smoke for 6 to 8 hours or until fish flakes easily. Cool and store tightly wrapped in refrigerator.

Sweet and Sour Barbecued Salmon

1 5-pound salmon, cut into filets
1/4 cup packed brown sugar
1/4 teaspoon salt
1/4 teaspoon pepper
1/2 cup butter

1/2 cup mayonnaise
1/4 cup catsup
2 tablespoons white vinegar
1/2 teaspoon Worcestershire sauce

Arrange filets skin side down on double layer of foil slightly larger than fish; sprinkle with brown sugar, salt and pepper. Dot with butter. Pierce foil at 2-inch intervals. Combine mayonnaise, catsup, vinegar and Worcestershire sauce in small bowl; mix well. Spread evenly over fish. Place foil on grill. Grill over hot coals until milky liquid forms on top of fish; cover with grill lid or foil. Grill for several minutes longer or until fish flakes easily. Yield: 8 servings.

Approx Per Serving: Cal 721; Prot 62 g; Carbo 8 g; Fiber <1 g;
T Fat 47 g; 60% Calories from Fat; Chol 237 mg; Sod 508 mg.

Dietary Exchanges: Lean Meat 9; Fruit 1/2; Fat 41/2

Verona Harper, Springfield, Tennessee

Fried Sauger

21/2 cups self-rising cornmeal
1 cup self-rising flour

1/4 cup Season-All salt
4 pounds sauger filets

Mix cornmeal, flour and salt in bowl. Rinse fish and coat with cornmeal mixture. Deep-fry in hot oil until golden brown; drain. Yield: 8 servings.

Approx Per Serving: Cal 429; Prot 50 g; Carbo 44 g; Fiber 3 g;
T Fat 4 g; 9% Calories from Fat; Chol 199 mg; Sod 2847 mg.

Dietary Exchanges: Bread 21/2; Lean Meat 4

Brenda Hicks, Springville, Tennessee

If worms are your bait of choice, start your own double-duty worm farm by building a mini-compost heap of leaves, grass clippings, coffee grounds and vegetable peelings. Add some worms and a top layer of leaves. Wet it down periodically, feed pile and worms with additional biodegradable material at least monthly; use the worms for fishing and the compost for gardening.

Salsa Sauger

1¹/₂ pounds sauger filets
¹/₂ cup salsa
2 tablespoons mayonnaise

2 tablespoons honey
2 tablespoons prepared mustard

Cut fish into 6 portions. Place in 9x13-inch baking dish. Bake at 450 degrees for 4 to 6 minutes or until fish flakes easily; drain. Pour mixture of salsa, mayonnaise, honey and mustard over filets. Bake for 2 to 3 minutes longer or until sauce is heated through. Remove fish to serving plates; spoon sauce over fish. Yield: 6 servings.

Approx Per Serving: Cal 170; Prot 23 g; Carbo 7 g; Fiber <1 g;
    T Fat 6 g; 30% Calories from Fat; Chol 102 mg; Sod 192 mg.

Dietary Exchanges: Lean Meat 2; Fruit ¹/₂; Fat 1

If you intend to cook your catch at waterside, be sure to select a site with plenty of available dead and downed dry firewood or carry along your own camp stove with its own heat source. Observe all safety rules for positioning, starting, maintaining and dousing the fire. A supply of high-energy no-cooking-needed snacks may be a good idea, too.

Sauger Divan Roll-Ups

¹/₄ cup lemon juice
¹/₄ cup melted margarine
Salt and pepper to taste
1 cup cooked rice

1¹/₄ cups chopped cooked broccoli
1 cup shredded Swiss cheese
8 sauger filets
Paprika to taste

Mix lemon juice, margarine, salt and pepper in bowl. Combine ¹/₄ cup lemon juice mixture with rice, broccoli and cheese in bowl; mix well. Spoon rice mixture onto sauger filets; roll fish to enclose filling. Place seam side down in shallow baking dish; sprinkle with paprika. Pour remaining lemon juice mixture over rolls. Bake at 375 degrees for 25 minutes or until fish flakes easily. Garnish with lemon wedges and parsley sprigs. Yield: 8 servings.

Approx Per Serving: Cal 252; Prot 28 g; Carbo 10 g; Fiber 1 g;
    T Fat 11 g; 40% Calories from Fat; Chol 112 mg; Sod 168 mg.

Dietary Exchanges: Bread ¹/₂; Lean Meat 2¹/₂; Vegetable ¹/₂; Fat ¹/₂

Campfire Stripe

1 tablespoon paprika	3/4 teaspoon black pepper
1 teaspoon salt	1/2 teaspoon thyme
1 teaspoon onion powder	1/2 teaspoon oregano
1 teaspoon garlic powder	3 pounds stripe filets
1 teaspoon red pepper	1/4 cup melted margarine
3/4 teaspoon white pepper	

Combine paprika, salt, onion powder, garlic powder, red pepper, white pepper, black pepper, thyme and oregano in small shallow bowl; mix well. Dip fish into melted margarine; coat with spice mixture. Preheat cast-iron skillet over grill or camp stove until very hot. Place fish in skillet. Cook for 2 minutes; turn fish. Cook for 1 minute longer. This is very smokey when prepared so it should be cooked outside or in a well-ventilated area. Yield: 8 servings.

Approx Per Serving: Cal 250; Prot 33 g; Carbo <1 g; Fiber 0 g;
T Fat 12 g; 45% Calories from Fat; Chol 118 mg; Sod 456 mg.

Dietary Exchanges: Lean Meat 3 1/2

Stripe with Mustard Sauce

2 pounds stripe filets	3 tablespoons margarine
1/4 cup white wine	3 tablespoons Dijon mustard
2 tablespoons lemon juice	3 tablespoons white wine
Garlic powder, salt and pepper to taste	1 teaspoon basil or tarragon
3 tablespoons minced onion	

Place fish in shallow bowl. Pour 1/4 cup wine and lemon juice over fish. Marinate for 1 hour. Sprinkle with garlic powder, salt and pepper. Sauté onion in margarine in small saucepan until transparent. Add mustard, remaining 3 tablespoons wine and basil; mix well. Cook until slightly thickened, stirring constantly. Place fish on perforated foil on grill. Grill over hot coals until fish flakes easily, basting frequently with sauce. Serve with remaining sauce. Yield: 4 servings.

Approx Per Serving: Cal 372; Prot 45 g; Carbo 2 g; Fiber <1 g;
T Fat 18 g; 44% Calories from Fat; Chol 158 mg; Sod 412 mg.

Dietary Exchanges: Lean Meat 5; Vegetable 1/2; Fat 1/2

You know it's illegal to drink and drive a car, but did you know it is also illegal to drink and drive a boat. Keep your skipper sober.

Skillet Stripe

1 pound new potatoes, unpeeled,
  thinly sliced
1 tablespoon olive oil
1 large onion, chopped
1 clove of garlic, minced
1 teaspoon cumin
1 tablespoon coarsely grated fresh
  ginger

1 large green bell pepper, coarsely
  chopped
2 tablespoons tomato paste
2 tablespoons balsamic vinegar
Salt to taste
1 pound stripe filets
4 small plum tomatoes, thinly sliced
1 cup chopped fresh coriander

Brown potatoes on both sides in olive oil in large nonstick skillet. Add onion, garlic, cumin and ginger; mix well. Sauté for 3 to 4 minutes or until onion is tender. Add green pepper. Cook for 3 to 4 minutes, stirring constantly. Stir in tomato paste, vinegar and salt. Arrange fish over vegetables; top with tomatoes. Cook, covered, for 10 minutes for each inch of fish thickness. Arrange fish and vegetables on serving plates; sprinkle with coriander. Yield: 3 servings.

Approx Per Serving: Cal 462; Prot 35 g; Carbo 49 g; Fiber 6 g;
    T Fat 14 g; 28% Calories from Fat; Chol 94 mg; Sod 186 mg.

Dietary Exchanges: Bread 2½; Lean Meat 4½; Vegetable 1½; Fat 1

Stripe with Vegetables

2 tablespoons melted margarine
2 tablespoons lemon juice
½ teaspoon dillweed
4 stripe filets
8 ¼-inch onion slices

2 medium potatoes
2 medium carrots
1 16-ounce can French-style green
   beans, drained

Combine margarine, lemon juice and dillweed in small bowl; mix well. Place fish filets in baking dish. Drizzle with margarine mixture. Top with onion slices. Peel potatoes and cut lengthwise into ¼-inch strips. Cut carrots into ⅛-inch slices. Place potatoes and carrots around fish. Top with beans. Cover with foil. Bake at 425 degrees for 30 to 35 minutes or until vegetables are tender. Yield: 4 servings.

Approx Per Serving: Cal 290; Prot 25 g; Carbo 25 g; Fiber 5 g;
    T Fat 10 g; 32% Calories from Fat; Chol 79 mg; Sod 449 mg.

Dietary Exchanges: Bread 1; Lean Meat 2½; Vegetable 1½

Trout Amandine

4 trout, skinned
1 cup buttermilk
1 egg
1 teaspoon almond extract

78 to 80 saltine crackers, crushed
Oil for frying
1/2 cup slivered almonds

Marinate filets in mixture of buttermilk, egg and almond flavoring in bowl for 1 to 2 hours; drain. Coat filets with cracker crumbs. Fry in hot oil in skillet until golden brown. Sprinkle with slivered almonds. Yield: 4 servings.

Approx Per Serving: Cal 607; Prot 44 g; Carbo 49 g; Fiber 4 g;
     T Fat 26 g; 38% Calories from Fat; Chol 149 mg; Sod 938 mg.
     Nutritional information does not include oil for frying.

Dietary Exchanges: Bread 3; Lean Meat 5; Milk 1/2; Fat 2

Trout au Gratin

2 tablespoons flour
Salt to taste
2 tablespoons melted margarine
2 cups milk

3/4 cup shredded Swiss cheese
1 tablespoon Worcestershire sauce
2 cups flaked cooked trout

Blend flour and salt into melted margarine in saucepan. Cook until bubbly. Add milk. Cook until thickened, stirring constantly. Add cheese, stirring until melted. Add Worcestershire sauce. Fold in fish. Spoon into baking ramekins. Bake at 350 degrees for 20 minutes or until golden brown. Yield: 4 servings.

Approx Per Serving: Cal 368; Prot 33 g; Carbo 10 g; Fiber <1 g;
     T Fat 21 g; 52% Calories from Fat; Chol 104 mg; Sod 277 mg.

Dietary Exchanges: Lean Meat 4; Milk 1/2; Fat 1 1/2

Beer Batter Trout

1 cup flour
1 cup cornstarch
1 teaspoon baking powder
1 teaspoon cayenne pepper

1   12-ounce bottle of beer
2 pounds trout filets
Oil for frying

Combine flour, cornstarch, baking powder and cayenne pepper in bowl. Add beer; mix well. Cut fish into 1-inch strips. Dip into batter. Fry in hot oil until golden brown. Yield: 6 servings.

Approx Per Serving: Cal 363; Prot 30 g; Carbo 38 g; Fiber 1 g;
     T Fat 7 g; 19% Calories from Fat; Chol 84 mg; Sod 128 mg.
     Nutritional information does not include oil for frying.

Dietary Exchanges: Bread 2 1/2; Lean Meat 4

Grilled Trout

4 1-pound trout
2 tablespoons olive oil
1/4 teaspoon grated lemon rind
1 tablespoon lemon juice

3/4 teaspoon oregano
1/2 teaspoon paprika
Salt and pepper to taste

Place fish in shallow dish. Combine olive oil, lemon rind, lemon juice, oregano and paprika in bowl; mix well. Pour over fish. Marinate in refrigerator for 2 hours or longer; drain, reserving marinade. Sprinkle fish with salt and pepper. Place on grill. Grill 4 to 6 inches from medium coals for 8 to 10 minutes, turning once, and brushing with reserved marinade several times. Yield: 4 servings.

Approx Per Serving: Cal 605; Prot 83 g; Carbo <1 g; Fiber <1 g;
         T Fat 28 g; 43% Calories from Fat; Chol 251 mg; Sod 203 mg.

Dietary Exchanges: Lean Meat 12; Fat 1 1/2

Greek-Style Trout

4 cloves of garlic, chopped
1/4 cup olive oil
2 tomatoes, chopped
1 green bell pepper, chopped

1 onion, chopped
1 lemon, thinly sliced
1 cup chopped parsley
2 pounds trout filets

Sauté garlic in olive oil in large skillet over low heat for several minutes. Add tomatoes, green pepper, onion, lemon and parsley. Simmer for 5 minutes. Add trout. Cook for 5 minutes. Turn trout. Cook for 1 minute or until fish flakes easily. Place fish on serving plate; spoon sauce over top. May microwave if preferred. Yield: 6 servings.

Approx Per Serving: Cal 290; Prot 29 g; Carbo 7 g; Fiber 2 g;
         T Fat 16 g; 51% Calories from Fat; Chol 84 mg; Sod 78 mg.

Dietary Exchanges: Lean Meat 4; Vegetable 1; Fat 2

Prepare your own garlic oil by chopping several cloves of garlic and adding vegetable or olive oil to cover. Store tightly covered in the refrigerator and use garlic and/or oil in cooking, marinades, salad dressings or sauces. Replenish garlic and oil as necessary. If fresh garlic is not available, get the flavor by using garlic flakes, powder or granules. Keep dry and tightly sealed until ready to use.

Zesty Cold Poached Trout

2 cups dry white wine
Salt to taste
8 peppercorns
1 small onion, coarsely chopped
6 sprigs of parsley
1 cup celery leaves
2 cups water

3 pounds trout filets
1/2 cup catsup
1/2 cup chili sauce
2 tablespoons lemon juice
1 1/2 teaspoons horseradish
1 teaspoon Worcestershire sauce
1/4 teaspoon pepper sauce

Combine wine, salt, peppercorns, onion, parsley, celery leaves and water in skillet. Simmer, covered, for 20 minutes. Arrange filets in single layer in skillet. Simmer, covered, for 10 minutes or until fish flakes easily. Drain and cool. Chill, covered, in refrigerator. Arrange on lettuce-lined plates. Combine catsup, chili sauce, lemon juice, horseradish, Worcestershire sauce and pepper sauce in bowl. Serve with trout. Garnish with cherry tomatoes. Yield: 10 servings.

Approx Per Serving: Cal 227; Prot 26 g; Carbo 8 g; Fiber 1 g;
T Fat 6 g; 26% Calories from Fat; Chol 75 mg; Sod 399 mg.
Nutritional information includes entire amount of poaching liquid.

Dietary Exchanges: Lean Meat 4; Fruit 1/2; Fat 1/2

Don't be confused by all those fronts and air masses and barometric readings you see on the weather map. Just remember that a "High" usually means good weather; a "Low" means poor.

Grilled Trout Dinner

4 trout filets
1 onion, sliced
2 potatoes, sliced
Juice of 1 lemon

2 tablespoons melted margarine
1/4 cup white wine
3 tablespoons chopped parsley
Salt and pepper to taste

Layer trout, onion and potatoes on piece of heavy-duty foil; drizzle with mixture of lemon juice and margarine. Pour wine over top; sprinkle with parsley, salt and pepper. Seal foil tightly; place on grill. Grill over hot coals until fish flakes easily. Yield: 4 servings.

Approx Per Serving: Cal 234; Prot 17 g; Carbo 19 g; Fiber 2 g;
T Fat 9 g; 36% Calories from Fat; Chol 43 mg; Sod 110 mg.

Dietary Exchanges: Bread 1; Lean Meat 2; Vegetable 1/2

Broiled Marinated Walleye

2¹/₂ pounds walleye filets
1¹/₂ cups white wine
¹/₂ cup lime juice
2 tablespoons melted margarine

Paprika, garlic powder, coriander, cayenne pepper and black pepper to taste

Combine fish with mixture of wine and lime juice in shallow dish. Marinate in refrigerator for several hours, turning to coat well; drain. Place on rack in broiler pan; brush with margarine. Sprinkle generously with paprika, garlic powder, coriander, cayenne pepper and black pepper. Broil for 5 to 10 minutes or until fish flakes easily. Garnish with lime slices. Yield: 6 servings.

Approx Per Serving: Cal 250; Prot 36 g; Carbo 2 g; Fiber <1 g;
T Fat 6 g; 21% Calories from Fat; Chol 145 mg; Sod 223 mg.
Nutritional information for this recipe includes entire amount of marinade.

Dietary Exchanges: Lean Meat 3; Fat 1

Baked Fish Filets

4 slices whole wheat bread, crumbled
¹/₃ cup grated Parmesan cheese
¹/₂ teaspoon thyme
2 teaspoons chopped fresh parsley

1 pound fish filets
1 tablespoon oil
Paprika, salt and pepper to taste

Mix bread crumbs with Parmesan cheese, thyme and parsley. Sprinkle into oiled 8x8-inch baking pan, coating well. Arrange fish in single layer in prepared pan. Brush with oil; sprinkle with paprika, salt and pepper. Bake at 375 degrees for 15 minutes or until fish flakes easily. Yield: 3 servings.

Approx Per Serving: Cal 348; Prot 38 g; Carbo 22 g; Fiber 3 g;
T Fat 12 g; 30% Calories from Fat; Chol 91 mg; Sod 579 mg.

Dietary Exchanges: Bread 1¹/₂; Lean Meat 3¹/₂; Fat 1¹/₂

Blackened Fish

1 tablespoon paprika
1 teaspoon onion powder
1¹/₂ teaspoons garlic powder
1 teaspoon red pepper
1 tablespoon chopped parsley

¹/₂ teaspoon each white pepper, black
  pepper, thyme and oregano
1 teaspoon salt
8 1-inch thick fish filets
¹/₂ cup melted unsalted margarine

Combine paprika, onion powder, garlic powder, red pepper, parsley, white pepper, black pepper, thyme, oregano and salt in small bowl; mix well. Dip fish into melted margarine; sprinkle on both sides with seasoning mixture. Cook in hot cast-iron skillet for 3 to 4 minutes on each side or until blackened. May add 1 tablespoon margarine to skillet if necessary to prevent sticking. Yield: 8 servings.

Approx Per Serving: Cal 250; Prot 31 g; Carbo <1 g; Fiber <1 g;
    T Fat 13 g; 49% Calories from Fat; Chol 86 mg; Sod 400 mg.

Dietary Exchanges: Lean Meat 3; Fat 2¹/₂

Barbecued Fish

¹/₂ cup lemon juice
¹/₄ cup vinegar
Tabasco sauce to taste
¹/₂ teaspoon garlic

¹/₂ teaspoon paprika
1¹/₂ teaspoons dry mustard
Salt and cayenne pepper to taste
2 pounds fish filets

Combine lemon juice, vinegar, Tabasco sauce, garlic, paprika, dry mustard, salt and cayenne pepper in saucepan. Bring to a boil. Place fish on grill; brush with sauce. Grill until fish flakes easily, brushing frequently with sauce. Yield: 4 servings.

Approx Per Serving: Cal 228; Prot 44 g; Carbo 4 g; Fiber <1 g;
    T Fat 3 g; 13% Calories from Fat; Chol 123 mg; Sod 190 mg.

Dietary Exchanges: Lean Meat 4¹/₂

Fishing Camp Hash

2 cups flaked cooked fish
¹/₄ cup minced onion
2 cups chopped cooked potatoes

2 eggs, beaten
Salt and pepper to taste
2 tablespoons oil

Combine fish, onion, potatoes, eggs, salt and pepper in bowl; mix well. Fry in oil in heated skillet until golden brown, stirring constantly. Yield: 4 servings.

Approx Per Serving: Cal 277; Prot 29 g; Carbo 15 g; Fiber 1 g;
    T Fat 11 g; 36% Calories from Fat; Chol 174 mg; Sod 140 mg.

Dietary Exchanges: Bread 1; Lean Meat 3; Fat 1¹/₂

Fish Gumbo

1 pound fish
2 cups water
1 onion, chopped
1 clove of garlic, minced
1/2 cup chopped celery
1/2 cup chopped green bell pepper
2 tablespoons oil

1 10-ounce can tomatoes with green
  chilies
1 10-ounce package frozen sliced okra
1/4 teaspoon thyme
1 bay leaf
Tabasco sauce to taste
Salt and pepper to taste

Cook fish in water in saucepan until it flakes easily; strain, reserving stock. Flake fish, discarding skin and bones. Sauté onion, garlic, celery and green pepper in oil in large saucepan. Add reserved stock, undrained tomatoes, okra, thyme, bay leaf, Tabasco sauce, salt and pepper. Simmer for 30 minutes. Add fish. Simmer, covered, for 20 minutes longer; discard bay leaf. Serve over rice. Yield: 4 servings.

Approx Per Serving: Cal 221; Prot 24 g; Carbo 12 g; Fiber 4 g;
    T Fat 9 g; 34% Calories from Fat; Chol 62 mg; Sod 395 mg.

Dietary Exchanges: Lean Meat 2; Vegetable 2; Fat 1 1/2

Foil-Baked Fish with Vegetables

4 4-ounce fish filets
1 cup chopped broccoli
1 cup carrot sticks
1 cup celery sticks

1/3 cup orange juice
2 tablespoons malt vinegar
2 tablespoons reduced-sodium soy
  sauce

Place each filet on 12-inch square of foil. Top with broccoli, carrot sticks and celery sticks. Spoon mixture of orange juice, vinegar and soy sauce over vegetables. Fold up foil, sealing top and sides. Place on baking sheet. Bake at 450 degrees for 30 minutes or until fish flakes easily. Serve with rice. Yield: 4 servings.

Approx Per Serving: Cal 145; Prot 23 g; Carbo 9 g; Fiber 2 g;
    T Fat 2 g; 10% Calories from Fat; Chol 62 mg; Sod 326 mg.

Dietary Exchanges: Lean Meat 2; Vegetable 1

Avoid insect bites by applying a good insect repellant but when the bugs break through your defenses be prepared to get some relief. Use a paste of meat tenderizer and water to break down toxins and soothe the itch. Ice, if available, baking soda paste or poultices or calamine or antihistamine lotion and creams will help, too.

Seviche

2 pounds firm white fish filets
Salt
1 cup finely chopped onion
2 hot peppers, finely chopped

1 clove of garlic, minced
1 cup lime juice
1/4 cup vinegar
1 teaspoon sugar

Cut fish into 3/8-inch pieces. Place fish in crock; sprinkle generously with salt. Cover with ice cubes. Chill in refrigerator overnight. Rinse thoroughly; drain. Place layer of fish 2 inches deep in bowl. Cover with 1/2 of the onion and all the peppers; sprinkle with garlic. Layer remaining fish and onion over top. Combine lime juice, vinegar and sugar in small bowl; mix well. Pour over layers. Let stand for 2 1/2 hours, stirring every 30 minutes. Chill until serving time. Yield: 4 servings.

Approx Per Serving: Cal 360; Prot 46 g; Carbo 13 g; Fiber 1 g;
    T Fat 14 g; 35% Calories from Fat; Chol 140 mg; Sod 121 mg.
    Nutritional information does not include salt.

Dietary Exchanges: Lean Meat 6 1/2; Fruit 1/2; Vegetable 1

Try Bill's **Special Frog Legs** by mixing about 1 cup of cornmeal with 1 teaspoon salt, 1/3 cup red pepper, 1 teaspoon black pepper and a cup of Cajun seasoning in a plastic bag. Add 6 or 8 large frog legs 1 or 2 at a time and shake bag until well coated. Deep-fry frog legs until golden and crisp (not hard). Drain well, place on serving plate and pour on a generous amount of picante sauce and serve with French fries and onion rings. Not for the faint at heart.

Fried Frog Legs

12 frog legs
Salt and pepper to taste
2 eggs

1/4 cup milk
1 cup flour
Oil for frying

Rinse frog legs and pat dry; cut larger tendons. Sprinkle with salt and pepper. Beat eggs with milk in bowl. Dip frog legs into egg mixture; coat with flour. Repeat process. Fry in heated oil in heavy skillet until golden brown and cooked through. Yield: 4 servings.

Approx Per Serving: Cal 319; Prot 43 g; Carbo 25 g; Fiber 1 g;
    T Fat 4 g; 12% Calories from Fat; Chol 217 mg; Sod 166 mg.
    Nutritional information for this recipe does not include oil for frying.

Dietary Exchanges: Bread 1 1/2; Lean Meat 3 1/2; Fat 1/2

To Fill the Bill

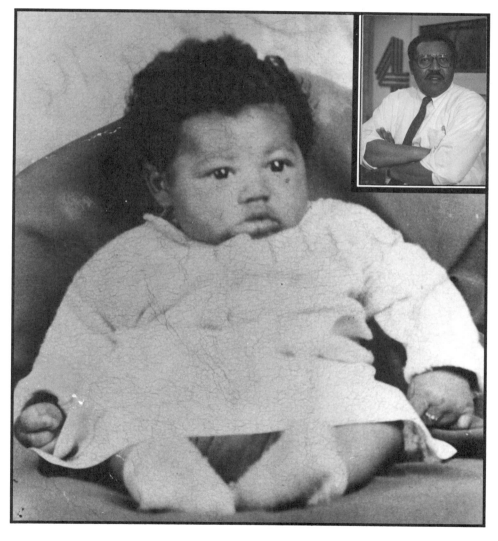

I was born to eat. I just got a late start cooking what I like.

Ambrosia Fruit Dip

1 cup fruit-flavored yogurt
1/2 cup cream of coconut

1/4 cup chopped toasted pecans

Combine yogurt and cream of coconut in small bowl; mix well. Stir in pecans. Chill in refrigerator. Serve with assorted favorite bite-sized fresh fruit for dipping. May also serve for dessert as dip or sauce over fruit in sherbet dishes. Yield: 16 (2-tablespoon) servings.

Approx Per Serving: Cal 21; Prot <1 g; Carbo 2 g; Fiber <1 g;
    T Fat 2 g; 63% Calories from Fat; Chol 0 mg; Sod 5 mg.

Dietary Exchanges: Fat 1/2

Cottage Cheese Dip

2 tablespoons milk
12 ounces small curd cottage cheese
1/4 cup mayonnaise-type salad dressing

Cayenne pepper to taste
1/4 teaspoon garlic powder
1 teaspoon onion salt

Combine milk, cottage cheese, salad dressing, cayenne pepper, garlic powder and onion salt in bowl; mix well. Chill until serving time. Serve with assorted bite-sized fresh vegetables for dipping. May process dip in blender if smooth dip is desired. Yield: 16 (2-tablespoon) servings.

Approx Per Serving: Cal 19; Prot 1 g; Carbo 1 g; Fiber 0 g;
    T Fat 1 g; 54% Calories from Fat; Chol 2 mg; Sod 106 mg.

Dietary Exchanges: Free

Dip with a Kick

1/2 cup catsup
1/2 cup nonfat plain yogurt
1/2 cup low-fat mayonnaise
2 tablespoons sweet pickle relish

1 tablespoon lemon juice
1 teaspoon Worcestershire sauce
1 teaspoon prepared horseradish

Combine catsup, yogurt, mayonnaise, pickle relish, lemon juice, Worcestershire sauce and horseradish in bowl; mix well. Chill until serving time. Serve with assorted bite-sized fresh vegetables for dipping. May substitute additional 1/2 cup low-fat yogurt for mayonnaise. Yield: 12 (2-tablespoon) servings.

Approx Per Serving: Cal 22; Prot <1 g; Carbo 3 g; Fiber <1 g;
    T Fat 1 g; 40% Calories from Fat; Chol 1 mg; Sod 102 mg.

Dietary Exchanges: Free

Fruit Salsa

1 large green bell pepper, chopped
1 large yellow bell pepper, chopped
1 large red bell pepper, chopped
1 medium jalapeño pepper, chopped

1 large papaya or mango, cubed
1 pineapple, cored, cubed
1/2 cup finely chopped cilantro
1 medium purple onion, chopped

Mix bell peppers, jalapeño pepper, papaya, pineapple, cilantro and onion thoroughly in large bowl. Serve with corn chips or over grilled fish or chicken breasts. May add more jalapeño pepper to make salsa hotter. Yield: 32 (1/4-cup) servings.

Approx Per Serving: Cal 15; Prot <1 g; Carbo 4 g; Fiber 1 g;
T Fat <1 g; 6% Calories from Fat; Chol 0 mg; Sod 1 mg.

Dietary Exchanges: Free

When trying to reduce fat content in your diet, a mixture of equal parts of nonfat yogurt and ricotta cheese blended in a food processor makes a good base for dips. For thicker dips or cheese balls, drain the yogurt in a strainer lined with cheesecloth or a coffee filter for several hours. The resulting yogurt cheese can be substituted for cream cheese in most recipes.

Garden Vegetable Dip

1 cup nonfat plain yogurt
2 tablespoons reduced-calorie
   mayonnaise
3 tablespoons finely shredded carrot
1 tablespoon minced onion

1 clove of garlic, minced
1 teaspoon dillweed
1/8 teaspoon salt
Pepper to taste

Combine yogurt and mayonnaise in small bowl; stir until blended. Add carrot, onion, garlic, dillweed, salt and pepper; mix well. Chill, covered, for 2 hours. Serve with assorted bite-sized fresh vegetables. Yield: 20 (1-tablespoon) servings.

Approx Per Serving: Cal 11; Prot 1 g; Carbo 1 g; Fiber <1 g;
T Fat <1 g; 26% Calories from Fat; Chol 1 mg; Sod 31 mg.

Dietary Exchanges: Free

Bill's Own Fire Franks

30 all beef franks
1 32-ounce bottle of barbecue sauce
1 4-ounce can jalapeño peppers,
    chopped
1/4 cup red pepper

1/4 cup black pepper
1 teaspoon onion powder
1 teaspoon garlic powder
1/2 cup Worcestershire sauce

Cook franks in boiling water to cover in large saucepan for several minutes; drain well. Slice franks into bite-sized pieces. Combine barbecue sauce, jalapeño peppers, red and black pepper, onion and garlic powder and Worcestershire sauce in saucepan. Mix well. Stir in sliced franks. Bring to a boil over medium heat. Serve hot. Yield: 30 servings.

Approx Per Serving: Cal 207; Prot 7 g; Carbo 6 g; Fiber <1 g;
     T Fat 17 g; 74% Calories from Fat; Chol 35 mg; Sod 931 mg.

Dietary Exchanges: Lean Meat 1; Vegetable 1/2; Fat 3

Bill Hall, Nashville, Tennessee

Fruit Compote

1 cup chopped unpeeled apple
1 1/2 cups orange juice
2/3 cup kumquat halves
2/3 cup cubed papaya

2/3 cup cubed cantaloupe
2/3 cup sliced kiwifruit
2/3 cup green grapes
2/3 cup strawberries

Combine apple and orange juice in small bowl; set aside. Combine kumquats, papaya, cantaloupe, kiwifruit, grapes and strawberries in large bowl. Add apple and orange juice mixture; mix gently. Chill, covered, in refrigerator. Serve in sherbet glasses as appetizer or light dessert. Yield: 10 servings.

Approx Per Serving: Cal 55; Prot 1 g; Carbo 14 g; Fiber 2 g;
     T Fat <1 g; 5% Calories from Fat; Chol 0 mg; Sod 3 mg.

Dietary Exchanges: Fruit 1

Help your family select nutritious snacks: keep cut-up fresh vegetables in the refrigerator with a supply of yogurt or bean dip; make frozen juice pops in an ice cube tray or freeze grapes, pineapple, banana chunks or other fresh fruit; stock up on snacks high in carbohydrates and low in fat, such as bagels, pretzels and English muffins.

Spinach-Stuffed Mushrooms

1 12-ounce package frozen spinach
   soufflé, thawed
1/3 cup herb-seasoned bread crumbs
1/3 cup grated Parmesan cheese

1/2 teaspoon lemon juice
Hot pepper sauce to taste
20 large fresh mushrooms
2 tablespoons melted butter

Combine spinach soufflé, bread crumbs, Parmesan cheese, lemon juice and hot pepper sauce in large bowl; mix well. Rinse mushrooms; remove stems. Dip mushroom caps in melted butter. Arrange stem side up in 9x13-inch baking dish. Spoon 1 heaping tablespoon of spinach mixture onto each mushroom; drizzle with remaining melted butter. Bake at 400 degrees for 15 to 20 minutes or until filling is puffed. Arrange on serving dish; serve hot. Yield: 20 servings.

Approx Per Serving: Cal 56; Prot 3 g; Carbo 2 g; Fiber 1 g;
    T Fat 4 g; 64% Calories from Fat; Chol 28 mg; Sod 183 mg.

Dietary Exchanges: Lean Meat 1/2; Vegetable 1/2; Fat 1/2

Watching your diet does not mean skipping fun foods or just watching other people eat. Wrap thin slices of smoked salmon around cucumber slices, or thin slices of prosciutto around melon slices, for easy and elegant appetizers.

New Potato Appetizers

1/2 cup sour cream
2 tablespoons chopped chives

24 small new potatoes
4 slices bacon, crisp-fried, crumbled

Mix sour cream and chives together in small bowl; set aside. Cook potatoes in boiling water in saucepan until tender; drain. Let stand until cool enough to handle easily. Cut into halves; scoop out centers with teaspoon or melon baller. Fill with sour cream mixture; sprinkle with bacon. Chill in refrigerator until serving time. May add 1/3 teaspoon garlic powder to sour cream mixture. Yield: 24 servings.

Approx Per Serving: Cal 61; Prot 1 g; Carbo 11 g; Fiber 1 g;
    T Fat 2 g; 23% Calories from Fat; Chol 3 mg; Sod 23 mg.

Dietary Exchanges: Bread 1/2; Fat 1/2

Snow Pea Canoes

8 ounces Chinese pea pods
3 cups water
Dash of salt
5 ounces cream cheese, softened
6 tablespoons yogurt

1/8 teaspoon pepper
1 teaspoon prepared horseradish
1/2 teaspoon prepared mustard
2 4-ounce packages thinly sliced
   spiced beef, finely chopped

Trim ends from pea pods. Bring water and salt to a boil in medium saucepan. Add pea pods. Simmer over medium heat for 1 minute or until tender-crisp; drain. Immerse in cold water; drain. Chill for 30 minutes or longer. Beat cream cheese with yogurt in small bowl. Add pepper, horseradish, mustard and beef; mix well. Slit 1 side of pea pods; fill with cream cheese mixture. Place cheese side up in serving dish. Chill for 1 hour before serving. Yield: 30 servings.

Approx Per Serving: Cal 34; Prot 3 g; Carbo 1 g; Fiber <1 g;
    T Fat 2 g; 55% Calories from Fat; Chol 9 mg; Sod 279 mg.

Dietary Exchanges: Lean Meat 1/2; Fat 1/2

Stuffed Cherry Tomatoes

24 cherry tomatoes
8 ounces cream cheese, softened
1 2-ounce jar stuffed green olives,
   drained, chopped

1 teaspoon Worcestershire sauce
1/4 teaspoon white pepper
1/4 cup finely chopped parsley

Slice tops from tomatoes. Remove pulp with small melon baller; invert on paper towels. Combine cream cheese, olives, Worcestershire sauce and pepper in bowl. Fill tomatoes with cream cheese mixture; roll tops in chopped parsley to coat. Place on serving dish. Chill, tightly covered with plastic wrap, until serving time. May store, tightly wrapped in plastic wrap, for up to 2 days. Yield: 24 appetizers.

Approx Per Appetizer: Cal 39; Prot 1 g; Carbo 1 g; Fiber <1 g;
    T Fat 4 g; 80% Calories from Fat; Chol 10 mg; Sod 81 mg.

Dietary Exchanges: Fat 1/2

Add fresh cucumber and carrot strips, green beans and cauliflower to liquid left in pickle jar. Refrigerate for several days for easy cocktail snacks. Serve the vegetables heaped high in a pretty dish or skewered on toothpicks stuck in half a cabbage head.

Zucchini Appetizers

4 eggs, slightly beaten
1/2 cup oil
3 cups shredded zucchini
1 cup baking mix
1/2 cup finely chopped onion
1/2 cup grated Parmesan cheese

2 tablespoons parsley
1 teaspoon salt
1/2 teaspoon oregano
1 clove of garlic, minced
1/8 teaspoon pepper

Combine eggs and oil in bowl; mix well. Add zucchini, baking mix, onion, Parmesan cheese, parsley, salt, oregano, garlic and pepper; mix well. Pour into greased 9x13-inch baking pan. Bake at 350 degrees for 30 minutes. Cut into 1x2-inch rectangles. Yield: 48 servings.

Approx Per Serving: Cal 45; Prot 1 g; Carbo 2 g; Fiber <1 g;
    T Fat 3 g; 67% Calories from Fat; Chol 19 mg; Sod 103 mg.

Dietary Exchanges: Fat 1/2

Imitation Champagne Punch

1 2-liter bottle of sugar-free
   lemon-lime soda, chilled

1 12-ounce can frozen apple juice
   concentrate, thawed

Mix soda with thawed apple juice concentrate in large punch bowl just before serving. Float ice ring in punch. Garnish with strawberries and thin slices of orange, lemon or lime. Yield: 10 servings.

Approx Per Serving: Cal 56; Prot <1 g; Carbo 14 g; Fiber <1 g;
    T Fat <1 g; 2% Calories from Fat; Chol 0 mg; Sod 48 mg.

Dietary Exchanges: Fruit 1

Cranberry-Pineapple Punch

1 quart cranberry juice cocktail
1 quart pineapple juice
1 1/2 cups sugar

1 tablespoon almond extract
2 quarts ginger ale

Combine cranberry juice cocktail, pineapple juice, sugar and almond extract in large pitcher; stir until sugar is dissolved. Store in airtight container in refrigerator until serving time. Pour cranberry mixture into punch bowl. Add ginger ale. Make ice ring with additional ginger ale to float in the punch bowl. Yield: 25 servings.

Approx Per Serving: Cal 118; Prot <1 g; Carbo 30 g; Fiber <1 g;
    T Fat <1 g; 1% Calories from Fat; Chol 0 mg; Sod 7 mg.

Dietary Exchanges: Fruit 2

Fruit Cider

2 6-ounce cans frozen grapefruit
    juice concentrate
3 cups water
2 6-ounce cans frozen lemonade
    concentrate
3 cups water
1 6-ounce can frozen orange juice
    concentrate

6 cans water
2 quarts apple cider, chilled
4 cups water
2 10-ounce packages frozen
    strawberries, thawed, drained
2 quarts ginger ale, chilled

Mix grapefruit juice concentrate with 3 cups water. Pour into ice cube tray. Freeze until firm. Mix lemonade concentrate with 3 cups water. Pour into ice cube tray. Freeze until firm. Chill punch bowl. Mix orange juice concentrate and 6 cans water in punch bowl. Add cider, 4 cups water and strawberries. Add grapefruit juice and lemonade ice cubes to punch 30 minutes before serving. Add ginger ale 10 minutes before serving. Yield: 56 servings.

Approx Per Serving: Cal 57; Prot <1 g; Carbo 14 g; Fiber <1 g;
    T Fat <1 g; 1% Calories from Fat; Chol 0 mg; Sod 4 mg.

Dietary Exchanges: Fruit 1

Use low-calorie diet versions of ginger ale and other sodas in punches. The resulting drinks are both lighter and more refreshing. Chill all ingredients before mixing to avoid excessive dilution as ice melts.

Mint Julep

Juice of 24 lemons
4 cups sugar
2 cups water

4 double-handfuls of fresh mint
    leaves, crushed
2 quarts ginger ale, chilled

Combine lemon juice, sugar, water and crushed mint leaves in large saucepan. Add 8 of the lemon rind halves. Bring to a boil, stirring until sugar dissolves; remove from heat. Bring to a boil once or twice more; remove from heat. Let stand, covered, until cool. Add ginger ale just before serving. Serve in tall glasses over crushed ice. Garnish each glass with a sprig of fresh mint and a cherry. Yield: 10 servings.

Approx Per Serving: Cal 403; Prot <1 g; Carbo 106 g; Fiber <1 g;
    T Fat <1 g; <1% Calories from Fat; Chol 0 mg; Sod 16 mg.

Dietary Exchanges: Fruit 6½

Elizabeth James, Springfield , Tennessee

Fresh Mint Tea

4 tablespoons loose tea
2 to 3 cups sugar
1 large handful (or more) fresh mint
   leaves

4 cups boiling water
1¼ cups lemon juice
6 tablespoons frozen orange juice
   concentrate

Steep tea, sugar and mint leaves in boiling water for 15 to 30 minutes. Strain into 1 gallon container. Add lemon juice and orange juice concentrate and enough water to measure 1 gallon. Serve over crushed ice. May use tea from 9 ripped-open tea bags if you do not use loose tea. Yield: 16 servings.

Approx Per Serving: Cal 161; Prot <1 g; Carbo 42 g; Fiber <1 g;
    T Fat <1 g; <1% Calories from Fat; Chol 0 mg; Sod 3 mg.

Dietary Exchanges: Fruit 2½

Erma Forkum, Madison, Tennessee

Strawberry Tea

4 tea bags
2 cups boiling water
6 cinnamon sticks
1 teaspoon ground cloves
1 6-ounce can frozen orange juice
   concentrate

1 6-ounce can frozen lemonade
   concentrate
1 46-ounce can pineapple juice
1 3-ounce package strawberry gelatin
2 cups water

Steep tea bags in boiling water in large saucepan for several minutes. Add cinnamon sticks, cloves, orange juice concentrate, lemonade concentrate, pineapple juice, gelatin and 2 cups water. Bring to a boil, stirring until gelatin dissolves. Keep hot, covered, over low heat or serve from slow cooker. Yield: 20 servings.

Approx Per Serving: Cal 82; Prot 1 g; Carbo 20 g; Fiber <1 g;
    T Fat <1 g; 1% Calories from Fat; Chol 0 mg; Sod 13 mg.

Dietary Exchanges: Fruit 1

Bettye Griffin, Centerville, Tennessee

Instead of a large ice ring, use muffin cups to freeze large ice cubes for a punch bowl. Add fresh fruit for a festive touch. The ice will be clearer if made with boiled and cooled water.

Strawberry Yogurt Shake

1/2 cup pineapple juice
11/2 cups frozen unsweetened
strawberries, thawed

3/4 cup plain low-fat yogurt
1 teaspoon sugar

Combine pineapple juice, strawberries, yogurt and sugar in blender container, adding in order listed and blending until smooth. Serve in chilled glasses. Yield: 2 servings.

Approx Per Serving: Cal 140; Prot 5 g; Carbo 27 g; Fiber 3 g;
    T Fat 2 g; 10% Calories from Fat; Chol 6 mg; Sod 67 mg.

Dietary Exchanges: Fruit 11/2; Milk 1/2

When tomatoes are plentiful in your garden, purée them in the food processor, strain and add lemon juice or seasonings such as basil, oregano, pepper sauce or cumin for a refreshing drink.

Zippy Vegetable Cocktail

1   46-ounce can mixed vegetable juice
    cocktail
Juice of 1 large lemon
Juice of 1/2 medium grapefruit
2 tablespoons Worcestershire sauce
11/2 teaspoons Tabasco sauce
11/2 teaspoons coarsely ground pepper

1 teaspoon celery salt
1 teaspoon instant beef bouillon
1 ounce warm water
Onion salt to taste
21/2 limes
5 teaspoons horseradish
10 stalks celery

Combine vegetable juice, lemon juice, grapefruit juice, Worcestershire sauce, Tabasco sauce, pepper and celery salt in 2-quart pitcher. Dissolve beef bouillon in warm water in bowl. Add to pitcher. Sprinkle with onion salt; stir to mix well. Cut limes into quarters. Squeeze juice of 1 quarter lime over ice in each of 10 glasses. Add 1/2 teaspoon horseradish to each glass. Fill with vegetable juice mixture. Stir and serve with celery stalks. Yield: 10 servings.

Approx Per Serving: Cal 45; Prot 1 g; Carbo 11 g; Fiber 2 g;
    T Fat <1 g; 4% Calories from Fat; Chol <1 mg; Sod 788 mg.

Dietary Exchanges: Vegetable 11/2

Pot Roast

1 3-pound beef roast, trimmed
Juice of 1 lemon
2 medium onions, thinly sliced
6 small carrots
2 medium potatoes, cut into quarters
1 clove of garlic, minced

1 teaspoon dry mustard
1 teaspoon ginger
1 teaspoon thyme
4 stalks celery, chopped
1 small green bell pepper, chopped
2 cups vegetable juice cocktail

Place roast in shallow dish. Squeeze lemon juice over roast; pierce with fork. Marinate, covered, in refrigerator overnight. Place roast in roasting pan. Arrange onions, carrots and potatoes around roast. Sprinkle with garlic, dry mustard, ginger and thyme. Top with celery and green pepper. Pour vegetable juice around roast. Roast, covered, for 3 hours or until very tender. Yield: 6 servings.

Approx Per Serving: Cal 394; Prot 45 g; Carbo 23 g; Fiber 4 g;
    T Fat 13 g; 30% Calories from Fat; Chol 128 mg; Sod 408 mg.

Dietary Exchanges: Bread 1/2; Lean Meat 41/2; Vegetable 2

Roast Beef California-Style

1 cup orange juice
1 cup tomato juice
1/4 cup oil
1 clove of garlic, crushed

1/2 teaspoon allspice
1/2 teaspoon chili powder
Salt to taste
1 3-pound rolled rump roast

Combine orange juice, tomato juice, oil, garlic, allspice, chili powder and salt in bowl; mix well. Add roast, coating well. Marinate, covered, in refrigerator overnight. Drain roast, reserving marinade. Place roast in roasting pan. Roast at 325 degrees for 11/4 hours or for 25 minutes per pound, basting with reserved marinade. Cool slightly; cut into thin slices. Yield: 6 servings.

Approx Per Serving: Cal 401; Prot 43 g; Carbo 6 g; Fiber <1 g;
    T Fat 22 g; 50% Calories from Fat; Chol 128 mg; Sod 216 mg.
    Nutritional information for this recipe includes entire amount of marinade.

Dietary Exchanges: Lean Meat 41/2; Fruit 1/2; Vegetable 1/2; Fat 2

Carving a roast is easier if it is allowed to "rest" for 15 to 20 minutes after removing it from the oven.

Sunday Roast

1 4-pound boneless beef chuck roast   1 envelope dry onion soup mix
2 cups brewed coffee

Place beef roast and coffee in slow cooker. Add enough water to cover. Add soup mix. Cook on Low for 6 to 8 hours or until tender. Yield: 12 servings.

Approx Per Serving: Cal 226; Prot 28 g; Carbo <1 g; Fiber <1 g;
      T Fat 12 g; 48% Calories from Fat; Chol 95 mg; Sod 117 mg.

Dietary Exchanges: Lean Meat 4

Baked Lemon Steak

3 pounds chuck or round steak   1 cup catsup
2 tablespoons margarine, softened   1 tablespoon reduced-sodium soy
Salt and pepper to taste   sauce
2 onions, sliced   1/4 cup water
1 large lemon, sliced

Place steak in large baking dish. Spread with margarine; sprinkle with salt and pepper. Top with onion and lemon slices. Combine catsup, soy sauce and water in bowl; mix well. Pour over steak. Bake, covered, at 325 degrees for 2 hours. Yield: 8 servings.

Approx Per Serving: Cal 292; Prot 33 g; Carbo 12 g; Fiber 1 g;
      T Fat 13 g; 39% Calories from Fat; Chol 96 mg; Sod 498 mg.

Dietary Exchanges: Lean Meat 3 1/2; Fruit 1/2; Vegetable 1/2

Oven-Barbecued Swiss Steak

1/3 cup flour   1 tablespoon vinegar
Salt and pepper to taste   2 8-ounce cans seasoned tomato sauce
1 2-pound round or chuck steak   Pepper sauce to taste
1 tablespoon Worcestershire sauce   1 medium onion, sliced

Mix flour, salt and pepper in bowl. Sprinkle over steak, coating well. Brown slowly on both sides in lightly greased Dutch oven; drain. Combine Worcestershire sauce, vinegar, tomato sauce and pepper sauce in bowl; mix well. Pour over steak. Add onion. Bake, covered, at 350 degrees for 1 to 1 1/4 hours or until tender. Yield: 6 servings.

Approx Per Serving: Cal 253; Prot 30 g; Carbo 13 g; Fiber 2 g;
      T Fat 9 g; 31% Calories from Fat; Chol 86 mg; Sod 531 mg.

Dietary Exchanges: Bread 1/2; Lean Meat 3; Vegetable 1

Oven-Barbecued Baby Beef Ribs

2 pounds baby beef ribs
4 green onions, chopped
2 tablespoons margarine
1 tablespoon flour
1 tablespoon Dijon mustard

1 cup beef broth
2 tablespoons lemon juice
3 tablespoons chili sauce
Freshly ground pepper to taste

Wipe ribs with damp paper towel; arrange in single layer in shallow baking pan. Bake at 450 degrees for 20 minutes; drain. Sauté green onions in margarine in skillet. Stir in flour and mustard. Cook for 1 to 2 minutes, stirring constantly. Add beef broth, lemon juice, chili sauce and pepper. Cook for 5 to 7 minutes or until thickened, stirring constantly. Brush over ribs. Bake for 30 minutes longer or until tender, basting occasionally with sauce. Yield: 4 servings.

Approx Per Serving: Cal 409; Prot 21 g; Carbo 7 g; Fiber 1 g;
     T Fat 33 g; 73% Calories from Fat; Chol 73 mg; Sod 539 mg.

Dietary Exchanges: Lean Meat 3; Fat 3$^1/2$

Pepper Steak

1 pound sirloin or round steak, cut
     into cubes
2 tablespoons shortening
$^1/4$ cup soy sauce
1$^1/2$ cups water

1 clove of garlic, chopped
2 medium onions, cut into strips
2 green bell peppers, cut into strips
2 tablespoons cornstarch

Brown steak on all sides in shortening in skillet. Add soy sauce and water. Simmer for 10 minutes. Add garlic, onions and green peppers. Cook until beef and vegetables are tender. Stir in mixture of cornstarch and a small amount of water. Cook until thickened, stirring constantly. Serve over rice. Yield: 3 servings.

Approx Per Serving: Cal 348; Prot 31 g; Carbo 17 g; Fiber 2 g;
     T Fat 17 g; 45% Calories from Fat; Chol 86 mg; Sod 1419 mg.

Dietary Exchanges: Bread $^1/2$; Lean Meat 3; Vegetable 1$^1/2$; Fat 1$^1/2$

Mary H. Horner, Centerville, Tennessee

If a roast is too large for one meal, don't slice all of it. A solid piece of meat will not dry out in the refrigerator as quickly as sliced meat. The chilled roast can also be sliced very thinly for sandwiches or other uses for saving calories, fat and cholesterol without losing flavor.

Beef Teriyaki

1¹/2 pounds flank steak
¹/2 cup reduced-sodium soy sauce
1 cup beef bouillon
¹/2 cup finely chopped onion

2 tablespoons lemon juice
2 tablespoons honey
¹/2 teaspoon garlic powder
Seasoned salt to taste

Cut beef into 1¹/2-inch pieces. Combine soy sauce, bouillon, onion, lemon juice, honey, garlic powder and seasoned salt in small bowl; mix well. Add beef. Marinate in refrigerator for 24 hours; drain. Thread beef onto skewers. Grill over hot coals for 6 to 8 minutes or until done to taste, turning to brown all sides. Yield: 2 servings.

Approx Per Serving: Cal 529; Prot 56 g; Carbo 28 g; Fiber 1 g;
T Fat 21 g; 35% Calories from Fat; Chol 135 mg; Sod 2120 mg.
Nutritional information includes entire amount of marinade.

Dietary Exchanges: Lean Meat 7¹/2; Fruit 1; Vegetable ¹/2

Stews and stir-fried dishes that use small amounts of meat combined with lots of tasty vegetables are an easy healthy alternative eating style.

Upside-Down Cauliflower and Beef with Rice

1 pound stew beef
2 to 3 cups water
1 head cauliflower, chopped
4 large carrots, chopped
1 large onion, chopped

¹/4 cup olive oil
2 cups uncooked rice
1 teaspoon allspice
Nutmeg, salt and pepper to taste

Cook beef in 2 to 3 cups water in saucepan for 30 to 45 minutes or until tender. Drain, reserving liquid. Sauté cauliflower, carrots and onion separately in 1¹/3 tablespoons olive oil each in skillet, removing to bowl. Layer beef and vegetables in 4-quart saucepan. Soak rice in warm water in bowl for 10 minutes; drain. Layer over vegetables. Sprinkle with allspice, nutmeg, salt and pepper. Strain 2 or more cups reserved cooking liquid over layers. Simmer for 15 minutes. Let stand for several minutes. Invert onto serving platter. May add eggplant or substitute eggplant for cauliflower. Yield: 6 servings.

Approx Per Serving: Cal 453; Prot 20 g; Carbo 59 g; Fiber 4 g;
T Fat 15 g; 29% Calories from Fat; Chol 45 mg; Sod 173 mg.

Dietary Exchanges: Bread 2; Lean Meat 2; Vegetable 1¹/2; Fat 2

Vegetable and Beef Soup

1 zucchini, cut into 1/2-inch pieces
1/4 cup oil
1 1/2 pounds stew beef
1 onion, chopped
3 stalks celery, chopped
2 carrots, sliced
1/2 head cabbage, shredded
5 potatoes, chopped

1 potato, shredded
1 28-ounce can tomatoes, chopped
1 16-ounce can green beans
1 8-ounce can lima beans
6 cups water
1/2 teaspoon basil
4 teaspoons salt

Sauté zucchini in oil in skillet until light brown; remove with slotted spoon. Add beef to skillet. Cook over high heat until brown. Combine beef, zucchini, onion, celery, carrots, cabbage, potatoes, tomatoes, green beans, lima beans, water, basil and salt in large saucepan. Simmer for 1 hour or until done to taste. May add any leftover vegetables desired or leave potatoes unpeeled. Yield: 8 servings.

Approx Per Serving: Cal 350; Prot 22 g; Carbo 38 g; Fiber 7 g;
    T Fat 13 g; 33% Calories from Fat; Chol 51 mg; Sod 1717 mg.

Dietary Exchanges: Bread 1 1/2; Lean Meat 2; Vegetable 2 1/2; Fat 1 1/2

Barbara Landis, Shelbyville, Tennessee

Texas-Style Chili

1 pound pork shoulder, cut into
    3/8-inch pieces
1/2 teaspoon ground cumin
1 pound beef flank steak, finely
    chopped
1/2 teaspoon ground cumin
6 stalks celery, chopped
1 medium white onion, chopped
1 tomato, chopped
1 8-ounce can green chili salsa

1 clove of garlic, minced
1 8-ounce can green chili peppers,
    seeded, chopped
1 teaspoon each oregano and hot red
    pepper sauce
1 tablespoon each hot chili powder,
    medium chili powder and mild chili
    powder
2 tablespoons water
Salt to taste

Brown pork in nonstick skillet, stirring constantly. Combine pork with 1/2 teaspoon cumin in bowl; drain skillet, reserving 2 tablespoons drippings. Brown beef in nonstick skillet, stirring frequently; drain, reserving 2 tablespoons beef drippings. Add 1/2 teaspoon cumin; mix well. Remove from heat. Combine celery, onion, tomato, salsa, garlic, chili peppers, oregano and pepper sauce in 6-quart saucepan. Add mixture of chili powders and water; mix well. Simmer, covered, for 20 minutes, stirring occasionally. Add pork, beef and reserved drippings to saucepan. Simmer for 1 to 1 1/2 hours or until meat is tender, stirring frequently. Add salt; mix well. Yield: 8 servings.

Approx Per Serving: Cal 196; Prot 22 g; Carbo 8 g; Fiber 2 g;
    T Fat 9 g; 40% Calories from Fat; Chol 63 mg; Sod 568 mg.

Dietary Exchanges: Lean Meat 3; Vegetable 1 1/2

Why Did I Do It Chili

1 large red onion, chopped
1 tablespoon oil
4 pounds ground beef
4   16-ounce cans chili beans
1   4-ounce can chopped jalapeño peppers

2   16-ounce cans whole tomatoes
1/2 cup (about) chili powder
1/2 cup red pepper
1/2 cup black pepper
Salt to taste

Sauté onion in oil in saucepan. Add ground beef. Cook until ground beef is brown and crumbly, stirring frequently; drain. Add remaining ingredients; mix well. Simmer for 1 hour; taste frequently. Yield: 12 servings.

Approx Per Serving: Cal 569; Prot 45 g; Carbo 30 g; Fiber 11 g;
    T Fat 32 g; 49% Calories from Fat; Chol 138 mg; Sod 1185 mg.

Dietary Exchanges: Bread 1; Lean Meat 5½; Vegetable 1½; Fat 3

Bill Hall, Nashville, Tennessee

Beef Patties Superb

2 pounds ground beef
2 teaspoons prepared horseradish

3/4 teaspoon chili powder
Salt and pepper to taste

Combine ground beef, horseradish, chili powder, salt and pepper in bowl; mix well. Shape into 8 patties. Place on rack in broiler pan. Broil until done to taste. May shape into meatballs if preferred. Yield: 8 servings.

Approx Per Serving: Cal 250; Prot 25 g; Carbo <1 g; Fiber <1 g;
    T Fat 16 g; 58% Calories from Fat; Chol 84 mg; Sod 64 mg.

Dietary Exchanges: Lean Meat 3½; Fat 1½

Meat Loaf

1 egg
3/4 cup milk
1/2 cup fine dry bread crumbs
1/4 cup finely chopped onion

1½ pounds ground beef
1/4 cup catsup
1/2 cup tomato sauce

Beat egg and milk in bowl. Stir in bread crumbs and onion. Add ground beef; mix well with hands like Mama does. Place in 4x8-inch baking pan. Bake at 350 degrees for 1¼ hours; drain well. Spread mixture of catsup and tomato sauce over top. Bake for 10 minutes longer. Yield: 6 servings.

Approx Per Serving: Cal 332; Prot 29 g; Carbo 12 g; Fiber 1 g;
    T Fat 18 g; 50% Calories from Fat; Chol 124 mg; Sod 402 mg.

Dietary Exchanges: Bread ½; Lean Meat 3½; Vegetable ½; Fat 1½

Tina Hall, Nashville, Tennessee

Jimmy's Birthday Meat Loaves

1 cup bread crumbs
2 cups milk
1 cup grated Parmesan cheese
4 eggs
2 tablespoons Worcestershire sauce

1 onion, chopped
3 tablespoons Italian seasoning
Salt, pepper and garlic salt to taste
4 pounds ground beef

Combine bread crumbs, milk, Parmesan cheese, eggs, Worcestershire sauce, onion and seasonings in bowl; mix well. Add ground beef; mix well. Shape into 2 loaves; place in baking pan. Top with catsup and parsley if desired. Bake at 350 degrees for 1 hour. May substitute skim milk and/or egg substitute for milk and eggs. Yield: 12 servings.

Approx Per Serving: Cal 457; Prot 42 g; Carbo 10 g; Fiber <1 g;
 T Fat 27 g; 54% Calories from Fat; Chol 195 mg; Sod 376 mg.

Dietary Exchanges: Bread 1/2; Lean Meat 51/2; Fat 21/2

Demetria Kalodimos, Nashville, Tennessee

Stuffed Zucchini

4 8-inch zucchini
8 ounces ground beef
8 ounces Italian sausage
1/2 cup ricotta cheese
1/2 cup shredded mozzarella cheese
1/4 cup grated Parmesan cheese

1 medium clove of garlic, minced
3/4 cup bread crumbs
1/4 cup chopped onion
1 egg
1 tablespoon basil
1 16-ounce jar spaghetti sauce

Cut zucchini into halves lengthwise. Scoop out pulp, leaving shells; reserve 1 cup pulp. Combine reserved pulp with ground beef, Italian sausage, ricotta cheese, mozzarella cheese, Parmesan cheese, garlic, bread crumbs, onion, egg and basil in bowl; mix well. Spoon into zucchini shells; place in large baking dish. Bake at 375 degrees for 30 minutes. Heat spaghetti sauce in saucepan until bubbly. Spoon over zucchini. Serve immediately. Yield: 8 servings.

Approx Per Serving: Cal 288; Prot 17 g; Carbo 20 g; Fiber 2 g;
 T Fat 16 g; 49% Calories from Fat; Chol 74 mg; Sod 608 mg.

Dietary Exchanges: Bread 1/2; Lean Meat 2; Vegetable 11/2; Fat 2

Enjoy the sweet and nutty flavor of wheat germ and get a nutritious bonus by substituting it for half the bread crumbs in meat loaf or meatballs. Grated potato and carrot are nutritious fillers for meat loaf.

Barbecued Pork Shoulder

1 4-pound pork shoulder roast
Salt to taste
1 cup catsup
1/2 cup packed brown sugar
6 tablespoons vinegar
2 tablespoons lemon juice

1/4 cup Worcestershire sauce
2 teaspoons prepared mustard
1 to 2 tablespoons chili powder
1 teaspoon salt
1 teaspoon pepper

Combine pork with water to cover and salt to taste in heavy saucepan. Simmer, covered, for 2 to 2 1/2 hours or until tender; drain. Cut into thin slices; place in shallow 2-quart baking dish. Combine catsup, brown sugar, vinegar, lemon juice, Worcestershire sauce, mustard, chili powder, 1 teaspoon salt and pepper in bowl; mix well. Spoon over pork, turning slices to coat well. Bake at 300 degrees for 45 minutes. May serve on buns. May cook roast in slow cooker if preferred. Yield: 12 servings.

Approx Per Serving: Cal 292; Prot 31 g; Carbo 15 g; Fiber 1 g;
    T Fat 12 g; 37% Calories from Fat; Chol 107 mg; Sod 597 mg.

Dietary Exchanges: Lean Meat 4; Fruit 1; Vegetable 1/2

Martha Jean Burris, Unionville, Tennessee

Glazed Pork Roast

1/2 teaspoon chili powder
1/2 teaspoon salt
1/2 teaspoon garlic salt
1 4-pound pork tenderloin, tied

2 tablespoons vinegar
1 cup apple jelly
1 cup catsup
2 teaspoons chili powder

Mix 1/2 teaspoon chili powder, salt and garlic salt together; sprinkle on roast. Place pork fat side up in roasting pan. Roast at 325 degrees for 3 1/4 to 3 3/4 hours or until tender. Combine vinegar, jelly, catsup and 2 teaspoons chili powder in saucepan. Bring to a boil; reduce heat. Simmer for 2 minutes. Spoon over roast. Roast for 15 minutes longer. Let stand for 10 minutes before slicing. Yield: 12 servings.

Approx Per Serving: Cal 242; Prot 27 g; Carbo 23 g; Fiber 1 g;
    T Fat 5 g; 17% Calories from Fat; Chol 74 mg; Sod 483 mg.

Dietary Exchanges: Lean Meat 3; Fruit 1 1/2

Mrs. Thomas Byrd, Nashville, Tennessee

Pork Chops with Apples

4 4-ounce center-cut pork chops
1 medium onion, chopped
1¼ cups water
¼ teaspoon pepper

1 teaspoon instant chicken bouillon
3 medium cooking apples
½ teaspoon cinnamon

Trim pork chops. Spray skillet with nonstick cooking spray. Brown pork chops with onion in skillet. Mix water, pepper and instant bouillon in bowl, stirring until bouillon is dissolved. Add to pork chops. Simmer, covered, for 15 to 20 minutes. Skim fat. Peel and slice apples. Add apples and cinnamon to skillet. Simmer, covered, for 15 minutes longer. Yield: 4 servings.

Approx Per Serving: Cal 230; Prot 23 g; Carbo 17 g; Fiber 2 g;
     T Fat 8 g; 30% Calories from Fat; Chol 69 mg; Sod 344 mg.

Dietary Exchanges: Lean Meat 3; Fruit 1; Vegetable ½

Baked Creole Pork Chops

4 pork chops
1 tablespoon oil
2 8-ounce cans tomato sauce
½ cup water
⅓ cup chopped celery

2 tablespoons brown sugar
Juice of ½ lemon
½ teaspoon dry mustard
½ teaspoon salt
⅛ teaspoon pepper

Brown pork chips in oil in skillet; remove to greased shallow baking dish. Combine tomato sauce, water, celery, brown sugar, lemon juice, dry mustard, salt and pepper in bowl; mix well. Pour over chops. Bake, covered, at 350 degrees for 1¼ hours or until tender. Yield: 4 servings.

Approx Per Serving: Cal 313; Prot 33 g; Carbo 13 g; Fiber 2 g;
     T Fat 14 g; 40% Calories from Fat; Chol 97 mg; Sod 1040 mg.

Dietary Exchanges: Lean Meat 4; Fruit ½; Vegetable 1½; Fat ½

Shirley Rankin, Columbia, Tennessee

Rib, blade, arm and loin end pork chops are just as delicious and nutritious as center cuts and cost less. Try to trim off excessive amounts of fat from chops before cooking and then drain or skim after cooking to reduce calories and fat. Cook pork thoroughly for safety and best flavor and tenderness.

Spanish Pork Chops

6 pork chops
1/4 cup catsup
1 teaspoon dry mustard
1 teaspoon salt

1 teaspoon pepper
1/2 cup water
1/4 cup vinegar
2 tablespoons sugar

Brown pork chops in skillet. Mix remaining ingredients in small bowl. Add to pork chops. Simmer, covered, for 45 minutes. Yield: 6 servings.

Approx Per Serving: Cal 197; Prot 23 g; Carbo 8 g; Fiber <1 g;
    T Fat 8 g; 36% Calories from Fat; Chol 71 mg; Sod 533 mg.

Dietary Exchanges: Lean Meat 3; Fruit 1/2

Fried Hash with Fried Eggs

2 large onions, coarsely chopped
3/4 cup chopped red bell pepper
3 cloves of garlic, minced
1/2 cup chopped red or green chilies
Salt and pepper to taste
6 tablespoons butter

3 cups chopped cooked lean pork
3 cups chopped cooked chicken
1/2 cup whipping cream
6 medium potatoes, cooked, peeled,
    chopped
6 eggs, fried

Sauté onions, bell pepper, garlic and chilies with salt and pepper in 4 tablespoons butter in 12-inch ovenproof skillet over low heat for 10 minutes. Combine with pork, chicken, cream, potatoes, salt and pepper in large bowl; mix well. Add to skillet with remaining 2 tablespoons butter; press down firmly. Cook over medium heat for 15 minutes. Bake at 350 degrees for 15 minutes. Invert onto serving plate. Place fried eggs on top. This is good for a picnic as it can be served hot or cold. Yield: 6 servings.

Approx Per Serving: Cal 639; Prot 43 g; Carbo 38 g; Fiber 4 g;
    T Fat 35 g; 50% Calories from Fat; Chol 368 mg; Sod 388 mg.

Dietary Exchanges: Bread 2; Lean Meat 5; Vegetable 1; Fat 4 1/2

Carrie Byrne Bartlett, Gallatin, Tennessee

Hoss Burns' Gumbo Recipe

Brown flour in oil in cast-iron skillet to make roux. Bring chicken or seafood stock to a boil in saucepan. Add enough roux to thicken slightly and color light brown. Add onion salt, garlic salt, salt and pepper, pepper and pepper. Stir in soy sauce and Tabasco sauce. Add vegetables such as onion, green pepper, green onions, celery, parsley, garlic or jalapeño peppers. Stir in meat such as sausage, chicken or other meat. Simmer over low heat for 30 minutes or until done to taste. Chill overnight. Reheat to serve.

Nutritional information for this recipe is not available.

Hoss Burns, WSIX-FM, Nashville, Tennessee

Oven-Barbecued Chicken

2 tablespoons (or more) oil
3 to 4 pounds chicken pieces
1/3 cup chopped onion
3 tablespoons margarine
3/4 cup catsup
1/3 cup vinegar

Artificial sweetener to taste
1/2 cup water
2 teaspoons prepared mustard
1 tablespoon Worcestershire sauce
1/4 teaspoon salt
1/8 teaspoon pepper

Heat oil in large skillet. Skin chicken pieces, rinse well and pat dry. Cook chicken in oil in skillet until brown; drain. Arrange chicken in 9x13-inch baking dish. Sauté onion in margarine in saucepan until tender. Add catsup, vinegar, sweetener, water, mustard, Worcestershire sauce, salt and pepper; mix well. Simmer, covered, for 15 minutes. Pour over chicken. Bake at 350 degrees for 1 hour, basting occasionally. Yield: 8 servings.

Approx Per Serving: Cal 313; Prot 33 g; Carbo 7 g; Fiber 1 g;
     T Fat 16 g; 47% Calories from Fat; Chol 100 mg; Sod 524 mg.

Dietary Exchanges: Lean Meat 4; Fruit 1/2; Vegetable 1/2; Fat 1/2

Gladys McGee, Greenbrier, Tennessee

Lime and Hot Pepper Chicken

3 tablespoons soy sauce
1 teaspoon grated lime rind
1 tablespoon lime juice

1/2 teaspoon hot pepper sauce
1/3 cup oil
1 whole chicken, cut up

Whisk soy sauce, lime rind, lime juice, hot pepper sauce and oil in bowl. Reserve 3 tablespoons for basting. Rinse chicken; pat dry. Combine with marinade in plastic bag. Marinate in refrigerator for 30 minutes or longer. Grill chicken over hot coals until done to taste, turning and basting frequently with reserved marinade. Yield: 6 servings.

Approx Per Serving: Cal 328; Prot 33 g; Carbo 1 g; Fiber <1 g;
     T Fat 21 g; 57% Calories from Fat; Chol 100 mg; Sod 614 mg.
     Nutritional information includes entire amount of marinade.

Dietary Exchanges: Lean Meat 4; Fat 2 1/2

To save time, buy chicken breast filets or bone chicken breasts ahead of time and refrigerate or freeze them. They will cook in about half the usual time. Be sure to skin chicken and remove all visible fat for maximum dietetic benefit.

Calabaza con Pollo

2¹/2 pounds chicken breasts
¹/4 cup oil
¹/2 green bell pepper, chopped
1 onion, chopped
2 to 3   1-inch serrano peppers, minced
2 cloves of garlic, crushed

2 tablespoons oil
1   16-ounce can tomatoes
¹/2 teaspoon cumin
Salt and pepper to taste
8 yellow squash, sliced

Rinse chicken and pat dry. Brown well in ¹/4 cup oil in large skillet. Add a small amount of water. Simmer for 15 minutes. Drain and bone chicken. Sauté green pepper, onion, serrano peppers and garlic in 2 tablespoons oil in skillet. Add tomatoes, cumin, salt and pepper. Cook for 5 minutes. Add chicken, squash and enough water to cook squash. Cook, covered, until squash is tender. Serve with corn or flour tortillas. May use chopped fresh tomatoes or substitute 1 can Ro-Tel tomatoes with chilies for tomatoes and serrano peppers. Yield: 8 servings.

Approx Per Serving: Cal 290; Prot 34 g; Carbo 6 g; Fiber 1 g;
    T Fat 14 g; 45% Calories from Fat; Chol 90 mg; Sod 173 mg.

Dietary Exchanges: Lean Meat 3; Vegetable 1; Fat 2

Baked or roasted chicken has fewer calories than stewed chicken. Remove skin to further reduce calories.

Chicken in the Garden

Flowerets of ¹/2 head cauliflower
1 pound broccoli spears
2 large carrots, sliced
2 tablespoons melted butter

1¹/2 cups chopped cooked chicken
1 cup cream of mushroom soup
¹/3 cup milk
¹/2 cup shredded Cheddar cheese

Steam cauliflower, broccoli spears and carrots separately in a small amount of water in saucepan until tender-crisp; drain. Toss with butter in bowl. Layer vegetables and chicken in 9x9-inch baking dish. Top with mixture of soup and milk. Sprinkle with cheese. Bake at 450 degrees for 15 minutes or until heated through. May microwave, loosely covered, on High for 6 minutes, rotating after 3 minutes. Yield: 4 servings.

Approx Per Serving: Cal 344; Prot 25 g; Carbo 18 g; Fiber 6 g;
    T Fat 20 g; 51% Calories from Fat; Chol 80 mg; Sod 767 mg.

Dietary Exchanges: Lean Meat 2¹/2; Vegetable 2¹/2; Fat 3

Chicken Tenders

1 pound chicken breast filets
1 onion, cut into quarters
1 green bell pepper, cut into squares
1 red bell pepper, cut into squares
8 ounces mushroom caps
1 clove of garlic, crushed
2 tablespoons lemon juice
1 teaspoon olive oil

1 small onion, chopped
1 tablespoon soy sauce
1/2 cup low-sodium soy sauce
1/2 teaspoon chili powder
1 teaspoon lemon juice
1/4 teaspoon crushed garlic
1/4 teaspoon finely chopped ginger

Cut chicken into 1-inch cubes. Thread onto skewers alternately with onion quarters, peppers and mushrooms. Place in shallow dish. Add mixture of next 5 ingredients. Marinate for 1 to 3 hours; drain. Mix 1/2 cup soy sauce and remaining ingredients in bowl. Grill chicken over hot coals until chicken is tender, basting frequently with sauce. Serve remaining sauce with chicken. Yield: 4 servings.

Approx Per Serving: Cal 210; Prot 29 g; Carbo 14 g; Fiber 2 g;
    T Fat 5 g; 20% Calories from Fat; Chol 72 mg; Sod 1104 mg.
    Nutritional information includes entire amount of marinade.

Dietary Exchanges: Lean Meat 2 1/2; Vegetable 1 1/2

Chicken Kabobs

1 cup vegetable oil
1/2 cup soy sauce
1/3 cup lemon juice
2 tablespoons Worcestershire sauce
2 tablespoons prepared mustard

2 cloves of garlic, minced
Pepper to taste
6 chicken breast filets
1 large red bell pepper
1 large green bell pepper

Combine oil, soy sauce, lemon juice, Worcestershire sauce, mustard, garlic and pepper in shallow dish; mix well. Rinse chicken and pat dry; cut into 1 1/2-inch pieces. Add to marinade. Marinate in refrigerator for 3 hours or longer, turning chicken occasionally. Preheat grill. Cut bell peppers into squares. Drain chicken, reserving marinade. Thread chicken and peppers onto skewers. Grill for 20 minutes, turning skewers and basting occasionally with reserved marinade. Serve over hot cooked rice or with favorite pilaf. May use vegetables of choice, parboiling vegetables for easier skewering if desired. Yield: 6 servings.

Approx Per Serving: Cal 493; Prot 28 g; Carbo 6 g; Fiber 1 g;
    T Fat 40 g; 72% Calories from Fat; Chol 72 mg; Sod 1554 mg.

Dietary Exchanges: Lean Meat 2 1/2; Vegetable 1/2; Fat 7

Lemon Chicken

4 chicken breast filets	8 ounces fresh mushrooms, sliced
1/4 cup flour	Juice of 2 lemons
3 tablespoons margarine	1/2 teaspoon oregano
2 cloves of garlic, minced	Salt and pepper to taste
1 small onion, chopped	1/2 cup chicken broth

Rinse chicken; pat dry. Coat lightly with flour; shake off excess. Heat margarine in skillet. Add chicken. Cook for 2 minutes on each side. Add garlic and onion. Cook until onion is tender, stirring occasionally. Add remaining ingredients. Cook, covered, over low heat until chicken is tender and sauce is thickened. Yield: 4 servings.

Approx Per Serving: Cal 279; Prot 30 g; Carbo 13 g; Fiber 1 g;
T Fat 12 g; 39% Calories from Fat; Chol 72 mg; Sod 264 mg.

Dietary Exchanges: Bread 1/2; Lean Meat 21/2; Vegetable 1

Dorothy Boyce, Nashville, Tennessee

Nutty Chicken Fingers

1/3 cup cornflake crumbs	1/8 teaspoon each garlic powder and salt
1/2 cup finely chopped pecans	12 ounces chicken breast filets
1 tablespoon parsley flakes	2 tablespoons skim milk

Mix first 5 ingredients in shallow dish. Rinse chicken and pat dry; cut into 1x3-inch strips. Dip strips in milk; roll in crumb mixture. Arrange in baking pan. Bake at 400 degrees for 7 to 9 minutes or until tender. Yield: 5 servings.

Approx Per Serving: Cal 185; Prot 17 g; Carbo 7 g; Fiber 1 g;
T Fat 10 g; 48% Calories from Fat; Chol 44 mg; Sod 146 mg.

Dietary Exchanges: Lean Meat 11/2; Fat 11/2

Chicken à l'Orange

4 chicken breast filets	1 6-ounce can frozen orange juice
2 tablespoons butter	concentrate, thawed
2 tablespoons oil	Tabasco sauce to taste
Salt and pepper to taste	

Rinse chicken and pat dry. Sauté in butter and oil in skillet for 1 to 3 minutes or until golden brown. Sprinkle with salt and pepper. Add orange juice concentrate and Tabasco sauce. Simmer, covered, for 30 minutes. Serve with rice. Yield: 4 servings.

Approx Per Serving: Cal 318; Prot 28 g; Carbo 16 g; Fiber <1 g;
T Fat 16 g; 45% Calories from Fat; Chol 88 mg; Sod 123 mg.

Dietary Exchanges: Lean Meat 21/2; Fruit 1; Fat 21/2

Pepper-Fettucini Chicken Toss

1 16-ounce package fettucini
6 chicken breast filets
2 large red bell peppers
2 large yellow bell peppers
1 large green bell pepper

1 medium onion, coarsely chopped
2 cups sliced mushrooms
1 teaspoon salt-free herb seasoning
1/4 cup olive oil

Cook fettucini using package directions; drain. Rinse chicken and pat dry; cut into strips. Cut peppers into strips. Sauté chicken, peppers, onion, mushrooms and herb seasoning in oil in large skillet for 8 to 10 minutes or until chicken is tender. Combine with fettucini in serving bowl; toss to mix well. Serve immediately. Yield: 12 servings.

Approx Per Serving: Cal 269; Prot 19 g; Carbo 33 g; Fiber 2 g;
     T Fat 7 g; 23% Calories from Fat; Chol 36 mg; Sod 36 mg.

Dietary Exchanges: Bread 2; Lean Meat 1; Vegetable 1; Fat 1

Chicken Piccata

2 egg whites
6 chicken breast filets
1/2 cup flour
2 tablespoons olive oil
1/2 onion, chopped
2 green onions, chopped
1/2 green bell pepper, chopped

Chopped parsley to taste
2 tablespoons olive oil
1 tablespoon flour
1/2 cup skimmed chicken broth
1/3 cup white wine
1 8-ounce can tomato sauce
Salt and pepper to taste

Beat egg whites just until foamy. Rinse chicken and pat dry. Pound with meat mallet to flatten. Coat with 1/2 cup flour; dip in egg whites. Brown on both sides in 2 tablespoons olive oil in skillet. Remove to warm platter. Sauté onion, green onions, green pepper and parsley in 2 tablespoons olive oil in separate skillet. Sprinkle with 1 tablespoon flour. Add chicken broth and wine. Stir in tomato sauce. Season with salt and pepper. Cook until thickened to desired consistency, stirring constantly. Add chicken. Cook until heated through. Serve with pasta and favorite vegetables. Yield: 6 servings.

Approx Per Serving: Cal 296; Prot 30 g; Carbo 14 g; Fiber 1 g;
     T Fat 12 g; 38% Calories from Fat; Chol 72 mg; Sod 435 mg.

Dietary Exchanges: Bread 1/2; Lean Meat 21/2; Vegetable 1/2; Fat 2

Did you know that most chicken recipes can be prepared using turkey breast slices, pork scallops or veal scallops? Chicken may be the most versatile of all the commonly used meats because it serves as a vehicle for seasonings and sauces without losing texture and flavor.

Thai Stir-Fry

1 pound chicken breast filets
3 tablespoons soy sauce
1 clove of garlic, minced
1/4 to 1/2 teaspoon crushed red pepper
   flakes
1/4 cup peanut butter
1 tablespoon oil

1 tablespoon brown sugar
1 tablespoon soy sauce
2 tablespoons oil
2 small onions, sliced
1/2 red bell pepper, cut into strips
1/2 green bell pepper, cut into strips
1/4 head cabbage, shredded

Rinse chicken and pat dry. Cut into bite-sized pieces. Combine with 3 tablespoons soy sauce, garlic and red pepper in shallow dish; mix well. Marinate for 15 minutes. Combine peanut butter, 1 tablespoon oil, brown sugar and 1 tablespoon soy sauce in bowl; mix well. Stir-fry chicken in 2 tablespoons oil in skillet for 4 minutes. Add onions and bell pepper strips. Stir-fry until vegetables are tender-crisp. Stir in cabbage and peanut sauce. Simmer, covered, for 2 minutes or until cabbage is tender. Serve over rice or egg noodles. Yield: 4 servings.

Approx Per Serving: Cal 378; Prot 33 g; Carbo 15 g; Fiber 3 g;
    T Fat 22 g; 50% Calories from Fat; Chol 72 mg; Sod 1179 mg.

Dietary Exchanges: Lean Meat 3; Fruit 1/2; Vegetable 1 1/2; Fat 3

Chicken Ranch Spaghetti

1 pound chicken tenders
Soy sauce to taste
1   7-ounce package spaghetti
1/2 cup shredded Cheddar cheese

1/2 cup shredded mozzarella cheese
1/4 cup grated Parmesan cheese
1/2 cup ranch salad dressing

Rinse chicken; pat dry. Cook chicken in skillet over medium heat for 10 to 15 minutes or until light brown, adding a hint of soy sauce. Cook spaghetti using package directions; drain. Place spaghetti on plates; add chicken tenders. Top with mixture of cheeses; drizzle ranch dressing over top. Yield: 6 servings.

Approx Per Serving: Cal 371; Prot 28 g; Carbo 26 g; Fiber 1 g;
    T Fat 17 g; 41% Calories from Fat; Chol 77 mg; Sod 302 mg.

Dietary Exchanges: Bread 2; Lean Meat 2 1/2; Fat 3

Jill Hutchison, Antioch, Tennessee

Add variety to pasta dishes by trying a different shape pasta (there are dozens to choose from) or try a flavor change with vegetable-flavored or whole wheat versions.

Grilled Turkey Steaks

1/2 cup soy sauce
1/4 cup oil
1 tablespoon honey

1 tablespoon ginger
1 teaspoon dry mustard
1 6-pound turkey breast

Combine soy sauce, oil, honey, ginger and dry mustard in glass dish; mix well. Let stand at room temperature overnight. Rinse turkey and pat dry. Slice cross grain into 1-inch steaks. Place turkey slices in marinade. Marinate in refrigerator for several hours to overnight. Grill over hot coals or on electric grill for 16 minutes, turning once. May ask butcher to bone turkey breast and cut into serving pieces. Yield: 8 servings.

Approx Per Serving: Cal 422; Prot 78 g; Carbo 4 g; Fiber 0 g;
    T Fat 9 g; 19% Calories from Fat; Chol 212 mg; Sod 1160 mg.
    Nutritional information includes entire amount of marinade.

Dietary Exchanges: Lean Meat 61/2; Fat 11/2

Freshly ground turkey is a fairly new addition to the supermarket meat counter. Try it as a substitute for ground beef as well as in specific recipes. For reduced-fat dishes it makes diet control almost painless but leaves the flavor.

Turkey with Ginger Salsa

1/4 cup vinegar
2 tablespoons dry sherry
2 tablespoons soy sauce
1 tablespoon grated gingerroot
1 clove of garlic, minced
1 teaspoon red pepper
4 4-ounce turkey breast tenderloins

1 medium tomato, peeled, seeded, chopped
1 green onion, chopped
1/4 cup chopped green bell pepper
1 tablespoon chopped cilantro
4 6-inch flour tortillas

Combine vinegar, sherry, soy sauce, gingerroot, garlic and red pepper in plastic bag; mix well. Reserve 2 tablespoons mixture. Rinse turkey; pat dry and place in marinade. Marinate in refrigerator for 1 hour. Combine reserved 2 tablespoons marinade with tomato, onion, green pepper and cilantro in bowl; mix well. Chill, covered, in refrigerator. Drain turkey, reserving marinade. Grill turkey over medium coals for 12 to 15 minutes, turning once and basting frequently with reserved marinade. Cut turkey into strips. Heat tortillas in single layer on grill for 15 seconds. Serve turkey with chilled salsa and warm tortillas. Yield: 4 servings.

Approx Per Serving: Cal 227; Prot 29 g; Carbo 20 g; Fiber 2 g;
    T Fat 3 g; 11% Calories from Fat; Chol 71 mg; Sod 689 mg.
    Nutritional information includes entire amount of marinade.

Dietary Exchanges: Bread 1; Lean Meat 2; Vegetable 1/2; Fat 1/2

Turkey Lasagna

8 ounces uncooked lasagna noodles
1 pound ground turkey
1 cup chopped onion
2 cloves of garlic, minced
1   16-ounce can low-sodium tomatoes, chopped
1   8-ounce can tomato sauce
1   6-ounce can tomato paste
2 teaspoons basil, crushed
1 teaspoon oregano, crushed

1 teaspoon fennel seed, crushed
1/8 teaspoon red pepper
1 egg, beaten
2 cups low-fat cottage cheese
3/4 cup grated Parmesan cheese
1 tablespoon parsley flakes
1/2 teaspoon black pepper
8 ounces low-moisture part-skim milk
   mozzarella cheese, sliced

Cook noodles using package directions, omitting oil; drain. Brown turkey with onion and garlic in saucepan, stirring until onion is tender; drain. Stir in tomatoes, tomato sauce, tomato paste, basil, oregano, fennel seed and red pepper. Simmer, covered, for 15 minutes, stirring frequently. Mix egg, cottage cheese, 1/2 of the Parmesan cheese, parsley and black pepper in bowl. Layer noodles, cottage cheese mixture, mozzarella cheese and meat sauce 1/2 at a time in lightly greased 9x13-inch baking dish. Sprinkle with remaining Parmesan cheese. Bake at 375 degrees for 30 to 35 minutes or until heated through. Let stand for 10 minutes before serving. Yield: 10 servings.

Approx Per Serving: Cal 348; Prot 30 g; Carbo 28 g; Fiber 2 g;
    T Fat 13 g; 33% Calories from Fat; Chol 78 mg; Sod 764 mg.

Dietary Exchanges: Bread 1; Lean Meat 31/2; Vegetable 1; Fat 1/2

Turkey and Zucchini Skillet

1 pound ground turkey
1 cup chopped onion
3 cups sliced unpeeled zucchini

1   16-ounce can tomatoes
Salt and pepper to taste
1 cup shredded Cheddar cheese

Brown ground turkey in electric skillet, stirring until crumbly; drain. Top with onion, zucchini and tomatoes. Sprinkle with salt and pepper. Cook over medium heat for 15 minutes. Top with cheese. Cook until cheese melts. Yield: 4 servings.

Approx Per Serving: Cal 365; Prot 33 g; Carbo 12 g; Fiber 3 g;
    T Fat 21 g; 52% Calories from Fat; Chol 116 mg; Sod 455 mg.

Dietary Exchanges: Lean Meat 41/2; Vegetable 2; Fat 11/2

Applesauce-Cheddar Quiche

1 cup plus 1 tablespoon rolled oats
1/4 cup wheat germ
1/4 cup packed light brown sugar
1/4 teaspoon cinnamon
3/4 tablespoon butter or margarine
4 ounces Cheddar cheese, sliced

1 cup unsweetened applesauce
3 large eggs, slightly beaten
1/4 teaspoon nutmeg
1/2 teaspoon cinnamon
11/2 tablespoons flour
1 cup half and half

Combine oats, wheat germ, brown sugar, cinnamon and butter in bowl. Press into 9-inch round baking dish. Bake at 375 degrees for 8 to 10 minutes. Cool. Place cheese slices over bottom of baked crust; cover with applesauce. Combine eggs, spices and flour; mix well. Add half and half; mix well. Pour mixture over applesauce. Bake at 350 degrees for 45 minutes. Cool for 5 minutes before slicing. Yield: 10 servings.

Approx Per Serving: Cal 181; Prot 8 g; Carbo 17 g; Fiber 2 g;
    T Fat 10 g; 48% Calories from Fat; Chol 87 mg; Sod 111 mg.

Dietary Exchanges: Bread 1/2; Lean Meat 1/2; Fruit 1/2; Fat 11/2

Breakfast Casserole

1 pound sausage links
5 slices sourdough bread, cubed
2 cups shredded Cheddar cheese
4 eggs
21/4 cups milk

3/4 teaspoon dry mustard
1   10-ounce can cream of mushroom
    soup
1/2 soup can milk

Brown sausage links in skillet; drain well. Cut sausage into pieces. Layer bread cubes, cheese and sausage in greased 9x13-inch baking pan. Beat eggs with 21/4 cups milk and mustard. Pour over layers. Chill, covered, overnight. Blend soup with 1/2 soup can milk. Pour over top. Bake, uncovered, at 350 degrees for 1 hour. Serve with fresh fruit for a perfect breakfast. Yield: 10 servings.

Approx Per Serving: Cal 308; Prot 16 g; Carbo 13 g; Fiber <1 g;
    T Fat 21 g; 62% Calories from Fat; Chol 136 mg; Sod 798 mg.

Dietary Exchanges: Bread 1/2; Lean Meat 11/2; Milk 1/2; Fat 3

Barbara Landis, Shelbyville, Tennessee

Eggs for Brunch

18 eggs
Salt to taste

2 4-ounce cans chopped green chilies
6 cups shredded Colby cheese

Beat eggs in mixer bowl. Beat in salt. Drain chilies, reserving liquid. Beat reserved liquid into eggs. Layer cheese and chilies in greased 9x13-inch baking dish. Pour egg mixture evenly over layers. Mix lightly with fork. Bake at 350 degrees for 30 minutes or until puffed and golden. This dish reheats well. Yield: 15 servings.

Approx Per Serving: Cal 270; Prot 18 g; Carbo 3 g; Fiber <1 g;
    T Fat 21 g; 69% Calories from Fat; Chol 297 mg; Sod 525 mg.

Dietary Exchanges: Lean Meat 2¹/₂; Fat 3

Jennifer Smith, Franklin, Tennessee

Fettucini and Broccoli in Parmesan Sauce

1 12-ounce package fettucini
3 cups broccoli flowerets
1 cup reduced-calorie sour cream

³/₄ cup grated Parmesan cheese
1¹/₃ cups cherry tomatoes, quartered

Cook pasta using package directions for half the time. Add broccoli to pasta. Cook for 5 to 10 minutes or until pasta is *al dente* and broccoli is tender-crisp. Drain, reserving ¹/₃ cup cooking liquid. Mix sour cream, Parmesan cheese and reserved liquid in bowl. Add pasta, broccoli and tomatoes; mix well. Serve immediately. Yield: 2 servings.

Approx Per Serving: Cal 1017; Prot 45 g; Carbo 144 g; Fiber 9 g;
    T Fat 29 g; 26% Calories from Fat; Chol 76 mg; Sod 802 mg.

Dietary Exchanges: Bread 9¹/₂; Lean Meat 2; Vegetable 2; Milk ¹/₂; Fat 4

Pasta Primavera

8 ounces uncooked spaghetti
2 tablespoons chopped onion
³/₄ cup diagonally sliced celery
1 cup diagonally sliced carrots
2 tablespoons olive oil
¹/₂ green bell pepper, sliced

12 fresh snow peas
8 broccoli flowerets
4 mushrooms, sliced
¹/₂ cup yogurt
Basil, garlic powder, salt and pepper
    to taste

Cook spaghetti using package directions; drain. Sauté onion, celery and carrots in olive oil in large skillet for 5 minutes. Add green pepper, snow peas, broccoli and mushrooms. Stir-fry until tender-crisp. Add spaghetti in stir-fried vegetables; toss well. Add remaining ingredients. Cook until heated through, stirring constantly. Yield: 4 servings.

Approx Per Serving: Cal 319; Prot 10 g; Carbo 50 g; Fiber 4 g;
    T Fat 9 g; 25% Calories from Fat; Chol 4 mg; Sod 51 mg.

Dietary Exchanges: Bread 3; Vegetable 1; Fat 1¹/₂

Spinach Lasagna

3/4 cup chopped onion
2 cloves of garlic, minced
1 tablespoon olive oil
1 16-ounce can tomato sauce
1/8 teaspoon pepper
1 teaspoon oregano
1/4 teaspoon basil

1 10-ounce package frozen chopped spinach, thawed, well drained
2 cups low-fat cottage cheese
3/4 cup grated Parmesan cheese
1 8-ounce package lasagna noodles
2 cups shredded mozzarella cheese

Sauté onion and garlic in olive oil in skillet just until tender. Add tomato sauce, pepper, oregano and basil. Simmer for 30 minutes. Combine spinach, cottage cheese and Parmesan cheese in bowl; mix well. Cook lasagna noodles using package directions. Place in cold water until ready to use; drain. Alternate layers of well drained noodles, sauce, spinach mixture and mozzarella cheese in greased 9x13-inch baking dish. Bake at 350 degrees for 30 to 40 minutes or until bubbly. Let stand for 10 minutes before cutting. Yield: 12 servings.

Approx Per Serving: Cal 217; Prot 15 g; Carbo 21 g; Fiber 1 g;
T Fat 8 g; 34% Calories from Fat; Chol 23 mg; Sod 586 mg.

Dietary Exchanges: Bread 1; Lean Meat 1 1/2; Vegetable 1; Fat 1

Eva Myers, Santa Fe, Tennessee

Spaghetti Squash Primavera

1 3-pound spaghetti squash
8 ounces medium zucchini
1 small red bell pepper
Flowerets of 8 ounces broccoli
1 shallot, minced
2 tablespoons olive oil

4 ounces snow peas
1 cup whipping cream
1/4 cup butter
3/4 cup grated Parmesan cheese
1/4 teaspoon salt
Pepper to taste

Pierce squash with fork. Bring to a boil in water to cover in large saucepan; reduce heat. Simmer, covered, for 50 to 55 minutes. Cool slightly. Cut into halves lengthwise; discard seed. Scrape carefully lengthwise with fork to separate into strands; set aside. Cut zucchini diagonally into 1/4-inch slices. Cut bell pepper into 1/4-inch strips. Sauté zucchini, bell pepper, broccoli and shallot in olive oil in large skillet over medium heat for 3 to 5 minutes. Add snow peas. Sauté for 1 minute; remove from heat. Heat cream and butter just to the boiling point in small saucepan. Stir in Parmesan cheese, salt and pepper. Toss with squash strands. Spoon onto serving platter. Top with sautéed vegetables. Serve with additional cheese. Yield: 8 servings.

Approx Per Serving: Cal 276; Prot 7 g; Carbo 12 g; Fiber 4 g;
T Fat 23 g; 74% Calories from Fat; Chol 64 mg; Sod 334 mg.

Dietary Exchanges: Bread 1/2; Lean Meat 1/2; Vegetable 1; Fat 4

Classy Grits

1¹/4 cups instant grits
5 cups water
¹/2 cup sour cream
1 4-ounce can chopped mild green
   chilies
2 tablespoons margarine

2 eggs, beaten
¹/4 teaspoon garlic powder
2 teaspoons salt
¹/2 teaspoon pepper
¹/2 cup shredded Cheddar cheese
¹/2 cup shredded Swiss cheese

Cook grits with water using package directions. Combine cooked grits, sour cream, green chilies and margarine in bowl; mix well. Add eggs, garlic powder, salt, pepper and Cheddar cheese; mix well. Pour into greased 9x13-inch baking dish; sprinkle with Swiss cheese. Bake at 350 degrees for 30 minutes. Yield: 10 servings.

Approx Per Serving: Cal 178; Prot 6 g; Carbo 17 g; Fiber 2 g;
     T Fat 9 g; 47% Calories from Fat; Chol 58 mg; Sod 654 mg.

Dietary Exchanges: Bread ¹/2; Lean Meat ¹/2; Fat 1

Mexican Hominy

2 15-ounce cans white hominy
1 15-ounce can yellow hominy
1 medium onion, finely chopped
3 tablespoons taco sauce

1 4-ounce can green chilies, chopped
1 cup sour cream
2 cups shredded Colby cheese

Cook hominy and onion in saucepan for 15 minutes, stirring frequently. Add taco sauce, green chilies, sour cream and cheese; mix well. Pour into greased 2-quart baking dish. Bake at 325 degrees for 30 minutes or until hot and bubbly. Yield: 10 servings.

Approx Per Serving: Cal 238; Prot 8 g; Carbo 22 g; Fiber 2 g;
     T Fat 13 g; 50% Calories from Fat; Chol 32 mg; Sod 569 mg.

Dietary Exchanges: Bread 1; Lean Meat ¹/2; Vegetable ¹/2; Fat 2

Gourmet Rice

1 cup quick-cooking brown rice
2 cups water
3 chicken bouillon cubes
¹/2 cup chopped green bell pepper

¹/2 cup chopped green onions
2 tablespoons butter
¹/2 cup sliced black olives
3 tablespoons chopped pimento

Mix rice, water and bouillon cubes in 2-quart saucepan. Cook, covered, for 25 minutes or until rice is tender. Sauté green pepper and green onions in butter in skillet until tender. Add to rice. Stir in olives and pimento. Heat to serving temperature. Yield: 4 servings.

Approx Per Serving: Cal 263; Prot 5 g; Carbo 40 g; Fiber 3 g;
     T Fat 10 g; 33% Calories from Fat; Chol 16 mg; Sod 1067 mg.

Dietary Exchanges: Bread 2; Vegetable ¹/2; Fat 1¹/2

Greek Stir-Fried Rice

1/2 cup broccoli flowerets
1/2 cup cauliflowerets
1/2 cup julienned carrots
2 tablespoons oil
1/2 cup coarsely shredded yellow
  squash
1/2 cup julienned zucchini

1/2 cup coarsely shredded red cabbage
1 to 2 teaspoons soy sauce
1 teaspoon hot sesame oil
2 cups cooked rice
1/4 cup unsalted cashews
Salt and pepper to taste

Blanch broccoli and cauliflower for 2 minutes; drain and keep warm. Stir-fry carrots in 2 tablespoons hot oil until tender-crisp. Add yellow squash, zucchini and cabbage. Cook until tender-crisp. Add soy sauce, 1 teaspoon hot sesame oil, broccoli and cauliflower. Stir in rice gently. Add cashews, salt and pepper. Heat to serving temperature. May add strips of tomato and chopped green onions. Yield: 6 servings.

Approx Per Serving: Cal 182; Prot 4 g; Carbo 24 g; Fiber 2 g;
  T Fat 8 g; 40% Calories from Fat; Chol 0 mg; Sod 124 mg.

Dietary Exchanges: Bread 1; Vegetable 1/2; Fat 1 1/2

Italian Green Rice

1 cup chopped onion
1 cup chopped parsley
1 1/2 cups chopped fresh spinach
2 tablespoons olive oil
2 tablespoons butter

2 cups uncooked rice
1 teaspoon salt
Pepper to taste
3 1/2 cups hot chicken stock
2 tablespoons butter

Cook onion, parsley and spinach in olive oil and 2 tablespoons butter in tightly covered saucepan over low heat for 5 minutes. Add rice. Cook until rice is translucent, stirring constantly. Add salt, pepper and 2 cups chicken stock. Simmer, covered, for 10 minutes. Add remaining 1 1/2 cups chicken stock. Simmer, covered, for 10 minutes. Add 2 tablespoons butter, mixing lightly with fork. Spoon into serving bowl. Garnish with sprinkle of freshly ground pepper and Parmesan cheese. Omit salt if using chicken bouillon. Yield: 6 servings.

Approx Per Serving: Cal 372; Prot 8 g; Carbo 53 g; Fiber 2 g;
  T Fat 14 g; 33% Calories from Fat; Chol 21 mg; Sod 907 mg.

Dietary Exchanges: Bread 2; Vegetable 1/2; Fat 2 1/2

Vary grain side dishes by trying different types of rice—brown rice (which is chewier and nutty), basmati, aromatica, long grain, short grain—the list is longer than you may think and each brings its own flavor and texture to a familiar recipe.

Risotto

1 cup uncooked brown rice
4 chicken bouillon cubes
1¹/₂ cups hot water
2 tablespoons chopped celery
¹/₄ cup chopped green bell pepper

3 tablespoons finely chopped onion
3 tablespoons chopped mushrooms
2 tablespoons chopped pimento
8 whole mushrooms

Sprinkle rice over bottom of baking dish. Dissolve bouillon cubes in hot water. Sauté celery, green pepper and onion in a small amount of bouillon liquid in skillet until brown. Stir sautéed vegetables, remaining bouillon liquid, mushroom pieces and pimento into rice. Bake at 425 degrees for 30 minutes. Stir until well mixed. Arrange whole mushrooms over top. Bake for 15 minutes longer or until rice is tender. Serve piping hot. Yield: 8 servings.

Approx Per Serving: Cal 99; Prot 3 g; Carbo 20 g; Fiber 1 g;
  T Fat 1 g; 8% Calories from Fat; Chol <1 mg; Sod 581 mg.

Dietary Exchanges: Bread 1; Vegetable ¹/₂

Sybil Crawford, Greenbrier, Tennessee

Did you know that only 6 ounces of beef is enough protein for the entire day? That makes stir-fry dishes using a small amount of meat and an assortment of vegetables and grains good tasting and good for you.

Best-Ever Wild Rice

1 carrot
3 cloves of garlic, chopped
¹/₂ cup chopped celery
1 small onion, chopped
¹/₄ cup sliced almonds

2 tablespoons margarine
¹/₂ cup uncooked wild rice
¹/₂ cup uncooked brown rice
3 cups water
¹/₄ cup finely chopped red bell pepper

Shred carrot into wide strips with vegetable peeler. Sauté with garlic, celery, onion and almonds in margarine in skillet until vegetables are tender. Add rices, water and half the red bell pepper; mix well. Bring to a boil. Reduce heat to low. Cook, covered, for 30 minutes or until rices are tender. Spoon into serving dish. Top with remaining red bell pepper. Yield: 6 servings.

Approx Per Serving: Cal 177; Prot 4 g; Carbo 26 g; Fiber 2 g;
  T Fat 6 g; 32% Calories from Fat; Chol 0 mg; Sod 61 mg.

Dietary Exchanges: Bread 1¹/₂; Vegetable ¹/₂; Fat ¹/₂

Eula's Love Biscuit Mix

6 cups self-rising flour   **¹/₂ cup nonfat dry milk powder**

Combine flour and dry milk powder in bowl; mix well. Store in airtight container at room temperature. Remove desired amount of mix as needed. Add enough water to make batter of consistency of cake batter. Spoon into greased muffin cups. I like to use heart-shaped ones. Bake at 450 degrees until golden brown. Yield: 18 servings.

Approx Per Serving: Cal 154; Prot 5 g; Carbo 32 g; Fiber 1 g;
      T Fat <1 g; 2% Calories from Fat; Chol <1 mg; Sod 539 mg.

Dietary Exchanges: Bread 2

Eula Steele, Lutts, Tennessee

Riz Biscuits

1 envelope dry yeast   **¹/₄ cup sugar**
¹/₄ cup warm water   **1 cup buttermilk**
2¹/₂ cups self-rising flour   **¹/₃ cup melted shortening**
¹/₂ teaspoon baking soda

Dissolve yeast in warm water. Combine flour, baking soda and sugar in bowl; mix well. Add buttermilk, shortening and yeast; mix well. Knead several times on floured surface. Pat to ¹/₄-inch thickness; cut with biscuit cutter. Arrange in greased baking pan. Let rise for 3 hours. Bake at 375 degrees until golden brown. Yield: 12 servings.

Approx Per Serving: Cal 169; Prot 3 g; Carbo 25 g; Fiber 1 g;
      T Fat 6 g; 33% Calories from Fat; Chol 1 mg; Sod 386 mg.

Dietary Exchanges: Bread 1; Fruit ¹/₂; Fat 1

Edna Annette Brannon, Culleoka, Tennessee

Alabama Corn Bread

2 eggs, beaten   **¹/₂ cup oil**
1   8-ounce can cream-style corn   **1 cup self-rising cornmeal**
1 cup sour cream

Combine eggs, corn, sour cream, oil and cornmeal in bowl; mix well. Preheat skillet in oven. Pour batter into hot greased skillet. Bake at 400 degrees for 20 minutes or until golden brown. May double recipe and bake in greased sheet cake pan. Yield: 6 servings.

Approx Per Serving: Cal 376; Prot 6 g; Carbo 26 g; Fiber 2 g;
      T Fat 28 g; 67% Calories from Fat; Chol 88 mg; Sod 458 mg.

Dietary Exchanges: Bread 1¹/₂; Lean Meat ¹/₂; Fat 5

Rose Gasser, Ashland City, Tennessee

Corn Loaf Bread

3 cups self-rising cornmeal
3/4 cup self-rising flour
1 cup sugar

2 1/2 to 2 3/4 cups milk
1 egg, beaten
1/2 cup oil

Combine cornmeal, flour and sugar in bowl. Add enough milk to beaten egg to measure 3 cups. Add egg mixture and oil to cornmeal mixture; mix well. Pour batter into 2 greased 5x9-inch loaf pans. Bake at 350 degrees for 45 minutes or until loaves test done. Cool in pans for several minutes. Turn onto plate or wire rack. Serve warm or cold. Yield: 24 servings.

Approx Per Serving: Cal 168; Prot 3 g; Carbo 25 g; Fiber 1 g;
T Fat 6 g; 32% Calories from Fat; Chol 13 mg; Sod 298 mg.

Dietary Exchanges: Bread 1; Fruit 1/2; Fat 1

Kevin Kovach, Clarksville, Tennessee

Cookin' Corn Bread in a Homemade Oven

3/4 cup milk
1/4 cup vegetable oil, preheated in
outdoor oven
2 eggs, beaten

2 tablespoons sugar
1 tablespoon salt
1 cup self-rising white corn bread mix

Combine milk, oil and eggs in bowl; mix well. Mix sugar, salt and corn bread mix in bowl. Add egg mixture; mix well. Pour into hot greased 8-inch cast-iron skillet. Place skillet on rack in outdoor oven. Cover oven with foil-covered box bottom. Bake for 20 minutes or until brown. Do not check corn bread frequently or heat will escape from oven. Yield: 6 servings.

Making the Outdoor Oven: Get a Jack Daniels 1-case cardboard box from your local liquor store. Remove and discard the top lid flaps. Cut bottom from box in one piece; do not discard. Cover inside of box with heavy duty aluminum foil, sealing edges with duct tape; do not leave any portion of box inside uncovered. Make rack of oven by bending 3 or 4 wire coat hangers to make rack that will position skillet in middle of oven. Cover reserved bottom of box with foil, sealing edges with duct tape, to use as lid for oven. Place 1/2 shovelful of oak coals or 2 or 3 charcoal briquettes from fire on square piece of foil. Position oven over coals; place rack in oven over coals. This oven is also suitable for baking cakes of all kinds; bundt cakes bake especially well.

Approx Per Serving: Cal 238; Prot 5 g; Carbo 24 g; Fiber <1 g;
T Fat 14 g; 52% Calories from Fat; Chol 75 mg; Sod 1350 mg.

Dietary Exchanges: Bread 1; Lean Meat 1/2; Fruit 1/2; Fat 2 1/2

Robert Parish, Tullahoma, Tennessee

Banana Bread

1/2 cup butter, softened
1 cup sugar
2 eggs
11/2 cups flour, sifted

1 teaspoon baking soda
1/4 teaspoon salt
1 cup mashed ripe bananas
1 cup chopped pecans

Cream butter and sugar in mixer bowl until light and fluffy. Beat in eggs. Sift flour, soda and salt together. Fold into creamed mixture. Stir in bananas and pecans. Pour into greased 5x9-inch loaf pan. Bake at 350 degrees for 40 to 50 minutes or until loaf tests done. Yield: 12 servings.

Approx Per Serving: Cal 285; Prot 4 g; Carbo 35 g; Fiber 1 g;
    T Fat 16 g; 47% Calories from Fat; Chol 56 mg; Sod 202 mg.

Dietary Exchanges: Bread 1/2; Lean Meat 1/2; Fruit 11/2; Fat 3

Carolyn R. Hall, Nashville, Tennessee

Healthful Date Bread

1 8-ounce package pitted whole
   dates, snipped
1 cup raisins
11/2 cups boiling water
2 cups whole wheat flour
1 teaspoon baking powder

1 teaspoon baking soda
1/4 teaspoon salt
2 egg whites, slightly beaten
1 teaspoon vanilla extract
1/4 cup oil
1/4 cup chopped pecans

Combine dates and raisins in large bowl. Pour boiling water over top; set aside to cool. Mix flour, baking powder, baking soda and salt in bowl. Add egg whites, oil and vanilla to date mixture; mix well. Add flour mixture and pecans; mix well. Mixture will be thick. Spread evenly in greased 5x9-inch loaf pan. Bake at 350 degrees for 40 to 50 minutes or until toothpick inserted in center comes out clean. May substitute applesauce for oil to reduce fat content if desired. Yield: 12 servings.

Approx Per Serving: Cal 221; Prot 4 g; Carbo 40 g; Fiber 5 g;
    T Fat 7 g; 26% Calories from Fat; Chol 0 mg; Sod 153 mg.

Dietary Exchanges: Bread 1; Fruit 11/2; Fat 1

Edna Annette Brannon, Culleoka, Tennessee

Changing all or part of the flour in a recipe will make it brand new. Try replacing a portion of all-purpose flour with whole wheat or rye flour. Just switching to bread flour or unbleached flour will change the texture and the fiber content.

Apple-Cinnamon-Bran Muffin Mix

_ cups packed brown sugar
5 teaspoons baking soda
1 teaspoon salt
2 teaspoons cinnamon
1 teaspoon nutmeg

1 cup dried buttermilk powder
1 cup shortening
1   15-ounce package wheat bran
    flakes with raisins
1¹/2 cups chopped dried apples

Combine flour, brown sugar, baking soda, salt, cinnamon, nutmeg and buttermilk powder in large bowl. Cut in shortening until crumbly. Add cereal and apples; mix well. Divide mix into four 4¹/2-cup portions; seal each portion in plastic bag. Store in refrigerator for up to 6 weeks. Yield: 4 (4¹/2-cup) packages.

Approx Per Package: Cal 2003; Prot 34 g; Carbo 350 g; Fiber 14 g;
    T Fat 56 g; 25% Calories from Fat; Chol 21 mg; Sod 2291 mg.

Dietary Exchanges: Bread 9¹/2; Fruit 11; Milk 1; Fat 10¹/2

Apple-Cinnamon-Bran Muffins

1   4¹/2-cup package Apple-Cinnamon-
    Bran Muffin Mix

1 egg, beaten
1 cup water

Combine Muffin Mix, egg and water in bowl; mix just until moistened. Spoon into 12 greased muffin cups. Bake at 400 degrees for 15 to 17 minutes or until baked through. Yield: 12 servings.

Approx Per Serving: Cal 173; Prot 3 g; Carbo 29 g; Fiber 1 g;
    T Fat 5 g; 26% Calories from Fat; Chol 19 mg; Sod 196 mg.

Dietary Exchanges: Bread 1; Fruit 1; Fat 1

Joanna McAtee, Nashville, Tennessee

Cheddar Muffins

2 cups flour
3¹/2 teaspoons baking powder
1 cup shredded Cheddar cheese
1 teaspoon paprika

¹/2 teaspoon salt
1 egg, beaten
1 cup milk
¹/4 cup melted butter

Combine flour, baking powder, cheese, paprika and salt in large bowl; mix well. Make well in center. Combine egg, milk and butter in small bowl; mix. Pour into well; mix just until moistened. Fill greased muffin cups 2/3 full. Bake at 425 degrees for 20 minutes. Remove immediately to wire rack. Yield: 12 servings.

Approx Per Serving: Cal 168; Prot 6 g; Carbo 17 g; Fiber 1 g;
    T Fat 8 g; 45% Calories from Fat; Chol 41 mg; Sod 298 mg.

Dietary Exchanges: Bread 1; Lean Meat ¹/2; Fat 1¹/2

Sourdough Flapjacks

1 envelope dry yeast
1 cup warm water
2¹/₂ cups (about) flour
1 or 2 eggs

¹/₄ teaspoon baking soda
³/₄ teaspoon salt
6 tablespoons sugar

Dissolve yeast in warm water in bowl. Add enough flour to make batter of consistency of waffle batter. Let stand, covered, at room temperature overnight. Add 1 egg for thick batter or 2 eggs for thin batter, baking soda, salt and sugar; mix well. Ladle onto hot greased griddle. Bake until brown on both sides, turning once. May reserve 3 tablespoons flour mixture before adding eggs and use in lieu of yeast, adding water and flour as above for the next day's breakfast. Yield: 8 servings.

Approx Per Serving: Cal 200; Prot 6 g; Carbo 40 g; Fiber 1 g;
 T Fat 2 g; 8% Calories from Fat; Chol 53 mg; Sod 243 mg.

Dietary Exchanges: Bread 2; Lean Meat ¹/₂; Fruit ¹/₂

Mary Colley, Donelson, Tennessee

Use low-fat versions of milk, yogurt and cheeses whenever possible. Save calories and fat grams for an occasional binge and improve your health and well being.

Three-Grain Waffles

1 cup oat bran
³/₄ cup yellow cornmeal
¹/₄ cup flour
2 tablespoons sugar
1¹/₂ teaspoons baking powder

¹/₂ teaspoon salt
2 eggs, beaten
1³/₄ to 2 cups skim milk
3 tablespoons oil
1 teaspoon vanilla extract

Process oat bran in food processor until pulverized. Add cornmeal, flour, sugar, baking powder and salt. Process just until mixed. Combine eggs, 1³/₄ cups milk, oil and vanilla in bowl; mix well. Add oat bran mixture; mix well. Add enough remaining ¹/₄ cup milk to make batter of desired consistency. Bake waffles on hot waffle iron using manufacturer's directions. Serve with maple syrup and fruit or yogurt. Yield: 6 servings.

Approx Per Serving: Cal 252; Prot 10 g; Carbo 36 g; Fiber 4 g;
 T Fat 10 g; 33% Calories from Fat; Chol 72 mg; Sod 324 mg.

Dietary Exchanges: Bread 1¹/₂; Lean Meat ¹/₂; Fruit ¹/₂; Milk ¹/₂; Fat 1¹/₂

Banana Pudding

5 egg yolks, beaten
1 cup sugar
1 tablespoon flour
1 tablespoon cornmeal
1 cup milk

1/2 cup butter, softened
1   10-ounce package vanilla wafers
2 large bananas, sliced
5 egg whites
10 tablespoons sugar

Beat egg yolks with 1 cup sugar, flour and cornmeal in saucepan. Stir in milk and butter. Cook over medium heat until of smooth custard consistency, stirring constantly. Layer vanilla wafers, banana slices and custard 1/2 at a time in baking dish. Beat egg whites in mixer bowl until foamy. Add 10 tablespoons sugar gradually, beating until stiff peaks form. Spread over custard. Bake at 325 degrees for 20 minutes or until golden brown. Yield: 10 servings.

Approx Per Serving: Cal 412; Prot 6 g; Carbo 61 g; Fiber 1 g;
    T Fat 17 g; 36% Calories from Fat; Chol 151 mg; Sod 226 mg.

Dietary Exchanges: Bread 1½; Lean Meat ½; Fruit 2½; Fat 2½

Ramona Crutcher, Lebanon, Tennessee

Enjoy desserts without as many empty calories by using some of the new products available in supermarkets. Try sugar-free gelatins and puddings; reduced-calorie whipped toppings or lightly sweetened non-fat sour cream; artificial sweetener or fruit juice on fresh fruit; and, of course, the many variations on frozen confections that emulate ice cream.

Caribbean Bananas

1/4 cup margarine
4 medium bananas
1/3 cup packed brown sugar

1 tablespoon lemon juice
1/2 teaspoon allspice
1/4 cup light rum

Melt margarine in 9x9-inch baking dish in 350-degree oven. Tilt and rotate dish to coat bottom with margarine. Cut bananas crosswise into halves; split lenthwise into halves. Arrange cut side down in baking dish. Mix brown sugar, lemon juice and allspice in small bowl; drizzle over bananas. Bake, uncovered, at 350 degrees for 15 minutes. Warm rum; ignite. Pour over bananas. Spoon into serving dishes. Yield: 8 servings.

Approx Per Serving: Cal 148; Prot 1 g; Carbo 21 g; Fiber 1 g;
    T Fat 6 g; 34% Calories from Fat; Chol 0 mg; Sod 71 mg.

Dietary Exchanges: Fruit 1½; Fat ½

Jill Hutchison, Antioch, Tennessee

Creamy Tofu-Berry Delight

2 envelopes unflavored gelatin
1/3 cup cold water
8 ounces tofu
Sweetener to taste
1 teaspoon vanilla extract
1 12-ounce can diet cream soda

1/8 teaspoon lemon juice
1/8 teaspoon salt
1/2 teaspoon orange extract
2 cups blueberries
2 cups strawberry halves

Soften gelatin in cold water in saucepan. Cook over medium heat until dissolved. Cool. Process tofu, sweetener and vanilla in blender. Add cream soda and gelatin gradually, processing until blended. Pour into bowl. Stir in lemon juice, salt and orange flavoring. Chill until set. Stir to mix well. Reserve 3 tablespoons mixture. Spoon remaining mixture over blueberries in large glass bowl. Top with strawberries and dollops of reserved tofu mixture. Chill until serving time. Yield: 4 servings.

Approx Per Serving: Cal 128; Prot 9 g; Carbo 19 g; Fiber 5 g;
    T Fat 3 g; 22% Calories from Fat; Chol 0 mg; Sod 97 mg.

Dietary Exchanges: Lean Meat 1/2; Fruit 1

Great Country Blackberry Cobbler

2 cups sugar
2 cups water
1 1/2 cups self-rising flour
1/2 cup oil

1/3 cup milk
2 cups blackberries
1 teaspoon cinnamon
1/2 cup margarine

Bring sugar and water to a boil in saucepan, stirring until sugar dissolves; set aside. Combine flour, oil and milk in bowl; mix well. Roll on floured surface into 10x12-inch rectangle. Mix blackberries with cinnamon; place on rectangle; roll as for jelly roll. Slice into 16 slices. Melt margarine in 9x13-inch baking dish in 350-degree oven. Arrange slices in baking dish. Pour syrup carefully over top. Bake at 350 degrees for 40 to 45 minutes or until golden brown. Let stand for 15 minutes. Spoon into dessert dishes. Serve with whipped topping or ice cream. May substitute chopped apples or peaches for blackberries. May double pastry for extra crust if desired. Yield: 16 servings.

Approx Per Serving: Cal 262; Prot 2 g; Carbo 36 g; Fiber 1 g;
    T Fat 13 g; 43% Calories from Fat; Chol 1 mg; Sod 218 mg.

Dietary Exchanges: Bread 1/2; Fruit 2; Fat 1 1/2

Rose Gasser, Ashland City, Tennessee

For a continental dessert, serve a plate of assorted fruits and cheese with individual knives for paring and slicing.

Punch Bowl Trifle

1   2-layer package yellow cake mix
1   6-ounce package vanilla instant
    pudding mix
3 cups milk
1   20-ounce can crushed pineapple,
    drained

1   20-ounce can cherry pie filling
16 ounces whipped topping
1 cup chopped pecans

Prepare and bake cake using package directions for 9x13-inch cake pan. Cool and crumble cake. Prepare pudding mix with milk using package directions. Layer cake crumbs, pudding, pineapple, pie filling, whipped topping and pecans 1/2 at a time in large clear glass bowl. Chill until serving time. Serve by scooping through all layers to serve in dessert dishes. Yield: 24 servings.

Approx Per Serving: Cal 270; Prot 3 g; Carbo 40 g; Fiber 1 g;
     T Fat 12 g; 39% Calories from Fat; Chol 5 mg; Sod 274 mg.

Dietary Exchanges: Bread 1/2; Fruit 2; Fat 2

Glinda Walker, Nashville, Tennessee

Chocolate Satin Cake

2/3 cup butter, softened
13/4 cups sugar
2 eggs
1 teaspoon vanilla extract
21/2 squares baking chocolate, melted

21/2 cups sifted cake flour
11/4 teaspoons baking soda
1/2 teaspoon salt
11/4 cups ice water
Chocolate Satin Frosting

Cream butter, sugar, eggs and vanilla in mixer bowl for 5 minutes or until light and fluffy. Beat in cooled chocolate. Add mixture of cake flour, baking soda and salt alternately with ice water, beating well after each addition. Pour into greased and floured 9x13-inch cake pan. Bake at 350 degrees for 25 to 30 minutes or until cake tests done. Cool. Frost with Chocolate Satin Frosting. Yield: 15 servings.

Chocolate Satin Frosting

3 cups confectioners' sugar
41/2 tablespoons hot water
1 egg

1/2 cup butter, softened
11/2 teaspoons vanilla extract
31/2 squares baking chocolate, melted

Blend confectioners' sugar and hot water in mixer bowl. Add egg, butter, vanilla and melted chocolate; beat until of spreading consistency. Yield: 15 servings.

Approx Per Serving: Cal 443; Prot 4 g; Carbo 63 g; Fiber 2 g;
     T Fat 22 g; 42% Calories from Fat; Chol 81 mg; Sod 300 mg.

Dietary Exchanges: Bread 1/2; Fruit 3; Fat 4

Fannie B. Smith, Nashville, Tennessee

Cake for Diabetics

1 16-ounce can unsweetened fruit
   cocktail
2 cups raisins
5 packets artificial sweetener
3/4 cup butter
1 cup unsweetened applesauce
2 eggs

2 teaspoons vanilla extract
1 1/4 teaspoons cinnamon
1/2 teaspoon nutmeg
1/2 teaspoon cloves
2 cups self-rising flour
1 cup chopped pecans

Drain fruit cocktail, reserving liquid. Add enough water to reserved liquid to measure 2 cups. Combine raisins with liquid in saucepan. Cook until liquid evaporates, stirring frequently. Stir in artificial sweetener, butter and applesauce. Let stand until cool. Pour into large bowl. Add eggs and vanilla; mix well. Add mixture of spices and flour; mix well. Stir in fruit cocktail and pecans. Pour into greased and floured tube pan. Bake at 375 degrees for 1 hour or until cake tests done. Yield: 16 servings.

Approx Per Serving: Cal 269; Prot 4 g; Carbo 34 g; Fiber 3 g;
    T Fat 15 g; 47% Calories from Fat; Chol 50 mg; Sod 299 mg.

Dietary Exchanges: Bread 1/2; Fruit 1 1/2; Fat 2 1/2

Gladys McGee, Greenbrier, Tennessee

Great Depression Cake

2 cups sugar
2 cups strong coffee
1 cup shortening
2 cups raisins
1 apple, peeled, grated
2 cups flour

1 teaspoon baking soda
2 teaspoons baking powder
1 teaspoon each cinnamon, allspice,
   cloves and nutmeg
1 cup chopped walnuts

Combine sugar, coffee, shortening, raisins and apple in large saucepan. Simmer for 10 minutes, stirring occasionally. Cool for 10 minutes. Add mixture of flour, baking soda, baking powder and spices; mix well. Stir in walnuts. Pour into greased and floured 9x13-inch cake pan. Bake at 350 degrees for 25 to 30 minutes or until cake tests done. Cool completely. Garnish with dusting of confectioners' sugar if desired. May substitute water for coffee if desired. May substitute candied fruit for apple to make an easy fruitcake. Yield: 15 servings.

Approx Per Serving: Cal 408; Prot 4 g; Carbo 60 g; Fiber 2 g;
    T Fat 19 g; 40% Calories from Fat; Chol 0 mg; Sod 103 mg.

Dietary Exchanges: Bread 1; Fruit 3; Fat 2 1/2

Elizabeth Frazier, Greenbrier, Tennessee

Whole Wheat Sugarless Cake

1/2 cup butter, softened
2 eggs
5 packets artificial sweetener
1 1/2 cups unsweetened applesauce
3 medium bananas, mashed
1 teaspoon vanilla extract
2 cups whole wheat flour

1 1/2 teaspoons baking soda
1 teaspoon baking powder
1 teaspoon salt
1/2 teaspoon cinnamon
1/4 teaspoon allspice
1/2 cup raisins
1 cup chopped pecans

Cream butter and eggs in bowl. Add artificial sweetener, applesauce, bananas and vanilla; mix well. Sift in flour, baking soda, baking powder, salt, cinnamon and allspice; mix well. Stir in raisins and pecans. Pour into well greased bundt pan. Bake at 300 degrees for 40 to 50 minutes or until cake tests done. Yield: 16 servings.

Approx Per Serving: Cal 207; Prot 4 g; Carbo 24 g; Fiber 3 g;
T Fat 12 g; 49% Calories from Fat; Chol 42 mg; Sod 301 mg.

Dietary Exchanges: Bread 1/2; Fruit 1; Fat 2

Faye Solomon, Decherd, Tennessee

Enjoy dessert occasionally and in moderation as a special treat but don't overlook the bountiful fresh fruit your supermarket provides all year. Fresh fruit is good and good for you.

Cranberry Bars

1 1/2 cups flour
1 1/2 cups oats
3/4 cup packed brown sugar
1 teaspoon grated lemon rind

1/4 teaspoon baking soda
3/4 cup melted butter
1 16-ounce can whole cranberry sauce
1/4 cup finely chopped walnuts

Combine flour, oats, brown sugar, lemon rind and baking soda in bowl; mix well. Add butter; mix until crumbly. Reserve 1 cup mixture. Press remaining mixture into ungreased 9x13-inch baking pan. Bake at 350 degrees for 20 minutes. Spread cranberry sauce over baked layer. Mix walnuts with reserved mixture; sprinkle over cranberry sauce. Bake for 30 minutes longer. Cool for several minutes. Cut into bars. Yield: 30 servings.

Approx Per Serving: Cal 125; Prot 2 g; Carbo 18 g; Fiber 1 g;
T Fat 6 g; 39% Calories from Fat; Chol 12 mg; Sod 60 mg.

 y **Exchanges:** Bread 1/2; Fruit 1/2; Fat 1

Demetria Kalodimos, Nashville, Tennessee

Old-Fashioned Tea Cakes

1 cup butter, softened
2 cups sugar
3 eggs, beaten
1 teaspoon baking soda

2 tablespoons buttermilk
1 teaspoon vanilla extract
5 cups flour

Cream butter and sugar in bowl until light and fluffy. Beat in eggs. Dissolve baking soda in buttermilk. Add to creamed mixture with vanilla; mix well. Add flour; mix well. Chill, covered, for several hours to overnight. Roll to desired thickness on floured surface; cut with 3-inch cutter. Arrange on lightly greased cookie sheet. Bake at 400 degrees for 7 to 8 minutes or for crisper cookies bake for 9 to 10 minutes. Store in covered container. Cookies are good for several weeks if they last that long. Yield: 48 servings.

Approx Per Serving: Cal 118; Prot 2 g; Carbo 18 g; Fiber <1 g;
    T Fat 4 g; 32% Calories from Fat; Chol 24 mg; Sod 61 mg.

Dietary Exchanges: Bread 1/2; Fruit 1/2; Fat 1

Bettye Griffin, Centerville, Tennessee

Sugarless Apple Pie

1   12-ounce can frozen apple juice
    concentrate, thawed
3 tablespoons cornstarch
1 teaspoon cinnamon
1/2 teaspoon nutmeg

1/4 teaspoon salt
5 cups sliced peeled apples
3 packets artificial sweetener
2 unbaked pie shells
2 tablespoons margarine

Combine apple juice concentrate, cornstarch and spices in saucepan. Cook until thickened, stirring constantly. Stir in salt, apples and artificial sweetener. Pour into one of the pie shells. Top with remaining pie shell, sealing edge and cutting vents. Dot with margarine. Bake at 400 degrees until golden brown. Yield: 8 servings.

Approx Per Serving: Cal 523; Prot 5 g; Carbo 65 g; Fiber 3 g;
    T Fat 28 g; 47% Calories from Fat; Chol 0 mg; Sod 498 mg.

Dietary Exchanges: Bread 2; Fruit 2 1/2; Fat 4 1/2

Rosemary Finch, Shelbyville, Tennessee

Make the switch to healthy snacks by stocking up on fresh and dried fruit, trail mix and popcorn. Forget the sweet and salty in favor of high energy, high fiber alternatives.

Susie's Apple Pie

1¼ cups flour
½ teaspoon salt
½ cup shortening
2½ tablespoons water
½ tablespoon vinegar
½ egg, slightly beaten
5 or 6 apples, peeled, chopped or sliced
¾ cup sugar
2 tablespoons butter

1 teaspoon vanilla extract
1 teaspoon lemon juice
¼ teaspoon almond extract
½ cup oats
½ cup flour
½ cup packed brown sugar
1 teaspoon cinnamon
2 tablespoons butter

Mix 1¼ cups flour and salt in bowl. Cut in shortening until crumbly. Add water, vinegar and egg; mix well. Roll on floured surface; fit into pie plate. Prick surface with fork. Bake at 450 degrees for 10 minutes. Cook apples in a small amount of water in saucepan until tender. Add next 5 ingredients. Pour into baked pie shell. Mix oats, ½ cup flour, brown sugar and cinnamon in small bowl. Sprinkle over apples. Dot with 2 tablespoons butter. Bake at 350 degrees for 15 minutes or until topping is brown. May double pastry and refrigerate or freeze until needed. Yield: 8 servings.

Approx Per Serving: Cal 458; Prot 4 g; Carbo 68 g; Fiber 3 g;
    T Fat 20 g; 38% Calories from Fat; Chol 29 mg; Sod 201 mg.

Dietary Exchanges: Bread 1½; Fruit 2½; Fat 3½

Susie Simmons, Warren, Arkansas

Banana-Butterscotch Pie

2 medium bananas, sliced
1 9-inch graham cracker pie shell
1 4-serving package sugar-free
   butterscotch instant pudding mix

2 cups skim milk
½ cup reduced-calorie whipped
   topping

Layer banana slices in pie shell. Prepare pudding mix with milk using package directions. Blend in whipped topping. Pour over bananas. Chill, covered, for 2 hours or until set. Garnish with additional whipped topping. Yield: 8 servings.

Approx Per Serving: Cal 269; Prot 4 g; Carbo 40 g; Fiber 2 g;
    T Fat 11 g; 35% Calories from Fat; Chol 1 mg; Sod 424 mg.

Dietary Exchanges: Bread 2; Fruit ½; Milk ½; Fat 1½

Gladys McGee, Greenbrier, Tennessee

Added Attractions

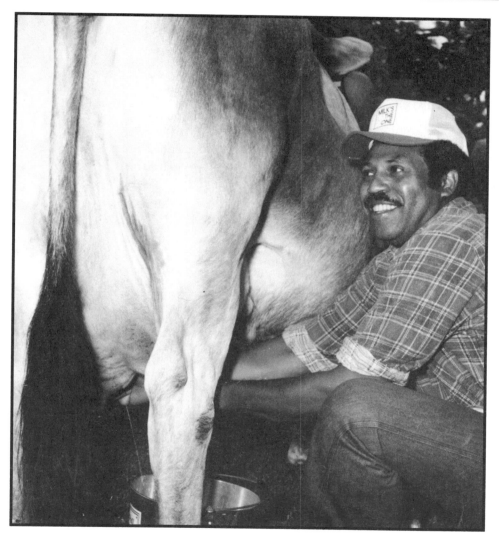

Can you believe that some folks showed up in a suit and tie to do this?

Equivalent Chart

	When the recipe calls for	Use
Baking	¹/₂ cup butter	4 ounces
	2 cups butter	1 pound
	4 cups all-purpose flour	1 pound
	4¹/₂ to 5 cups sifted cake flour	1 pound
	1 square chocolate	1 ounce
	1 cup semisweet chocolate chips	6 ounces
	4 cups marshmallows	1 pound
	2¹/₄ cups packed brown sugar	1 pound
	4 cups confectioners' sugar	1 pound
	2 cups granulated sugar	1 pound
Cereal – Bread	1 cup fine dry bread crumbs	4 to 5 slices
	1 cup soft bread crumbs	2 slices
	1 cup small bread cubes	2 slices
	1 cup fine cracker crumbs	28 saltines
	1 cup fine graham cracker crumbs	15 crackers
	1 cup vanilla wafer crumbs	22 wafers
	1 cup crushed cornflakes	3 cups uncrushed
	4 cups cooked macaroni	8 ounces uncooked
	3¹/₂ cups cooked rice	1 cup uncooked
Dairy	1 cup shredded cheese	4 ounces
	1 cup cottage cheese	8 ounces
	1 cup sour cream	8 ounces
	1 cup whipped cream	¹/₂ cup heavy cream
	²/₃ cup evaporated milk	1 small can
	1²/₃ cups evaporated milk	1 13-ounce can
Fruit	4 cups sliced or chopped apples	4 medium
	1 cup mashed bananas	3 medium
	2 cups pitted cherries	4 cups unpitted
	2¹/₂ cups shredded coconut	8 ounces
	4 cups cranberries	1 pound
	1 cup pitted dates	1 8-ounce package
	1 cup candied fruit	1 8-ounce package
	3 to 4 tablespoons lemon juice plus 1 tablespoon grated lemon rind	1 lemon
	¹/₃ cup orange juice plus 2 teaspoons grated orange rind	1 orange
	4 cups sliced peaches	8 medium
	2 cups pitted prunes	1 12-ounce package
	3 cups raisins	1 15-ounce package

When the recipe calls for	Use
Meats 4 cups chopped cooked chicken 3 cups chopped cooked meat 2 cups cooked ground meat	1 5-pound chicken 1 pound, cooked 1 pound, cooked
Nuts 1 cup chopped nuts	4 ounces shelled 1 pound unshelled
Vegetables 2 cups cooked green beans 2½ cups lima beans or red beans 4 cups shredded cabbage 1 cup grated carrot 8 ounces fresh mushrooms 1 cup chopped onion 4 cups sliced or chopped potatoes 2 cups canned tomatoes	½ pound fresh or 1 16-ounce can 1 cup dried, cooked 1 pound 1 large 1 4-ounce can 1 large 4 medium 1 16-ounce can

Measurement Equivalents

1 tablespoon = 3 teaspoons
2 tablespoons = 1 ounce
4 tablespoons = ¼ cup
5⅓ tablespoons = ⅓ cup
8 tablespoons = ½ cup
12 tablespoons = ¾ cup
16 tablespoons = 1 cup
1 cup = 8 ounces or ½ pint
4 cups = 1 quart
4 quarts = 1 gallon

1 6½ to 8-ounce can = 1 cup
1 10½ to 12-ounce can = 1¼ cups
1 14 to 16-ounce can = 1¾ cups
1 16 to 17-ounce can = 2 cups
1 18 to 20-ounce can = 2½ cups
1 29-ounce can = 3½ cups
1 46 to 51-ounce can = 5¾ cups
1 6½ to 7½-pound can or Number 10 = 12 to 13 cups

Metric Equivalents

Liquid	Dry
1 teaspoon = 5 milliliters 1 tablespoon = 15 milliliters 1 fluid ounce = 30 milliliters 1 cup = 250 milliliters 1 pint = 500 milliliters	1 quart = 1 liter 1 ounce = 30 grams 1 pound = 450 grams 2.2 pounds = 1 kilogram

NOTE: The metric measures are approximate benchmarks for purposes of home food preparation.

Substitution Chart

	Instead of	Use
Baking	1 teaspoon baking powder	¼ teaspoon soda plus ½ teaspoon cream of tartar
	1 tablespoon cornstarch (for thickening)	2 tablespoons flour or 1 tablespoon tapioca
	1 cup sifted all-purpose flour	1 cup plus 2 tablespoons sifted cake flour
	1 cup sifted cake flour	1 cup minus 2 tablespoons sifted all-purpose flour
	1 cup dry bread crumbs	¾ cup cracker crumbs
Dairy	1 cup buttermilk	1 cup sour milk or 1 cup yogurt
	1 cup heavy cream	¾ cup skim milk plus ⅓ cup butter
	1 cup light cream	⅞ cup skim milk plus 3 tablespoons butter
	1 cup sour cream	⅞ cup sour milk plus 3 tablespoons butter
	1 cup sour milk	1 cup milk plus 1 tablespoon vinegar or lemon juice or 1 cup buttermilk
Seasoning	1 teaspoon allspice	½ teaspoon cinnamon plus ⅛ teaspoon cloves
	1 cup catsup	1 cup tomato sauce plus ½ cup sugar plus 2 tablespoons vinegar
	1 clove of garlic	⅛ teaspoon garlic powder or ⅛ teaspoon instant minced garlic or ¾ teaspoon garlic salt or 5 drops of liquid garlic
	1 teaspoon Italian spice	¼ teaspoon each oregano, basil, thyme, rosemary plus dash of cayenne
	1 teaspoon lemon juice	½ teaspoon vinegar
	1 tablespoon mustard	1 teaspoon dry mustard
	1 medium onion	1 tablespoon dried minced onion or 1 teaspoon onion powder
Sweet	1 1-ounce square chocolate	¼ cup cocoa plus 1 teaspoon shortening
	1⅔ ounces semisweet chocolate	1 ounce unsweetened chocolate plus 4 teaspoons granulated sugar
	1 cup honey	1 to 1¼ cups sugar plus ¼ cup liquid or 1 cup corn syrup or molasses
	1 cup granulated sugar	1 cup packed brown sugar or 1 cup corn syrup, molasses or honey minus ¼ cup liquid

No-Salt Seasoning

Salt is an acquired taste and can be significantly reduced in the diet by learning to use herbs and spices instead. When using fresh herbs, use 3 times the amount of dried herbs. Begin with small amounts to determine your favorite tastes. A dash of fresh lemon or lime juice can also wake up your taste buds.

Herb Blends to Replace Salt

Combine all ingredients in small airtight container. Add several grains of rice to prevent caking.

No-Salt Surprise Seasoning — 2 teaspoons garlic powder and 1 teaspoon each of dried basil, oregano and dehydrated lemon juice.

Pungent Salt Substitute — 3 teaspoons dried basil, 2 teaspoons each of summer savory, celery seed, cumin seed, sage and marjoram, and 1 teaspoon lemon thyme; crush with mortar and pestle.

Spicy No-Salt Seasoning — 1 teaspoon each cloves, pepper and coriander, 2 teaspoons paprika and 1 tablespoon dried rosemary; crush with mortar and pestle.

Herb Complements

Beef — bay leaf, chives, cumin, garlic, hot pepper, marjoram, rosemary

Pork — coriander, cumin, garlic, ginger, hot pepper, savory, thyme

Poultry — garlic, oregano, rosemary, savory, sage

Cheese — basil, chives, curry, dill, marjoram, oregano, parsley, sage, thyme

Fish — chives, coriander, dill, garlic, tarragon, thyme

Fruit — cinnamon, coriander, cloves, ginger, mint

Bread — caraway, marjoram, oregano, poppy seed, rosemary, thyme

Salads — basil, chives, tarragon, parsley, sorrel

Vegetables — basil, chives, dill, tarragon, marjoram, mint, parsley, pepper

Basic Herb Butter

Combine 1 stick unsalted butter, 1 to 3 tablespoons dried herbs or twice that amount of minced fresh herbs of choice, 1/2 teaspoon lemon juice and white pepper to taste. Let stand for 1 hour or longer before using.

Basic Herb Vinegar

Heat vinegar of choice in saucepan; do not boil. Pour into bottle; add 1 or more herbs of choice and seal bottle. Let stand for 2 weeks before using.

Dietary Fiber in Foods

		Amount	Weight (grams)	Fiber (grams)
BREADS	Graham cracker	2 squares	14.2	0.4
	Pumpernickel bread	3/4 slice	24	1.4
	Rye bread	1 slice	25	1.7
	Whole wheat bread	1 slice	25	1.9
	Whole wheat cracker	6 crackers	19.8	2.1
	Whole wheat roll	3/4 roll	21	1.5
FRUIT	Apple	1/2 large	83	2.1
	Apricots	2	72	1.4
	Banana	1/2 medium	54	1.1
	Blackberries	3/4 cup	108	7.3
	Cantaloupe	1 cup	160	1.6
	Cherries	10 large	68	1.0
	Dates, dried	2	18	1.5
	Fig, dried	1 medium	20	2.2
	Grapes, green	10	50	0.6
	Grapefruit	1/2	87	1.1
	Honeydew	1 cup	170	1.8
	Orange	1 small	78	1.9
	Peach	1 medium	100	1.7
	Pear	1/2 medium	82	2.3
	Pineapple	1/2	78	1.2
	Plums	3 small	85	1.7
	Prunes, dried	2	15	1.4
	Raisins	1 1/2 tbsp.	14	0.8
	Strawberries	1 cup	143	3.7
	Tangerine	1 large	101	2.0
	Watermelon	1 cup	160	0.6
GRAINS	All Bran	1/3 cup	28	8.5
	Bran Chex	1/2 cup	21	3.9
	Corn Bran	1/2 cup	21	4.0
	Cornflakes	3/4 cup	21	0.4
	Grape Nuts Flakes	2/3 cup	21	1.4
	Grape Nuts	3 tbsp.	21	1.4
	Oatmeal	3/4 pkg.	21	2.3
	Shredded Wheat	1 biscuit	21	2.2
	Wheaties	3/4 cup	21	2.0

		Amount	Weight (grams)	Fiber (grams)
RICE	Rice, brown, cooked	1/3 cup	65	1.1
	Rice, white, cooked	1/3 cup	68	0.2
MEAT, MILK, EGGS	Beef	1 ounce	28	0.0
	Cheese	3/4 ounce	21	0.0
	Chicken/Turkey	1 ounce	28	0.0
	Cold cuts/Frankfurters	1 ounce	28	0.0
	Eggs	3 large	99	0.0
	Fish	2 ounces	56	0.0
	Ice cream	1 ounce	28	0.0
	Milk	1 cup	240	0.0
	Pork	1 ounce	28	0.0
	Yogurt	5 ounces	140	0.0
VEGETABLES	Beans, green	1/2 cup	64	1.5
	Beans, string	1/2 cup	55	2.1
	Beets	1/2 cup	85	1.7
	Broccoli	1/2 cup	93	3.1
	Brussels sprouts	1/2 cup	78	3.5
	Cabbage	1/2 cup	85	2.0
	Carrots	1/2 cup	78	2.5
	Cauliflower	1/2 cup	90	2.3
	Celery	1/2 cup	60	1.0
	Cucumber	1/2 cup	70	0.8
	Eggplant	1/2 cup	100	3.4
	Lentils, cooked	1/2 cup	100	5.1
	Lettuce	1 cup	55	0.7
	Mushrooms	1/2 cup	35	0.6
	Onions	1/2 cup	58	0.9
	Potato, baked	1/2 medium	75	1.8
	Radishes	1/2 cup	58	1.3
	Spinach, fresh	1 cup	55	1.8
	Sweet potato, baked	1/2 medium	75	2.3
	Tomato	1 small	100	1.5
	Turnip greens	1/2 cup	93	2.9
	Winter squash	1/2 cup	120	3.4
	Zucchini	1/2 cup	65	0.7

Nutritional Guidelines

The editors have attempted to present these family recipes in a form that allows approximate nutritional values to be computed. Persons with dietary or health problems or whose diets require close monitoring should not rely solely on the nutritional information provided. They should consult their physicians or a registered dietitian for specific information.

Abbreviations for Nutritional Profile

Cal — Calories   Fiber — Dietary Fiber   Sod — Sodium
Prot — Protein   T Fat — Total Fat   g — gram
Carbo — Carbohydrates   Chol — Cholesterol   mg — milligrams

Nutritional information for these recipes is computed from information derived from many sources, including materials supplied by the United States Department of Agriculture, computer databanks and journals in which the information is assumed to be in the public domain. However, many specialty items, new products and processed foods may not be available from these sources or may vary from the average values used in these profiles. More information on new and/or specific products may be obtained by reading the nutrient labels. Unless otherwise specified, the nutritional profile of these recipes is based on all measurements being level.

- **Artificial sweeteners** vary in use and strength so should be used "to taste," using the recipe ingredients as a guideline. Sweeteners using aspartame (NutraSweet and Equal) should not be used as a sweetener in recipes involving prolonged heating which reduces the sweet taste. For further information on the use of these sweeteners, refer to package information.
- **Alcoholic ingredients** have been analyzed for basic ingredients, although cooking causes the evaporation of alcohol thus decreasing caloric content.
- **Buttermilk, sour cream** and **yogurt** are the types available commercially.
- **Cake mixes** which are prepared using package directions include 3 eggs and ½ cup oil.
- **Chicken**, cooked for boning and chopping, has been roasted; this method yields the lowest caloric values.
- **Cottage cheese** is cream-style with 4.2% creaming mixture. Dry curd cottage cheese has no creaming mixture.
- **Eggs** are all large. To avoid raw eggs that may carry salmonella as in eggnog or 6-week muffin batter, use an equivalent amount of commercial egg substitute.·
- **Flour** is unsifted all-purpose flour.
- **Garnishes**, serving suggestions and other optional additions and variations are not included in the profile.
- **Margarine** and **butter** are regular, not whipped or presoftened.
- **Milk** is whole milk, 3.5% butterfat. Lowfat milk is 1% butterfat. Evaporated milk is whole milk with 60% of the water removed.
- **Oil** is any type of vegetable cooking oil. Shortening is hydrogenated vegetable shortening.
- **Salt** and other ingredients to taste as noted in the ingredients have not been included in the nutritional profile.
- If a choice of ingredients has been given, the nutritional profile information reflects the first option. If a choice of amounts has been given, the nutritional profile reflects the greater amount.

Index

Mail Order Form

Bill Hall's Land and Lakes Cookbook
C/O Amanda Solomon
Post Office Box 4
Nashville, Tennessee 37202
(615) 353-2405

Name _____

Address _____

City/State/Zip _____

Please send me _____ copies of
  Land and Lakes Cookbook @12.95 each $ _____

Tennessee residents add $1.06 sales tax $ _____

Add postage and handling @2.50 each $ _____

                        Total enclosed $ _____

Make checks payable to: Bill Hall's Land and Lakes Cookbook

Mail Order Form

Bill Hall's Land and Lakes Cookbook
C/O Amanda Solomon
Post Office Box 4
Nashville, Tennessee 37202
(615) 353-2405

Name _____

Address _____

City/State/Zip _____

Please send me _____ copies of
  Land and Lakes Cookbook @12.95 each $ _____

Tennessee residents add $1.06 sales tax $ _____

Add postage and handling @2.50 each $ _____

                        Total enclosed $ _____

Make checks payable to: Bill Hall's Land and Lakes Cookbook